Living the Catholic Social Tradition

Living the Catholic Social Tradition

Cases and Commentary

Edited by
Kathleen Maas Weigert
and Alexia K. Kelley

A SHEED & WARD BOOK
ROWMAN & LITTLEFIELD PUBLISHERS, INC.
Lanham • Boulder • New York • Toronto • Oxford

A SHEED & WARD BOOK

ROWMAN & LITTLEFIELD PUBLISHERS, INC.

Published in the United States of America
by Rowman & Littlefield Publishers, Inc.
A wholly owned subsidary of The Rowman & Littlefield Publishing Group, Inc.
4501 Forbes Boulevard, Suite 200, Lanham, Maryland 20706
www.rowmanlittlefield.com

PO Box 317
Oxford
OX2 9RU, UK

British Library Cataloguing in Publication Information Available

Library of Congress Cataloging-in-Publication Data

Living the Catholic social tradition : cases and commentary / edited by
Kathleen Maas Weigert and Alexia K. Kelley.
     p. cm.
"A Sheed & Ward book."
Includes index.
ISBN 0-7425-3187-2 (hardcover : alk. paper)—ISBN 0-7425-3188-0
(pbk. : alk. paper)
  1. Christian sociology—Catholic Church. 2. Church and social problems—
Catholic Church. 3. Catholic Church—Case studies. I. Weigert, Kathleen
Maas, 1943—II. Kelley, Alexia K., 1966–

BX1753.L58 2005
261.8'088'282—dc22

                              2004017290

Printed in the United States of America

♾™The paper used in this publication meets the minimum requirements of
American National Standard for Information Sciences—Permanence of Paper for
Printed Library Materials, ANSI/NISO Z39.48-1992.

In gratitude to the Raskob Foundation and the Catholic Campaign for Human Development (CCHD) for their grant support of this project, and to our colleagues at Georgetown University, the University of Notre Dame, the Catholic Campaign for Human Development, and the United States Conference of Catholic Bishops who cheered us on during the work.

Kathleen dedicates this book to Andy, Karen and Ernie, and Sheila: much love and peace!

Alexia dedicates this book to Jack, Madeleine, and William, and her former CCHD colleagues.

Contents

Foreword   ix
Bishop John J. Leibrecht

Preface   xi
Monika K. Hellwig

Part I: Framing Essays   1

1   Living the Catholic Social Tradition:
    Introduction and Overview   3
    Kathleen Maas Weigert

2   Social Change Strategies for the Future of
    Metropolitan Areas   15
    David Rusk

3   From Industrialization to Globalization: Church
    and Social Ministry   41
    Thomas J. Massaro

4   Catholic Social Teaching: Starting with the Common Good   59
    Todd David Whitmore

Part II: Case Studies   87

5   Introduction to Case Studies   89
    Rev. Robert J. Vitillo

6	Young Visionaries in the South Bronx					93
	Alexia K. Kelley

7	The Resurrection Project					105
	William P. Bolan

8	The Neighborhood Development Center					115
	Steven M. Rodenborn

9	Oakland Community Organizations' "Faith in Action":
	Locating the Grassroots Social Justice Mission					125
	Joseph M. Palacios

10	COPS: Putting the Gospel into Action in San Antonio					139
	Patrick J. Hayes

11	Coalition of Immokalee Workers					151
	Kathleen Dolan Seipel

12	Baltimore: BUILD and the Solidarity Sponsoring Committee					163
	Kathleen Dolan Seipel

13	Students Against Sweatshops					175
	Christopher C. Kelly

Appendix: Resources					197

Index					205

About the Contributors					217

Foreword

Bishop John J. Leibrecht

"And who is my neighbor?"

A lawyer asked that question of Jesus. It was answered recently in four Missouri counties by several women who helped at-risk mothers take better hold of their own lives as well as their children's. It was also answered in a poor Missouri county by an alliance of churches, with the leadership of the local Catholic parish, to form a community organization assisting neighbors in their basic human needs. Both these efforts began with local seed money from the Catholic Campaign for Human Development. Both were ways of fulfilling Catholic social teaching, which is, in sum, all about our neighbors.

U.S. bishops affirm that Catholic social teaching "is a central and essential element of our faith." Catholic social teaching describes both what Catholics *believe* and who they *are* as followers of Christ. It is based on charity and justice. Some people seem to content themselves, in their relationships to neighbors in need, with charity. But that is only part of the call to follow Christ. Justice is also essential in meeting the needs of neighbors.

Catholic social teaching is based on the belief that human life is sacred and that each person has an innate dignity. In addition, each person is a social being, that is, he or she stands in relationship to one's self and to all other human beings. This makes economic, political, and legal issues of essential concern for Christ's followers. Pope John Paul II keeps reminding the world about the virtue of solidarity, by which people must be committed to the common good, because "we are all really responsible for all" (*Sollicitudo rei socialis*, 38).

Catholic social teaching balances personal responsibility with social responsibility, individual rights with the common good. It draws attention to the most vulnerable members of society, as does the gospel story about the Last Judgment (Matthew 25:31–46).

To those eager to live out their faith in the world, I highly recommend this book coedited by Kathleen Maas Weigert and Alexia Kelley. As past chairperson of the U.S. bishops' Catholic Campaign for Human Development (CCHD), my understanding of and commitment to my neighbor has been deepened by witnessing CCHD's good works. My hope is that this book will lead its readers to new commitments, in charity and justice, toward all our neighbors.

Preface

Curricular Contexts and Challenges for Catholic Social Thinking

Monika K. Hellwig

There is no lack of good will about passing on the social teaching of the church at Catholic colleges and universities. There is, however, pervasive uncertainty as to how to go about it, for several reasons:

first of all, it is essentially an interdisciplinary project, requiring some background knowledge in several distinct academic disciplines;

second, the source documents in official church teaching are written in a style quite alien to that to which our students are accustomed;

third, the specific positions taken by Catholic social teaching rest on a deeper and more comprehensive understanding of Scripture and tradition than our college students generally possess;

in the fourth place, the curricular time given to the religious component in undergraduate studies has shrunk in most Catholic colleges to a skimpy total of six semester hours (two one-semester courses), while graduate programs offer no time at all;

and finally, in many cases professors in the germane fields, including theology and Scripture, have themselves only the most superficial knowledge of the Catholic social teachings.

While this entire volume is devoted to making the task of handing on the heritage of the Catholic social teachings more manageable, this preface will address the five above-listed obstacles specifically, and will make some suggestions as to how one might begin to overcome them or circumvent them.

THE INTERDISCIPLINARY DEMANDS

In our conventional understanding of undergraduate curricula, the subject matter of Catholic social teaching belongs in the theology or religious studies department. At a certain level, it is possible to treat the subject matter of the social-justice teachings simply as religious principles. And this in itself is worth doing. For example, moral theology need not confine itself to the private behavior of individuals, but can well address social principles. Examples follow: people are always more important than things, profit, or boosting the GNP; the dignity of the human person and the value of human life are inalienable properties of all human beings, no matter what their condition; all have the right to eat, to be housed in properly human conditions, to find dignified and properly compensated work, to be educated at least to the minimum standards required to participate in their society, to be free of violence and toxic damage; the global and cosmic environment is in trust from the creator for the benefit of all, including future generations. These same principles can be dealt with when discussing the meaning of the doctrine of creation, the nature and effects of sin, and the meaning and scope of the redemption.

At this level of general principles, anyone in the theology or religious studies department is competent to propose the principles, to have the students discuss their implications, and to show their intrinsic link to the basic doctrines of our faith. This is not complicated and does not rest on esoteric knowledge. Difficulties begin when these general principles are applied, for instance, to a critique of liberal capitalism (as it continues to evade regulation for the common good in the United States and in the multi-national companies); or Marxist Communism as we have known it; or wasteful, unproductive use of huge tracts of land by private owners (as in parts of Latin America); or one-crop soil despoliation by entrepreneurs (as in parts of Central America); or dumping of toxic and radioactive waste from industrial countries into Third World countries; or the operation of avowedly Catholic repressive governments; or the various ethnic independence movements now active in various parts of the world.

As soon as the principles are applied to any of the highly complex socio-economic situations that call for critical evaluation and action in our world, more factual knowledge and analytical competence is needed in matters usually acknowledged to belong to other academic disciplines. In this context, the theology professors may well be shy of getting involved. In the first place there is a certain territorial defensiveness in those other disciplines that one is hesitant to breach. Then there is also the fear of over-simplifying complex issues and misleading students. There is also the fear of getting involved so deeply in personal efforts to understand the economic, political, ecological, and social factors that the pursuit of these may become a distraction from the professor's own field. And when all is said and done, some are simply afraid of making fools of themselves, dabbling in scholarly territories where they are not at home.

What can be done? Certainly, as a starting point, we should not despise the simple setting forth of the principles of Catholic social teaching in the context of courses dealing with doctrinal or moral theology. This would be true also in Scripture courses, as the Scriptures are, after all, classic source texts from which basic Catholic social teaching is drawn. It will also be appropriate to invite students to identify and discuss situations in which the principles apply. The examples they choose may well be beyond the professor's ability to analyze with total competence, but it is possible to admit this while agreeing that the situation cited is a case in point that deserves attention. It may even be possible to suggest that students in the class who are currently taking classes in economics or political science approach the professors in those fields with the questions that have arisen out of the discussion—a request that may in some cases interest those professors sufficiently to engage them in study of and reflection on texts containing the social teachings.

We should not forget that all of us who read the better daily newspapers and various journals on public affairs are already somewhat informed on current issues. We are required to be informed in order to be responsible citizens of a democracy where we vote, lobby, and help as educated people to shape public opinion in various ways. It is one of the ills of the academic world to assume that only those who are highly specialized in a particular academic discipline can make intelligent discernments about matters touching on that discipline. This attitude in fact leads to a kind of paralysis of judgment in public affairs. All issues in public affairs touch a variety of the academic disciplines. We cannot have a society in which in practical matters none will give advice, make decisions, or take action because each finds that the questions touch on various other specializations. Our students will one day be responsible, mature citizens like ourselves. We have the obligation to model for them the kind of data search, reflection, and judgment on which responsible citizenship rests.

When all this is said, it must be admitted that in the ideal Catholic college or university one would expect vigorous and sustained conversation on current issues of peace, social justice, and the common good among professors in various disciplines. And one would expect that the cumulative wisdom of the Catholic tradition on such issues would be part of the conversation. In fact, there is often great reticence among the professors both on the issues and on the Catholic perspectives on the issues, even when the students are deeply involved in a quest to understand. This is not really due to the fact that we have an ecumenical mix on most faculties; the non-Catholic faculty members are often more open to such discussion than the Catholics. It seems rather to be due to a lingering ethos that demands "value-free" scholarship and teaching. This is an ethos that arrived relatively late on the Catholic campuses and lingers there while already discredited in some of the most prestigious schools. There may be another reason for reticence in issues of justice, peace, and the common good. This is simply that persistent narrow specialization seems to garner all the academic rewards because it more easily leads to publication in prestigious refereed journals. Dedication to such narrow specialization may preclude time and energy and even interest in pursuing broader questions.

Some institution-wide leadership is required to redirect these forces on a given campus. Public lectures can be helpful in prompting faculty conversation on a topic of public concern. Faculty seminars by invitation will draw some, especially if they are concerned with teaching the subject matter. Reading circles led by people who are knowledgeable, well-liked, and good facilitators can be an enjoyable and very productive way of engaging faculty in conversation across disciplinary lines, especially where these facilitators are top administrators or prestigious figures on campus. Another possible approach is to fund experiments in interdisciplinary courses in which two or more professors from different disciplines are committed to be present together at all sessions. There is a luxury or elitist dimension to this that assures it will not be the general norm for classroom instruction, though a few professors may continue the experiment on an overload basis for the sheer satisfaction of it. Nevertheless, that such classes exist at all on a campus will affect the general ethos, widen the range of competence of the participating professors, and encourage the addressing of cross-disciplinary issues.

THE DIFFICULT STYLE OF THE OFFICIAL TEXTS

There is no doubt that official church documents are written in a ponderous style. We have the papal and other Roman documents in officially authorized translations. The translators are often so anxious to stay close to the original text that the translation does not read like English. Even documents from our own bishops have a tendency to be verbose because they come usually not from individual writers but from committees accommodating everyone's objections, suggestions, and interventions. However, there are several collections of official documents, such as papal encyclicals and conciliar pronouncements, with excellent introductions, summaries, and explanatory notes.

A straightforward study of the documents should be helpful to the professor in preparing courses, and may be a possible approach with graduate students. It is, however, less well suited to undergraduate teaching because the limited time available in a three-credit one-semester course might be exhausted with the serious study of one long document such as the ground-breaking Vatican II pastoral constitution, *Gaudium et spes*. While that document is crucially important in understanding Catholic social teaching in our time, most under-graduates will find it tedious. Moreover, the time would not be well spent be-cause there would be no time to bring the course to a point of integrating the theoretical with the practical and the large picture with situations in which the students can act both now and later in their lives.

This volume itself in fact suggests another approach more likely to engage most undergraduate students—namely an approach through case studies and exploration of resources through which practical contacts and collabo-ration can be reached. This approach has many advantages. In the first place, it is concrete enough to engage students immediately, draw their reflection and input, link with their practical experience, and acquaint them with the context and agencies that we hope will set the direction of their future en-gagement. Second, it allows for the integration of the social teachings in a context in which their relevance is immediately evident. Third, the case stud-ies may be a good opportunity to call on professors from various academic disciplines to contribute their observations, insights, and analyses.

In this context, the professor can introduce the argument from the source texts of Catholic social teaching at appropriate junctures of the case studies, and perhaps bring to the class excerpts from the documents themselves that are par-ticularly apt for the occasion or particularly thought provoking about further im-plications of the situations and actions that have been studied. The combination of case studies and theoretical texts will also offer excellent opportunities for proceeding from the known to the unknown by analogies. There are possibil-ities in this to extend the reach of imagination and empathy to embrace a larger sense of community, common destiny, and social responsibility.

This last point is important. One of the great problems of the world in our times is that globalization of economies, political powers, and cultural influ-ences are not matched with practical concern for those others whom we do not know, whose lives we cannot easily imagine, and whose fate does not easily rouse our practical concern and compassion. Through the case studies and their extension by analogies, it should be possible to summon the human fac-ulty of empathy for widening circles of human beings and human communities, to the point of realization of community of destiny. The official texts of Catholic social teaching are important, and it is important that the students should know that such texts exist and that they deal with the real world. However, it is not important that the students should begin with the study of the texts. They have a better beginning through narratives that evoke empathy with real people.

THE NEED FOR BIBLICAL AND DOCTRINAL BACKGROUND

It is well known that most of our undergraduate students today have a very poor background in both Scripture and doctrine. In most of our Catholic

colleges the enrollment in any undergraduate class, even in a class dealing
with Catholic theology, will include somewhere between 10 and 50 percent of
students from other religious traditions or none. Even among the Catholic students, relatively few come from Catholic high schools and grade schools. If
they attend parish instruction at all, it often ends with confirmation at a young
age.

In the ideal setting students would come to a course on Catholic social
teaching well acquainted with Scripture and with a basic formation in Christian doctrine. We do not have the ideal setting. We can make no assumptions
about prior knowledge and have to incorporate a good deal of this background formation into the course itself. The question is how to do this without using all the available time in the semester. One way to incorporate
Scripture is to assign an initial reading of Luke's Gospel and the early chapters of Acts of the Apostles followed by a class discussion of what seem to be
the concerns of Jesus in his public life and how the early community of his
followers interpreted the implications for themselves. Taking very little time
from the class, the professor could sketch in the general structure of the
Bible, the relationship of the New Testament to the Hebrew Scriptures,
and the structure and relationship of the four Gospels. With some preparation on the part of the professor, this discussion can be enriched by reading
apt passages from the prophets of the Hebrew Scriptures, from the letters of
Paul and John, and from the letter of James.

The purpose of this foundation would be to connect later case studies directly with the person and concerns of Jesus and to be able to refer back to
particular stories or sayings appropriate to the situation in the case study.
Generally, young people, coming fresh to the issues, are very open to such
an approach. It is important to make this link because in the Catholic community at large we still suffer from centuries of individualization of the message of salvation. Ever since the Constantinian establishment of the fourth
century, there has been the tendency to assume that Christian nations do not
need radical transformation in the light of the Gospel, though individuals
need conversion and salvation. This has led to assumptions about Christian
spirituality in which social-justice concerns appear not as essential but as a
kind of "elective," perhaps a special vocation for some few, or even as a distraction from the proper concerns of religion. Connecting the social-justice
concerns directly to the person and concerns of Jesus in the Gospels offers
a foundation for a quite different perception of what is essential in being a
Christian.

Perhaps, rather than immediately adding a doctrinal foundation to the
scriptural one before moving into the case studies, it would be well to embark on the latter prepared to interject at an appropriate moment, "By the
way, you know that this rests on the basic beliefs of Christians?" Those basic
beliefs that need to be sketched out briefly and succinctly are as follows: cre-

ation, sin, redemption, Jesus Christ, grace, church, and the reign of God. This might best be done at least in part in a Socratic fashion. Most students have assimilated popular and quite distorted ideas of the basic Christian doctrines. One can draw these out and ask, "But does it make sense? Can you really believe this, knowing what you do from science?"

Basic to everything is the doctrine of creation, of dependence on the creator, of the responsibilities and boundaries of human freedom. From that point, one can draw out the real meaning of the doctrine of creation: the gift quality of life, personal existence, resources, and the like; the meaning of human life and interdependence of human beings and other creatures as depending on the creator of all; responsibility for what we do with life, opportunities, relationships, and resources. This leads naturally to a discussion of sin: if it is a good creation by a benign creator, what went wrong? Why is there so much suffering, injustice, oppression, war, and so on? This is a good way of leading to the complex interrelationships of social sin with individual destructive actions or failures to act. Good insights can be drawn from personal experiences and observations of the students.

This can again be related to what was read and discussed in relation to Luke's Gospel: what Jesus seemed to be about, the redemption that he envisaged for people. And it can be related to Acts: how the community of disciples seems to have seen its function as a church, and its continuing hope for the future. It would not be necessary in this context to go into the complex discussions and formulations of Christology that date from the fourth and fifth centuries. It would, however, be necessary to indicate that at the heart of being Christian is the conviction that Jesus is the definitive self-revelation of God. In other words, that Christians are those who believe that the essential meaning of human life, the key to the fundamental purpose of our existence, is to be read by a constant return to the testimonies we have about Jesus.

It may also be very fruitful to explore the idea of the reign of God that formed such a constant concern of Jesus in the Gospels: what would our world be like if God truly reigned in all human affairs? What would be different in the distribution of wealth? How would public resources be spent? What would be different about the relationships among nations? Such questions, like those mentioned above, can be introduced when they are pertinent to the particular case study in hand. With a quick reference to the over-arching structure of Christian doctrine, namely creation, sin, and redemption, the doctrinal foundation can be explored in each case. One may hope that the cumulative effect would be that students become accustomed to relating specific situations and questions to the doctrinal foundation of Christian life and action, and that this will give them criteria for judging and acting upon whatever they observe. The goal is to elicit a habit of reflection, based on adequate Christian foundations, and leading to practical judgments and actions. What can be done as described here is meager, but what is important is that it goes to the core of the Bible and tradition.

THE LACK OF SPACE IN THE CURRICULUM

We are situated in a context in which all participants in the education of undergraduates are complaining that they do not have a large enough share of the available time. All have very persuasive arguments. The heart of the conflict is this: Catholic colleges are committed to continuing the liberal arts tradition in an age in which demands for technical knowledge are increasing at the same time as is the pressure to finish one's education more quickly and begin earning money to pay back education loans. Liberal education depends on the leisure to read, reflect, converse, and engage in some creative pursuits. This puts liberal education into head-on opposition with the forces for rapid acquisition of technical competence in a chosen field. In this struggle, the attempt to initiate undergraduates into understanding and internalizing the tradition of Catholic social teaching is located inexorably at the liberal arts pole of the spectrum. Although some technical information and expertise is always involved in analysis of social-justice issues, the main task is in relating particular situations and challenges to the whole meaning of human existence and to the values and goals that should be dominant.

For the individual student, a course in the social-justice teachings of the Catholic Church does not constitute career advancement, except in the rare case in which the course contributes to a research project or in which the student plans to work in a church organization. We do not intend such courses only for such exceptional students. The purpose of offering such courses is to influence the formation of the Catholic conscience and consciousness very widely among those who, because of their education, will tend to be the critics and the shapers of society. That wider influence will quite probably be limited to relatively few students and to one course only for most or all of those. It is critically important to make the most of the possibilities that exist within the curriculum constraints.

Realistically, one cannot expect a substantial enrollment if the Catholic social-justice teaching course competes among many elective offerings within a theology or religious studies requirement of two three-credit courses, the first of which is often predetermined. One may expect even less enrollment in those cases in which philosophy and theology share a requirement of three three-credit courses. One possibility is to make a course such as the one suggested by the casebook approach of this volume integral to a theology or Catholic studies undergraduate minor. As the idea of a Catholic studies minor has spread among the Catholic colleges, such inclusion may draw more students into the course. Another possibility is to promote the course as a humanities elective in the upper division.

An enterprising chaplain might organize something on a non-credit basis, which might be just as influential. For instance, one might build a Lenten project around the case studies, combining practical involvement with serious weekly discussions. Nevertheless it is highly desirable to insert social-justice studies into the curriculum itself. This conveys the message that there is an intellectual as well as a practical challenge to be met.

In those colleges in which various patterns of interdisciplinary majors are established, there is of course an excellent opportunity to identify the programs in which the study of Catholic social-justice teaching can fittingly be included. In this case, it may actually be possible to build a sequence of courses, thereby giving time to wrestle with some of the key primary texts. The collection of case studies offered here could be expanded by the students' themselves undertaking inquiries into local situations, bringing back an account of problems and challenges, and "brainstorming" about possible solutions.

So far, this discussion has supposed that the real opportunities to spread knowledge of the Catholic social-justice teachings arise among undergraduates at the Catholic colleges. It is true, however, that where an administration and faculty take the exigence of promoting that teaching seriously, it would be possible to integrate it into graduate studies—even into requirements in graduate studies—in philosophy, theology, political theory, economics, sociology, ecology, law, medicine, business administration, modern history, and various other fields. At the graduate level there would be an opportunity to go more thoroughly into the theoretical issues and controversial applications. If some of our universities could reach this level of commitment, there would be a real possibility of sustained influence on public policy.

Not only in graduate schools, but also in various types of adult and continuing education, a significant impact could be made by courses in the social-justice teaching of the Catholic Church. At the very least it would help to disseminate among thinking Catholics the realization that the church's social concerns are broader than abortion, contraception, and sterilization. In many urban universities we have discovered significant numbers of professional and working adults who, now that they are established in their field of work, feel an urge to pursue a broad range of interests far beyond the utilitarian means to earning a livelihood. It would be a good policy to catch them, so to speak, the second time around, offering opportunities they missed in their undergraduate years. A course structured for such students has a huge range of possibilities. It can extend through a sequence of offerings. It can depend heavily on reading. It can call on more life experience and contain better-informed and more realistic discussions of both causes and solutions. In most cases, continuing education is taken less seriously in

terms of academic rigor, but there is no good reason for this. Very penetrat-
ing and consequential study can be undertaken by people who are interested in the subject matter and not concerned about amassing credits and
earning an academic degree.

THE NEED FOR QUALIFIED FACULTY

Perhaps the greatest concern in providing solid courses in Catholic social-
justice teaching is that of having a qualified faculty. Most faculty members in
the social sciences are concerned to stay within their particular discipline
and to avoid advocacy. Courses on the social-justice teaching of the Catholic
Church must be in some measure interdisciplinary and cannot avoid an advocacy approach on certain general principles, though they will generally
distance themselves from endorsing specific practical proposals wherever
the options are debatable. It will take a significant reversal of academic expectations to arrive at a stage where it is taken for granted that Catholic institutions of higher education will promote the cumulative wisdom of their
own tradition. That tradition is rich with two millennia of well-informed and
highly sophisticated reflection on political, economic, cultural, and other societal issues. Apart from current, widely accepted prejudices in the American
academy, there is no reason to be ashamed of promoting and further exploring and developing that tradition in Catholic higher education and scholarship.

The question, of course, is how to break through the double barrier of
general ignorance of the tradition and of prejudice against its prominent
presence in the curriculum. In practice, more thorough acquaintance tends
to overcome the barrier of prejudice. In the years since the promulgation of
the Apostolic Constitution *Ex corde ecclesiae,* most of the Catholic colleges
and universities of the United States have, in fact, gone to considerable pains
to understand what is and should be characteristic of the Catholic higher-ed-
ucation institutions. What we have found in that time is that so much was
taken for granted because we still relied on the leadership and formative influence of the sponsoring congregations. Everyone was aware of the dwindling numbers of representatives of those congregations. But this was seen
in quantitative terms with less awareness of the qualitative difference this
dwindling of numbers might be making in the tacit understanding of the role
and functions of the Catholic universities and colleges.

While the interest in exploring, maintaining, and if necessary retrieving the
Catholic character of the institutions has been very strong among top administrators, the same cannot be said of faculty. The latter had been hired for
some decades with primary, if not exclusive, concern for their competence
in their field of specialization. The loyalties and self-assessment of faculty

members since the 1960s have turned to the standards and expectations of the professional organizations rather than to the traditional or declared mission of the institution. Thus, in practice, the concern for the Catholic character of the institution has more often been a special concern of administration, campus ministry, and student-life personnel and services, than of the faculty. On the part of the students, interest was indeed more easily aroused for the social justice teachings of the church, and especially for actual volunteer involvement with helping the poor, the oppressed, and the excluded, than for any other aspect of Catholic faith and life.

For administrators concerned to emphasize the Catholic character of the institution, this often became a focal point, but it was the domain of specially appointed moderators, supervisors, and sponsors, never quite taking root in the faculty as faculty. The obvious consequence was that the enthusiasm and first-hand experience of the students has generally not been linked to adequate reflection on systemic causes of mass suffering or to the church's social-justice teachings and the basic tenets of the faith. Yet it is precisely at this level that Catholic higher education should intervene. It is clearly the role of higher education to form responsible leaders in society—people who are able to assess critically what is taken for granted in their milieu, are able to analyze causes and effects, relate the parts to the whole, and devise strategies for improvement. In Catholic higher education we must surely aim to do this drawing on the wealth of our own tradition, which has so much to offer on social questions.

To achieve such goals, however, clearly involves faculty participation as faculty and in their scholarly pursuits and normal teaching activities. Because of the criteria by which faculty were hired in most U.S. Catholic colleges, and especially in the universities, in the decades immediately after the Second Vatican Council, we have faculties largely unprepared for this involvement while highly qualified in their own fields. It is, of course, possible to reset hiring priorities in the light of *Ex corde ecclesiae*, but this requires departmental collaboration because in most cases hiring was decentralized in the late 1960s or early 1970s. The faculty members now serving on the hiring committees will in some cases be quite unsympathetic to this change in hiring priorities. It is also possible to create special chairs or lectureships with the explicit purpose of making the social-justice teaching of the Church present and influential on the campus. How much influence such a person can actually exert will depend on the chairholder's personal characteristics and scholarly standing in the wider academy. A member of the sponsoring community with a lively, outgoing personality and an established scholarly reputation may go far to change the prevailing reluctance to be too involved with the Catholic tradition.

Some of the more effective projects initiated on some campuses have involved continuing education for faculty members, to turn their interests to those consistent with the mission of the institution. The obvious easy choice is to provide public lecture series. In rural and less prestigious institutions, these are well attended by faculty who are glad to broaden their contacts and horizons. In the urban and more prestigious institutions, faculty members already have so many contacts and opportunities that their schedules are overfilled, and faculty attendance is likely to be very sparse, though professionals and educated adults of the city may flock to such lectures in great numbers. This outcome in itself is of course a useful result because the message is being disseminated among opinion leaders.

An alternative to public lectures is to invite faculty members into reading circles that meet regularly and discuss material they have all read. The social encyclicals and the pastoral letters of U.S. and other bishops' conferences would make very suitable material for such reading circles either within a discipline or across disciplines. Participating faculty would have much to contribute precisely out of their own expertise while reading and hearing social critique from an angle with which they are less familiar. Good leadership can make this a most enjoyable experience for all, especially if it takes place in a relaxed atmosphere of good fellowship, in comfortable chairs, and with suitable refreshments. Besides the intellectual content of such meetings, which can be very stimulating, there is the opportunity to create that sense of belonging that will tend to turn the loyalties and attention of participant faculty members more toward the mission and identity of the institution.

A variant of this last suggestion is the summer seminar, usually more attractive to younger and newer faculty. It usually requires funding from special sources to provide stipends that compensate younger faculty for the loss of a summer-session salary. The advantages of the summer seminar are many. Those who participate are free of other commitments at that time. It is possible to require some preparatory reading before the group meets and discusses the subject matter. Moreover, in choosing a director for the seminar it is possible to guarantee leadership by a person fully competent in the subject matter, someone who may have to be sought in a wide search outside the campus. Similar experiments in setting up faculty seminars during the year have been successful, especially when they can compensate for the time spent with a course reduction.

While it is possible for any institution to organize such programs for itself, it should also be pointed out that the already well-established and flourishing intercollegiate program known as *Collegium* has a continuing summer faculty formation program for newly hired faculty on Catholic campuses. Operating out of Fairfield University, this ambitious and highly successful program covers various aspects of Catholicism in a wide sweep, including the social justice dimension. It is able to cover as much as it does because it has a very carefully chosen and substantial required preparatory reading list, which sets newly hired faculty well on the way to immersion in Catholic tradition.

CONCLUSION

Given the present context both in the wider academy and in the Catholic campuses as they now are, it is certainly possible to offer a vigorous program in Catholic social teaching, even if its place in the curriculum is not large. It is, however, necessary to plan an appropriate strategy so that such a program can be accepted as legitimate by the faculty, can have adequate faculty participation, and can offer a sufficient foundation for a responsible Catholic presence in the larger society. That strategy can be stronger if it has an intercollegiate dimension.

I

FRAMING ESSAYS

1

Living the Catholic Social Tradition: Introduction and Overview

Kathleen Maas Weigert

> *"The focus of this statement is the urgent task to incorporate Catholic so-*
> *cial teaching more fully and explicitly into Catholic educational pro-*
> *grams. . . . Recognizing the importance of this broader goal of Catholic*
> *education and formation, we call for a renewed commitment to integrate*
> *Catholic social teaching into the mainstream of all Catholic educational*
> *institutions and programs."[1]*

What is the relationship between faith and daily life? How do believers try to
understand the world and their place in it? What can—what should—they
do to bring their faith alive in working with all those of good will to make
this world of ours a more just, more caring one?

These age-old questions call for contemporary examination. The rubric
under which Catholic believers have usually raised these questions goes by
various names; for example, Catholic social tradition, Catholic social teach-
ings, social ministry, the "social question." Whatever its name, the key issues
and concerns at the heart of the matter call believers to reflect on their faith
and to decide how to make it real in their everyday lives. The tradition is
long, stemming from the prophets of the Old Testament through, most par-
ticularly, the life and teachings of Jesus Christ, up to and including a series
of papal, conciliar, and episcopal writings, as well as the very lives of be-
lieving, acting Catholics.[2]

What does this tradition include? Who actually knows about it? DeBerri
and colleagues have labeled it "our best kept secret."[3] A concern that this la-
bel is still too accurate inspired the United States bishops to write their doc-
ument, "Sharing Catholic Social Teaching: Challenges and Directions,"[4]
from which the opening quotation is taken. Among the challenges they pose

is one for educational institutions: these institutions must do more to make opportunities available for the current generation to learn about the tradition—not just in some detached way, but in a way that opens the heart as well as excites the mind.

This book is one response to that challenge. We have invited members of older and younger generations to collaborate with us as we explore the theoretical as well as practical riches of the Catholic social tradition in asking how the tradition is being lived out in some of the communities of contemporary America. We envision this book primarily as a resource for courses in institutions of Catholic higher education taught in various colleges and schools, departments and divisions, but also for adult education and seminary programs. Faculty from different departments will bring their own expertise to the discussion. Part I of the book begins with a portrait of the contemporary metropolitan world that shapes the empirical studies, then offers one essay providing an overview of the Catholic social tradition and another essay that offers a detailed examination of key concepts and documents in the tradition. Part II offers eight "case studies" that document various attempts to bring about positive social change in the context of the Catholic social tradition. Each of the case studies tells a story—a story of dreams and motivations, of obstacles and resources. The relationship between the Catholic social tradition and the work of people in the case studies is not always a simple, straightforward one. It will be up to faculty and students to examine that relationship, to see where the tradition informs the work quite explicitly, where it is more implicit, and where it is at best a distant backdrop. It is our hope that such examination will engage the current generation in thinking about the tradition, their role in it, and the necessity for the ongoing development of the tradition.

Before providing an overview of the essays in Part I, we want to discuss three important topics that frame this book: first, the "global–local" world in which we all live and some issues related to our spatial location (i.e., urban, rural, metropolitan); second, issues related to pedagogy and social change; and third, issues dealing with the Catholic social tradition.

THE GLOBAL–LOCAL WORLD

> Today the principal fact that we must all recognise is that the social question has become world-wide.
>
> —(Paul VI, *Populorum progressio* 1967, 3)

Our world has more than 6 billion people living in more than 190 countries. About 290 million live in the United States of America. The connections between U.S. citizens and others are multiple, from family and religious ties to financial and business relationships. As at the beginning of the last century, so too now at the beginning of the twenty-first, immigrants are flocking to the United States. Many of them come to our cities in search of jobs, and they struggle, as did immigrants before them, to adapt to their new country, learning its language, politics, economics, culture, and the like; many keep alive their ties to the "old country." As the reader will see, some of these immigrants rely on churches, among other institutions, to help them make the transition, a transition that is often accompanied by the challenges of discrimination, prejudice, and xenophobia. The marginalized of this new century face many of the same conditions as did those of the previous century. But added to the mix now are the realities of the increasingly "globalized" world.

Historians debate the current conditions of globalization, comparing it with the globalization that occurred a century ago.[5] No doubt, globalization is a complicated and contested word with multiple definitions and realities.[6] Those who find it a positive development cite such factors as increases in trade accompanied by increases in choices for consumers worldwide; advances in communications; the possibilities that greater global economic integration can enhance the likelihood of greater political stability; the potential for increasing solidarity; and the likelihood of decreasing inter-state violence.

Those who find globalization to be troubling cite other factors, such as the increasing inequality between rich and poor both within countries and between countries; the decreasing strength of the "workers" in face of the seemingly limitless power of the "corporations"; the "race to the bottom," by which good jobs in the industrialized segments of the globe are fast disappearing, only to reappear in less-developed areas (and in turn, to even lesser-developed regions) at a fraction of the pay; the trafficking in humans; and what they consider to be the careless approach to the earth's limits or, worse, the systematic depletion of the earth's resources.

Whether one applauds or decries globalization, there are some "facts" that seem incontrovertible. One has to do with urbanization; a second is related—immigration. Urbanization seems to accompany globalization. Increasing numbers of people are leaving rural areas around the globe, making cities that are bursting at the seams. The United States went from a predominantly rural to a predominantly urban/metropolitan society as it industrialized from the mid-nineteenth to the mid-twentieth century. Globally, it is expected that 52 percent of the developing world's population will be in cities by the year 2020,[7] up from slightly over one-quarter in 1975,[8] not because of industrialization but because of the influx to the cities due in large part to economic conditions.[9] We now speak of "global cities."[10]

When examining the situation of the United States, what do we find? Brookings Institution researchers report that eighty-one of the nation's top one hundred cities gained population in the 1990s, in contrast to the 1980s when sixty-two of these cities grew.[11] If the five largest cities in the United States were "countries," they would be in the top thirty countries of the world in terms of gross output of goods and services. New York City, the largest American city, with more than eight million residents, would be sixteenth on that list, followed by Los Angeles and Chicago (tied at 23), Boston (25), and Washington D.C. (28).[12] Some researchers contend that in spite of their size and economic value, cities are a low priority item. Bruce Katz, for example, states, "The marginalization of urban policies is in part a response to the diminishing political influence of cities after decades of depopulation and suburban growth." He contends, "cities continue to lose ground to their suburbs in the competition for jobs and middle-class households and the tax revenues that they represent."[13]

A core issue in urbanization is immigration (a topic directly addressed in the essay by David Rusk in Part I). Kenneth T. Jackson argues that "inner-city revitalization is being fueled by immigrants, who are flocking to American cities," and that the influx is giving new life to once-decaying neighborhoods.[14] For some, this is good news; for others, it is not. In the 2000 elections, some groups placed ads that linked immigration to suburban sprawl. Daniel Stein, the director of the Federation for American Immigration Reform, an organization that ran the ads, stated, "Immigration policies and its population impacts are direct contributors to suburban sprawl."[15] Rank Sharry, the executive director of the National Immigration Forum (an advocacy group for immigrants), countered, "It's a militant anti-immigrant agenda trying to attach itself to a legitimate environmental issue."[16] What does immigration mean for our society and our globe? Is there a trade-off between growing cities and depleting natural resources? What kind of globalization is "good"?

Where is the reader on these issues? Whatever the reader's leanings, it is important to understand that the local–global nexus shapes much of our lives and we need some understanding of it to be effective citizens. We do, indeed, live in a "glocal" world. Almost all of the case studies that follow are nested in these issues, so the reader will have ample opportunity to explore them in some detail.

PEDAGOGY AND SOCIAL CHANGE

> The major purpose of the book is to promote and advance dialogue about education for transformation.[17]

Given these important changes, how do we teach and learn about social change? Over the years, people have experimented with different ideas and methods. One approach is called the "case method," one very famous version being that associated with the Harvard Business School and used quite regularly in the professional schools such as business and law. There are, however, many types of "cases," ranging "from a hypothetical problem, to a one-page 'critical incident' or 'verbatim' which reports a specific actual incident, to a four-hundred-page case history describing in detail an event or situation."[18] We are using a modified version of the case method in Part II of this book. We commissioned several people to undertake research on contemporary communities that are seeking to improve the life chances of their members—to increase their economic well-being while simultaneously affirming their cultural and familial ties. The emerging "cases" offer students some opportunities to examine social change and its relationship to Catholic social teachings in a number of sites that are drawn from different regions of the country, different ethnic groups, and different employment arenas. Each case is preceded by an introduction to offer some guidance in making connections between what is going on in the case and in relationship both to other cases in the section and to the frameworks and ideas offered in Part I.

The researchers had a common task. After learning as much as they could about the area, history, and current situation of the organization (or movement) under study, the researchers then conducted interviews with key figures. Six of the case studies are based on a standard interview protocol. The researchers tried to learn about the interviewees' relationship to the history and current structures of the organizations involved, while also learning about personal motivations for doing the work. One final topic of each interview dealt with the role of Catholic social teachings in the person's understanding of his/her work and motivation for it. The reader will discover how various respondents interpret and apply ideas and principles from the Catholic social tradition. The eighth researcher studied what many simply call "the sweatshop movement," interviewing a number of students from Catholic colleges and universities around the country to provide a picture of strategies, challenges, and results from this growing movement. The fourth researcher was already working on his project in Oakland, California, as we were beginning this book, but since the project overlapped so well with ours, we invited him to adapt his work to our format.

A second approach to teaching and learning about social change is "experiential education." A simple definition is offered by what is now called the National Society for Experiential Education: "'Experiential education' refers to learning activities that engage the learner directly in the phenomena being studied."[19] A work based on experiential education in the context of religious groups (and in this way, similar to this book) is *Pedagogies for the Non-Poor*.[20] The authors of that work urged that what is needed is "transformative education": if the "non-poor" of the world are to have a better understanding of the lives and opportunities of the poor, an understanding that will lead them to collaborative action to help alter the conditions that impinge on the life-chances of poor people, the way to do it is through experiential education. Go to poor people; listen to them; learn from them; work with them. It is the hope of the editors and authors of this book that the readers will have opportunities to "experience" local versions of these cases. Perhaps visits to local social change organizations can be undertaken, or maybe dialogues with organizational representatives can be arranged. In the resource section the reader will find some organizations that may be useful in thinking about such local opportunities.

If the case method and experiential education are some "means" to learning about social change, what do we mean by that concept itself? The term is often used to describe the broad sweep of history where we witness, for example, the change from the medieval world of feudalism to the modern world of capitalism or the changes that get subsumed under terms like "globalization." A definition in this vein is "the fundamental alterations that occur over time in patterns of culture, structure, and social behavior."[21] The level of analysis is society-wide or global. But social change is about more than such macro-changes. It is also about small groups and local communities drawing together to rid their neighborhoods and cities of illegal drugs and industrial pollution or about partnerships between nonprofit organizations and local government to create new job opportunities or about parents, teachers, and city administrators collaborating to make the schools better. The empirical cases that follow provide the reader with the opportunity to examine the ingredients of social change at a more micro-level: people working together to bring about positive social change in a defined area. Examining these cases will elicit this question: "What is my theory of social change?" In formulating a response to that question, ingredients might include the following: your view of human nature; your understanding of power; your sense of appropriate resources; and your vision of the better world.[22]

Given that this book is written especially with college students in mind, it might be useful here to comment on data from the annual survey of incoming first-year college students that is conducted by the Higher Education Research Institute at the University of California at Los Angeles. Each year the study asks students about their goals and objectives as well as about their attitudes and beliefs on a number of issues. The top four objectives have remained fairly consistent over the last few years: being very well-off financially and raising a family are the top two; helping others who are in difficulty and becoming an authority in one's field are the next two. Included in the list of objectives are what might be called social action items—for example, becoming involved in programs to clean up the environment, influencing the political structure, helping to promote racial understanding. While the top four objectives typically garner between 60 and 75 percent support, the social action items generally attract between 15 and 40 percent. How can we account for the differences? Certainly economic conditions are relevant. Job security seems to be a relic from the past, so concern with making money can be viewed as a way of trying to create a more secure future for oneself and one's family. Students, like generations before them, still want to help. For the class who entered in the fall of 2002, for example, 83 percent reported they had performed volunteer work the year prior to coming to college.[23] And they believe they can make a difference. Seventy-three percent disagreed with this statement: "Realistically, an individual can do little to bring about changes in our society."[24] But their willingness to help and their sense of efficacy do not seem to translate into interest in the political arena. Just 19 percent reported they had "discussed politics" the year before, and only 33 percent said that "keeping up to date with political affairs" is very important or essential to them.[25] Current data, however, suggest there is a slight change, with interest in the political world inching up.[26] What inspires someone to move into that larger, political arena? We return to this issue in the next section. The case studies that follow offer some insight into it as well.

CATHOLIC SOCIAL TRADITION

" . . . unless the Christian message of love and justice shows its effectiveness through action in the cause of justice in the world, it will only with difficulty gain credibility with the people of our times."

(*Justice in the World*, 1971, 35)

While Catholic social teaching has its roots in the Old Testament and most decisively in the life of Jesus Christ, the "modern" beginnings are often dated from Leo XIII's 1891 encyclical, *Rerum novarum.*[27] Documents from popes, councils, and synods of the church, along with episcopal statements, provide a growing and evolving body of material that addresses "the social question." The lives of ordinary and extraordinary believers contribute to its life and development. Professor Massaro will help acquaint the reader with major parts of that tradition as they relate to the challenges of our contemporary society. Here we simply want to point out four issues.

First, it is not the case that earlier generations of "ordinary Catholics" read, understood, critiqued, and "applied" the social documents. As Andrew Greeley pointed out in his 1967 overview, for the fifty years following *Rerum novarum*, at most it could be said that some "elites" of the Church were familiar with the documents; we lack evidence that demonstrates widespread knowledge of the social documents.[28] No "golden age" existed when ordinary Catholics were steeped in the Catholic social tradition. The challenge

for contemporary Catholics is to engage the tradition in light of their own society. As the American bishops proclaimed, "We need to build on the good
work already underway to ensure that every Catholic understands how the
Gospel and church teaching call us to choose life, to serve the least among
us, to hunger and thirst for justice, and to be peacemakers. The sharing of
our social tradition is a defining measure of Catholic education and formation."[29] This leads to the second issue.

How do we "engage" the tradition? Taking it seriously—studying it, questioning it—is certainly required. Applying it is important as well. *Gaudium
et spes*, the historic "Pastoral Constitution on the Church in the Modern
World," issued by Vatican Council II in 1965 (4) offered this advice:

> In every age, the church carries the responsibility of reading the signs of the
> times and of interpreting them in the light of the Gospel, if it is to carry out its
> task. In language intelligible to every generation, it should be able to answer the
> ever-recurring questions which people ask about the meaning of this present
> life and of the life to come, and how one is related to the other. We must be
> aware of and understand the aspirations, the yearnings, and the often dramatic
> features of the world in which we live.

"Reading the signs of the times" means asking questions about the world
(local, national, and global) around us today.[30] How is it structured in politics and economics; what do the various cultures prize; who benefits and
who suffers from different policies and decisions? In order to reflect on the
links between faith and action, that context must be examined. As the famous opening lines of *Gaudium et spes* (1) claim, "The joys and hopes, the
grief and anguish of the people of our time, especially those who are poor
or afflicted, are the joys and hopes, the grief and anguish of the followers of
Christ as well. Nothing that is genuinely human fails to find an echo in their
hearts." The cases in this book are of real people, in real settings, with real
hopes and joys. How do they interpret their setting? How do they read the
signs of the times? How do they seek to engage the tradition?

Third, reading the signs of the times can lead people into the world of politics. It is there that laws and policies are made, there that many resources are
gathered and distributed. For many Americans, as evidenced by voter
turnout, for example, the political arena is not typically where they put their
energies or spend their time. As noted above, the current generation of college students is not enthusiastic about the political arena either. That is not
to say younger citizens are apathetic or uninvolved in their communities—to
the contrary, as we discussed. The data do suggest, however, that by and
large Americans feel distant from the political arena.

For some religious people, the political arena is to be avoided; for others,
it is to be entered as a "citizen" but not as a "believer." They see their faith as
focusing on their personal relationship with God, inclusive of their family

and its need, but not of some larger entity like society. Believing that one's faith is a "private" affair means the arena of politics is to be entered, if at all, without reference to one's faith. For many Catholics this has been the case as well. Yet at the very core of the Catholic social tradition is concern for the larger society and its structural arrangements. It is the case that earlier documents, for example, *Rerum novarum,* "warned against official involvement in politics."[31] While not seeking to truncate that conversation, one could argue that the believer today must enter the larger world of politics—in the fullest meaning of that term—because that is where decisions are made that impact the lives and opportunities of our sisters and brothers. This does not mean the pursuit of unbridled partisan behavior or the rancor that sometimes seems to pervade the halls of government. It does mean, however, that for structural changes to occur at a broader level, believers have to get involved if a more just society is to be created. How does the believer respond to the challenging statement offered by the 1971 Synod of Bishops' document, *Justice in the World* (6): "Action on behalf of justice and participation in the transformation of the world fully appear to us as a constitutive dimension of the preaching of the Gospel, or, in other words, of the Church's mission for the redemption of the human race and its liberation from every oppressive situation"? This, then, leads to the final topic.

How does justice fit into this picture? As the title of a seminal book suggests, one way of stating the relationship is "the faith that does justice."[32] That title is rooted in the deliberations of the 1974–1975 Thirty-Second General Congregation of the Society of Jesus, which contributed the expressions "the service of faith" and "the promotion of justice" to this discussion. It is the case, of course, that the relationship between faith and justice has been central from the days of the Old Testament. God's people were in a covenant relationship with the Creator. As John Donahue, S.J., remarks about this relationship in the Old Testament, "Acting justly consists in avoiding violence and fraud and other actions which destroy communal life and in pursuing that which sustains the life of the community. Yahweh is just not only as a lawgiver and Lord of the covenant; his saving deeds are called 'just deeds' because they restore the community when it has been threatened."[33]

In contemporary America, this notion of the communal framing of justice gets short shrift. Individuals seem to be interested in what is "just" for them and their loved ones but not necessarily for what is just in the larger context. Yet as noted above, in the Catholic social tradition that larger context calls for our attention and action. In addition to concepts such as solidarity, subsidiarity, and the common good (see the essays by Professors Massaro and Whitmore), another important concept that deals with this issue is "structures of sin." In his 1991 encyclical *Centesimus annus* (38), John Paul II said, "The decisions which create a human environment can give rise to specific structures of sin which impede the full realization of those who are in any way oppressed by them. To destroy such structures and replace them with more authentic forms of living in community is a task which demands courage and patience." How can we work to bring about better structures? In a representative democracy like ours, it is especially through the political arena—where decisions are made that affect the whole—that such action is called for.

OVERVIEW

With these framing issues in mind, let us turn now to an overview of the essays in Part I. David Rusk provides the empirical context for the case studies, offering the reader insights into some of the structural challenges facing local groups that want to bring about positive social change. He explores issues of economic and racial segregation and focuses attention especially on the "rules of the game" for land use. Thomas J. Massaro, S.J., provides the historical context of the role of religious institutions in metropolitan settings, explores the particular response of the Catholic Church through the social teaching tradition, and examines both key approaches—such as the "see-judge-act" model and "reading the signs of the times"—and key figures, such as Mother Teresa and Dorothy Day. Finally, Todd David Whitmore offers the reader a way into the tradition through the foundational concept of the common good, which he examines in close detail; he then proceeds to elaborate on five key related themes: human rights and duties, the option for the poor, private property and consumer society, subsidiarity, and peace.

Part II features the case studies. Reverend Robert Vitillo, director of the Catholic Campaign for Human Development, provides an introduction to the case studies. Each case study itself is preceded by a brief editorial introduction to highlight some of the case's key Catholic social tradition themes and to suggest relationships to Part I's framing essays and to the other case studies. Following the case studies is a resource section that lists website references to the Catholic social tradition and to key organizations operating within that framework. The section also describes community-organizing networks in the United States, a list of current books on the Catholic social tradition, and database sites for service and justice opportunities.

It is our hope that this book will contribute to the growing body of literature that describes, analyzes, and critiques the principles, concepts, documents, and practices of the Catholic social tradition. It is a rich, vibrant tradition that belongs to all of us. And, indeed, all of us have the responsibility to carry it on in our daily lives as we work with others to make this a more just, more peaceful, more humane world—nothing less.

NOTES

1. National Conference of Catholic Bishops, *Sharing Catholic Social Teaching: Challenges and Directions—Reflections of the U.S. Catholic Bishops* (Washington, D.C.: United States Catholic Conference, 1998), 2.

2. David A. Boileau, "Introduction" in *Principles of Catholic Social Teaching*, ed. David A. Boileau, 9–24 (Milwaukee, WS: Marquette University Press, 1998); Marvin L. Krier Mich, *Catholic Social Teaching and Movements* (Mystic, Conn.: Twenty-Third Publications, 1998).

3. Edward P. DeBerri and James E. Hug with Peter J. Henriot and Michael J. Schultheis, *Catholic Social Teaching: Our Best Kept Secret*, 4th Revised and Expanded Edition (Maryknoll, NY: Orbis Books, 2003).

4. National Conference of Catholic Bishops, *Sharing Catholic Social Teaching*.

5. See, for example, the overview by Alexander Stille, "Globalization Now, A Sequel of Sorts," *New York Times*, 11 August 2001, A15, A17.

6. For different views of globalization, see such works as Richard Falk, *Predatory Globalization: A Critique* (Blackwell, 1999); Thomas L. Friedman, *The Lexus and the Olive Tree, Newly Updated and Expanded Edition* (New York: Anchor Books, 2000); John Micklethwait and Adrian Wooldridge, *A Future Perfect: The Challenge and Hidden Promise of Globalization* (Crown Publishing Group, 2000); and Joseph E. Stiglitz, *Globalization and Its Discontents* (New York: Norton, 2002).

7. Cited in Bread for the World Institute, *Foreign Aid to End Hunger: Hunger 2001, Eleventh Annual Report on the State of World Hunger* (Washington, D.C.: Bread for the World Institute, 2001), 64.

8. United Nations Development Programme, *Human Development Report* (New York: Oxford University Press, 2000), 226.

9. Ingomar Hauchler and Paul M. Kennedy, *Global Trends: The World Almanac of Development and Peace* (New York: Continuum, 1994), 114–116.

10. Saskia Sassen, *Globalization and Its Discontents* (New York: The New Press, 1998).

11. Cited in Eric Schmitt, "Most cities in U.S. expanded rapidly over last decade," *New York Times*, 7 May 2001, A1, A13.

12. The Globalist, "Can Cities Be as Large as Nations?" http://www.theglobalist. com/nor/chartroom/2002/01-12-01.shtml (accessed 2 December 2003).

13. Bruce Katz, "Enough of the Small Stuff! Toward a New Urban Agenda," *Brookings Review* 18, no. 3 (Summer 2000), http://brook.edu/press/REVIEW/summer2000/ katz.htm (accessed 18 June 2004).

14. Kenneth T. Jackson, "Once Again, the City Beckons," *New York Times*, 30 March 2001, A23.

15. Cited in Haya El Nasser, "Ads Blame Immigrants for Sprawl," *USA TODAY*, 6–8 October 2001, 1A.

16. Cited in Nasser, "Ads Blame Immigrants for Sprawl."

17. Alice Frazer Evans, Robert A. Evans, and William Bean Kennedy, *Pedagogies for the Non-Poor* (Maryknoll, NY: Orbis, 1987), 10.

18. Alice Frazer Evans, "Models in Case Form," in Alice Frazer Evans, Robert A. Evans and William Bean Kennedy, *Pedagogies for the Non-Poor* (Maryknoll, NY: Orbis, 1987), 14.

19. Jane Kendall et al., *Strengthening Experiential Education Within Your Institution* (Raleigh, NC: National Society for Internships and Experiential Education, 1986), 21.

20. Alice Frazer Evans, Robert A. Evans, and William Bean Kennedy, *Pedagogies for the Non-Poor* (Maryknoll, NY: Orbis, 1987), 14.

21. James W. Vander Zanden, *The Social Experience: An Introduction to Sociology* (New York: Random House, 1988), 590.

22. See, for example, Paul Rogat Loeb, *Soul of a Citizen: Living with Conviction in a Cynical Time* (New York: St. Martin's Griffin, 1999) and Virginia Coover, Charles Esser, Ellen Deacon, and Christopher Moore, *Resource Manual for a Living Revolution* (Philadelphia: New Society Publishers, 1985).

23. Linda Sax et al., *The American Freshman National Norms for Fall 2002* (Los Angeles, CA: Higher Education Research Institute, Graduate School of Education & Information Studies, University of California, Los Angeles, 2002), 23.

24. Sax et al., *American Freshmen National Norms*, 23.

25. Sax et al., *American Freshmen National Norms*, 23 and 33, respectively.

26. See Linda Sax, "Citizenship and Spirituality Among College Students: What Have We Learned and Where Are We Headed?" *Journal of College & Character* 2 (2003), http://www.collegevalues.org/articles.cfm?id=1023&a=1 (accessed 2 January 2004).

27. Although, as Michael J. Schuck has argued, the tradition can in fact be dated from at least the eighteenth century; see his *That They Be One: The Social Teaching of the Papal Encyclicals, 1740–1989* (Washington, D.C.: Georgetown University Press, 1991).

28. Andrew J. Greeley, *The Catholic Experience: An Interpretation of the History of American Catholicism* (Garden City, NY: Doubleday, 1967), 221–222.

29. National Conference of Catholic Bishops, *Sharing Catholic Social Teaching*, 3.

30. See Joe Holland and Peter Henriot, S.J., *Social Analysis: Linking Faith and Justice*, Revised and Enlarged Edition (Maryknoll, NY: Orbis, 1983).

31. David J. O'Brien and Thomas A. Shannon, eds., *Renewing the Earth: Catholic Documents on Peace, Justice and Liberation* (Garden City, NY: Image Books, 1977), 34.

32. John C. Haughey, ed., *The Faith That Does Justice: Examining the Christian Sources for Social Change* (New York: Paulist Press, 1977).

33. John R. Donahue, S.J., "Biblical Perspectives on Justice," in *The Faith That Does Justice: Examining the Christian Sources for Social Change*, ed. John C. Haughey, S.J. (New York: Paulist Press, 1977), 69.

2

Social Change Strategies for the Future of Metropolitan Areas

David Rusk

Urban areas, Professor Michael Parkinson has written,

> *are the best of places and the worst of places—a Janus-like phenomenon. We see prosperity, energy, creativity, and innovation cheek by jowl with poverty, exclusion, and deteriorating neighborhoods. The concentration of economic, physical and intellectual resources makes many of them centers of prosperity, creativity, culture, communication and innovation—the dynamos of the [global] economy. . . . But at the same time many [urban areas] are experiencing declining economic competitiveness, growing social exclusion, and physical and environmental deterioration—making them a drain on [their nation's] potential economic performance and its social stability. The key social face of cities and their [surrounding] regions is the emergence of social exclusion that is growing in rich as well as poor areas, in growing as well as declining areas. The growth in social exclusion is intimately connected to, and partly caused by, the search for economic competitiveness. But at the same time the growth in social exclusion is limiting the economic competitiveness of our cities and regions.*

The challenges faced by urban regions, Professor Parkinson further warns, "are caused by a number of structure changes taking place outside them and are primarily beyond their control:

- *economic globalization—with power going upwards from the nation state and the loss of local control;*
- *economic restructuring—which is creating divided labor markets and the 'Porsche-hamburger' economy;*
- *competition among cities, regions, and nations as well as firms; and*

- *the restructuring of welfare states, [reducing the social safety net in favor of more market-driven income and benefits]."[1]*

Professor Parkinson was actually writing about European cities and regions, but, slightly modified and Americanized, his comments apply equally to American cities and metropolitan areas. Indeed, despite different history and national policies, many European urban areas increasingly reflect American-style trends. As another distinguished European scholar has said in commenting on a comparative analysis of Dutch and American regions, "Europe is the Netherlands' past, but America may be our future."[2]

This chapter will focus on American urban trends and issues with occasional references to European contrasts and parallels. It will not discuss urban trends outside the context of the West. The issue of social exclusion within the world's more advanced economies[3] (where the poor are few and the middle class are many) takes on a different dimension in Third World countries (where the poor are many and the middle class are few).

Nor will economic globalization be put on trial for "causing" social exclusion. American democracy's original sin—the enslavement and then segregation of African Americans—has a four-hundred-year history. Discrimination and privation that many new immigrants currently face (particularly, many Hispanic immigrants) are substantially less than those encountered by earlier immigrant generations. For millions, the "Good Ol' Days" were never very good.

When I was mayor of Albuquerque, I would visit a local junior or senior high school every month to talk with students. Once a seventh grader rather timidly raised his hand to ask, "Sir, was there ever a worse time than now and, if so, when was it?" After momentary reflection, I answered, "Well, probably just about every time leading up to now was worse. Your challenge will be to make the world you inherit even better."

It is in that spirit that this chapter focuses on the issue of what Professor Parkinson terms "social exclusion" but which might more harshly be labeled racial and economic segregation. Quite simply, we can do better.

AMERICA: THE FIRST GLOBAL SOCIETY

Americans are always on the move. The 2000 Census charts our constant external and internal migration: newcomers from abroad, Rust Belt to Sun Belt, and rural to urban (especially African Americans). As of April 2000, census enumerators counted 281 million Americans (making the United States the world's third most populous nation behind China and India).

And America had become an even more racially and ethnically diverse society. Americans classified themselves as about 69 percent white, 12 percent black, 12 percent Hispanic, 4 percent Asian, 1 percent American Indian, and 2 percent multi-racial (a new category in the 2000 Census). Multi-ethnic California had become the first state without a majority group. Before 2050, demographers estimate, the entire nation will have become so diverse that there will be no majority group. For the first time in our history, whites of European descent will constitute a "minority" group in the United States.

The nation's population grew 13.2 percent in the 1990s, far outstripping the growth rate of the rest of the Western world. It was the United States' highest growth rate since the baby boom of the 1950s (18.4 percent). Growth was largely fueled by increased immigration. After receiving tens of millions of largely European immigrants during the late nineteenth and early twentieth centuries, a series of xenophobic, anti-immigration laws largely slammed the door shut in the 1920s. Only after more liberal immigration laws were enacted in 1968 did significant immigration begin again, accelerating during the booming 1990s. About 1 million legal immigrants enter the United States each year, about two-thirds from Mexico, Central America and the Caribbean, and Asia. Based on the new enumeration, the Census Bureau now estimates that another 8 million illegal immigrants have come to the United States (primarily, Hispanics).

America now is becoming the world's first truly global society—a fact looked upon with both ambivalence and some envy by Northern European societies.

International mobility is matched by internal mobility. Between 1950 and 2000, the South's share of the population increased from 31 to 36 percent, and the West increased from 13 percent to 22 percent. Meanwhile, despite overall population growth in each of the past five decades, the Midwest's share of total population fell from 29 to 23 percent and the Northeast's proportion declined from 26 percent to 19 percent.

THE REAL CITY = THE WHOLE METRO AREA

America is also among the world's most urbanized countries. In 1950, slightly over half of the U.S. population (84 million, or 56 percent) lived in 168 metropolitan areas. By 2000, the number of metro areas (331) had almost doubled, containing 226 million, or over 80 percent of the total population.

An even higher proportion of the nation's economy is generated within metropolitan areas. Some 43 percent of the United States' 3.5 million square miles may be devoted to farming, but farming only accounts for less than 3 percent of the labor force and barely 1 percent of gross domestic product (though 10 percent of American exports). By contrast, economic activity carried out within the sixty-one thousand square miles of urbanized land within metro areas (less than 2 percent of the United States' land area) accounts for almost 85 percent of gross domestic product.

In effect, the real "city" is now the entire metropolitan area—the traditional central city and its suburbs. That is the relevant economic, social, and cultural unit—a fact too often ignored by some American but particularly by many European politicians and scholars with their emotional and political focus on the historic core cities.[4]

Though the origins of suburbanization lie decades earlier, the last five decades have seen the constant suburbanization of America's cities. In 1950 the Census Bureau identified 157 "urbanized areas" (the central city and its contiguous suburbs). Overall density (city and suburb combined) was 5,391 persons per square mile. By 2000, the density of the same 157 urbanized areas had declined by 45 percent to 2,949 persons per square mile. In fact, overall density declined in all but nine of the 157 urbanized areas.[5] America's urban areas sprawled outward (becoming less compact), instead of growing upward (becoming more compact).

ELASTIC VS. INELASTIC CITIES

What happened to the cities in the Age of Sprawl? Let us imagine the following conversation. You are the mayor of a large American city in 1950. You call in your planning director and say, "I want you to give me a policy that will guarantee that our city continues to grow in population over the coming decades." With perfect foresight (which all planning directors have), the planning director would respond, "Well, Mayor, there are only three things that we can do. We can acquire more land, more Hispanic immigrants, or more college students." Those three, in effect, were the only conditions under which American cities would gain population over the next fifty years.

Almost 80 percent of 521 central cities[6] added more land. Between 1950 and 2000, these cities overall grew from 10,389 square miles to 30,710 square miles through either annexation (15,275 square miles) or city-county consolidation (5,046 square miles). Cities that expanded their boundaries through annexation (like Houston, Texas and Phoenix, Arizona) or through city-county consolidation (like Nashville-Davidson County or Indianapolis-Marion County) were what I have called *elastic cities*.[7] Elastic cities defended themselves against suburban sprawl by capturing a substantial share of new residential, commercial, and industrial development. By contrast, other cities entered the postwar era already densely populated and unable to expand their boundaries at all. New York, Detroit, Baltimore, Cleveland, and Washington, D.C. fell into this category. These *inelastic cities* could not defend themselves against suburban sprawl. They not only did not capture their share of new growth; they contributed to suburban expansion. Inelastic cities steadily lost middle-class households, retail stores, offices, and factories to their new suburbs. Despite the revival of many downtown business districts and regentrification of some historic neighborhoods in the 1980s and 1990s, more and more inelastic city neighborhoods became warehouses for the region's poor, particularly blacks and Hispanics.

The 2000 Census has been greeted as evidence that the decades-long decline of many cities has ended. Even the Census Bureau itself noted that eight of the United States' ten largest cities gained population for the first time since the 1950 census. But that is misleading, as Table 2.1 shows. The list of the ten largest cities in 2000 is not the same list that it was in 1950. Dropping down the list were inelastic Philadelphia (from 3rd to 5th) and Detroit (from 5th to 10th). Dropping completely off the list were inelastic Baltimore (from 6th to 17th), Cleveland (from 7th to 33rd), St Louis (from 8th to 50th!), Washington, D.C. (from 9th to 21st), and Boston (from 10th to 20th). All but Boston lost substantial population during the 1990s.

Their places were taken by highly elastic Houston (which expanded from 160 sq. mi. in 1950 to 579 sq. mi. by 1990), Phoenix (from 17 sq. mi. to 475 sq. mi.), San Diego (from 99 sq. mi. to 324 sq. mi.), Dallas (from 112 sq. mi. to 342 sq. mi.), and San Antonio (from 69 sq. mi. to 408 sq. mi.). Houston, Phoenix, and San Antonio continued to annex more land during the 1990s, and all received many more Hispanic immigrants.

Immigration drove the population upward in low-elastic Los Angeles, and zero-elastic New York City and Chicago. Indeed, Asian and Hispanic immigration accounted for all their population growth in the 1990s as these cities continued to lose white, native-born residents (and some suburbanizing African Americans as well).

In effect, what the 2000 Census illustrates is the continuing validity of that mythical planning director's observation: to gain population a city must acquire more land, more Hispanic immigrants, or more college students.[8]

CONCENTRATED POVERTY

Concentrated poverty is urban America's core problem—both socially and geographically. Concentrated poverty creates push-pull factors. Push factors—high crime rates, failing schools, falling property values, often higher tax rates—push middle class families out of poverty-impacted neighborhoods in central cities and many older suburbs. Pull factors—safer neighborhoods, better schools, rising home values, often lower tax rates—pull such families to newer suburban areas.

It is not any superior virtue of suburban governments that is responsible for suburban pull factors. Pull factors simply reflect the fact that most suburbs are low-poverty areas. Indeed, they were designed that way. Both push

Table 2.1. Population Ranking of the Ten Largest U.S.A. Cities in 1950 and 2000

	1950			2000		1990-2000
Rank	City	Population	Rank	City	Population	% Population Change
1	New York, NY	7,891,957	1	New York NY	8,008,278	9.4
2	Chicago IL	3,620,962	2	Los Angeles CA	3,694,820	6.0
3	Philadelphia PA	2,071,605	3	Chicago IL	2,896,016	4.0
4	Los Angeles CA	1,970,358	4	Houston TX	1,953,631	19.8
5	Detroit MI	1,849,568	5	Philadelphia PA	1,517,550	-4.3
6	Baltimore MD	949,708	6	Phoenix AZ	1,321,045	34.3
7	Cleveland OH	914,808	7	San Diego CA	1,223,400	10.2
8	St Louis MO	856,796	8	Dallas TX	1,188,580	18.0
9	Washington DC	802,178	9	San Antonio TX	1,144,646	22.3
10	Boston MA	801,444	10	Detroit MI	951,270	-7.5
14	Houston TX	596,163	17	Baltimore MD	651,154	-11.5
22	Dallas TX	434,462	20	Boston MA	589,141	2.6
25	San Antonio TX	408,442	21	Washington DC	572,059	-5.7
31	San Diego CA	334,387	33	Cleveland OH	478,403	-5.4
nr	Phoenix AZ	16,790	50	St Louis MO	348,189	-12.2

Source: U.S. Bureau of the Census (1950 and 2000).

and pull factors are largely opposite sides of the same coin—the concentration of poverty.

Concentrated poverty is not "color-blind." Nationally, almost twice as many residents of our metro areas are poor and white as those who are poor and black or poor and Hispanic. Yet poor whites rarely live in poor neighborhoods (where poverty rates exceed 20 percent). Only one quarter of poor whites live in slums; three quarters live in working class or middle class neighborhoods scattered all over our metropolitan areas. By contrast, half of poor Hispanics and three quarters of poor blacks live in poor ghettos and barrios in cities and inner suburbs.

What does this mean? For one thing, if you are poor and white, the odds are three out of four that at your neighborhood school your own children's classmates will be primarily middle-class children. If you are poor and black, the odds are three out of four that your own children will be surrounded by other poor school children. The socioeconomic backgrounds of a child's family *and of a child's classmates* are the strongest influences shaping school outcomes.

JIM CROW BY RACE–JIM CROW BY INCOME

Using a common dissimilarity index (100 = total segregation), Table 2.2 ranks the nation's sixty largest metro areas by black residential segregation in 2000 (column B). The level of housing segregation of African Americans declined in all but the New York City area from earlier levels. Overall, for thirty-seven regions with both 1970 and 2000 data available, the mean racial segregation level declined from 80 (very high) to 67 (high). In general, Southern and Western regions made progress about 50 percent faster than did Northeastern and Midwestern regions (though the latter picked up the pace in the 1990s, while Southern progress slowed).

For Hispanics, residential segregation increased from an average index of 41 in 1980 to an average index of 47 in 2000. During these two decades the Hispanic population of the United States more than doubled. Increased residential segregation, in part, reflects the traditional "ponding" together of newly arrived immigrants for mutual aid and support. Historically, such immigrant neighborhoods have been a transitional phenomenon as second- and third-generation, hyphenated-Americans move steadily into the mainstream. In such a fashion several older, formerly industrial regions with little job growth to attract new immigrants (such as Cincinnati, Dayton, and Rochester) saw their small Hispanic populations steadily move out of the barrio. Elsewhere, however, under the pressure of new immigration, the barrio expanded rapidly. However, even by 2000, average Hispanic segregation indices remained about 20 points below black levels.[9]

Table 2.2. 60 Largest U.S.A. Metropolitan Areas (More than 750,000 Residents) Ranked by Black Residential Segregation from Highest to Lowest in 2000 (100 = Total Segregation)

	Segregation Indices					
	Black		Hispanic		Economic	
	A	B	C	D	E	F
Metro Area	1970	2000	1980	2000	1970	1990
Milwaukee WI	91	82	55	60	39	55
Hartford CT	83	65	66	64	39	53
Anaheim-Santa Ana CA	46[a]	37	43	56	23	35
Buffalo NY	87	79	48	56	33	45
Detroit MI	88	85	41	46	39	50
New Haven CT	70[a]	69	59	55	36	46
Philadelphia PA-NJ	80	72	63	60	38	48
Rochester NY	73	66	56	54	33	42
Albany-Schenectady-Troy NY	64[a]	61	34	41	27	35
San Diego CA	64[a]	54	42	51	24	32
Chicago IL	92	81	64	62	42	50
Cleveland OH	91	80	58	58	43	51
Birmingham AL	76[a]	73	36	48	29	36
Dayton-Springfield OH	78[a]	70	29	27	33	40
Providence RI	73[a]	59	50	68	30	36
Boston MA	81	66	55	59	31	37
Newark NJ	81	80	67	65	42	48
Baltimore MD	82	68	35	36	40	46
Indianapolis IN	82	71	29	44	34	40
Cincinnati OH-KY-IN	77	75	31	30	37	43
Minneapolis-St. Paul MN	69	58	37	47	35	40
Richmond VA	65[a]	57	36	41	39	44
Columbus OH	82	63	28	38	39	44
St. Louis MO-IL	85	74	29	29	39	44
New York NY	81	82	65	67	38	43
Sacramento CA	59[a]	56	35	38	27	31
Austin TX	65[a]	52	46	46	34	38
Kansas City MO-KS	87	69	41	46	36	40
Los Angeles CA	91	68	57	63	31	35
Pittsburgh PA	75	67	30	30	30	34
Riverside-San Bernardino CA	55[a]	46	39	43	22[a]	25
Salt Lake City-Ogden UT	56[a]	37	35	43	27	30
Oakland CA	80	63	37	47	33	36
Denver CO	69[a]	62	49	50	36	39
Nassau-Suffolk NY	78[a]	74	37	47	27	30
Seattle WA	68[a]	50	20	43	27	30
Tampa-St. Petersburg FL	80[a]	64	51	45	28	31
San Francisco CA	80	61	46	54	33	36
Norfolk-Virginia Beach-Newport News VA	76	46	30	32	35	37
Portland OR	81	48	22	35	25	27

(continued)

TABLE 2.2 *Continued*

	Black		Hispanic		Economic	
	A	B	C	D	E	F
Metro Area	1970	2000	1980	2000	1970	1990
Fort Lauderdale FL	84[a]	62	28	32	30	32
San Jose CA	49[a]	41	46	52	29	31
Phoenix AZ	62[a]	44	53	53	36	37
Louisville KY-IN	72	64	26	36	38	39
Washington DC-MD-VA	81	63	33	48	37	38
Atlanta GA	82	66	31	52	40	40
Las Vegas NV	64[a]	43	23	43	30	29
West Palm Beach FL	84[a]	67	45	43	35	34
Greensboro-Winston-Salem NC	65	59	33	51	30	29
Dallas-Ft Worth TX	87	59	49	54	38	37
Houston TX	78	67	50	56	37	36
Memphis TN-AR-MS	76	69	42	48	44	43
San Antonio TX	77	50	58	51	39	38
Miami FL	85	74	53	44	33	31
Oklahoma City OK	90	54	29	44	36	33
New Orleans LA	73	69	27	36	41	38
Nashville TN	65	57	23	46	37	33
Jacksonville FL	69[a]	54	22	26	37	33
Orlando FL	74[a]	57	31	41	33	27
Charlotte NC-SC	67	55	32	50	38	32
Averages	80*	67*	41	47	34	38

Sources: Racial segregation indices: (1970 data) Douglas S. Massey and Nancy A. Denton, *American Apartheid: Segregation and the Making of the Underclass* (Cambridge, MA: Harvard University Press, 1993); and author's calculations;. (1980 and 2000 data) Lewis Mumford Center for Comparative and Regional Research at the State University of New York at Albany, (http://www.albany.edu/mumford/).

Economic segregation indices: Peter A. Tatian and Alisa Wilson, *Segregation of the Poor in U.S. Metropolitan Areas*, Neighborhood Change in Urban America Research Series (Washington, D.C.,: The Urban Institute, forthcoming).

Notes: [a]Data for 1980; *Averages for only 37 metro areas with both 1970 and 2000 black segregation indices available.

Columns E and F track changes in economic segregation, using the same scale (100 = total segregation). By contrast with segregation trends for African Americans, from 1970 to 2000, economic segregation increased in 34 of the 60 metro areas.[10] The Milwaukee region (55) was the most economically segregated; the Riverside-San Bernadino CA (25) was the least segregated.

Why were economic segregation indices (averaging 37 in 2000) so much lower than either Hispanic indices (47) or Black indices (67)? The answer is already provided above. Poor whites are usually not isolated in slum neighborhoods. In general, the higher the proportion of a region's poor that are white, the lower the economic segregation index (e.g. Portland, Seattle, Salt

Lake City-Ogden). Conversely, racial segregation and economic segregation are highly correlated. The most racially segregated metro areas are also the most economically segregated metro areas.

Beginning in the 1920s but accelerating dramatically during World War II and the immediate postwar years, the Great Migration was carrying millions of African Americans out of the rural South and into Southern and, especially, Northern cities. In one sense, American blacks—almost all of whom could trace their roots in America back to the seventeenth and eighteenth centuries—were a new wave of immigrants into America's cities. However, no immigrant group ever experienced the degree of isolation from white society that was imposed on African Americans. Unparalleled levels of racial segregation were the result of deliberate public policies that implemented (and reinforced) private racism. Beyond the South's Jim Crow laws, Northern apartheid was created de facto by

- city zoning codes that set up neighborhoods restricted to different racial groups (not outlawed by the U.S. Supreme Court until 1917);
- racially restrictive deed covenants (finally declared unenforceable by the Supreme Court in 1948);[11]
- banks' refusing to make mortgage loans for black or integrated neighborhoods ("red-lining") in compliance with official Federal Housing Administration policies (until the mid-1960s);
- the threat by Boards of Realtors to revoke realtors' licenses if they tried to sell blacks homes in white neighborhoods;[12]
- legally segregated public housing projects (until the mid-1960s);
- more recently, the implicit bias that poor blacks (mostly city dwellers) are generally offered space in large public housing projects (built and run by city public housing authorities) while poor whites (mostly suburbanites) receive rent vouchers from suburban housing assistance agencies (that never built big projects); and,
- of course, many acts of intimidation, even violence, against blacks who tried to integrate white neighborhoods while city officials and local police turned a blind eye to such outrages (or even sometimes arrested the victims for "disturbing the peace").

Since the civil rights revolution, the systems of legally sanctioned discrimination and segregation have been dismantled. More subtle discriminatory practices remain (racial steering by some real estate agents, for example) but are slowly dying out.

In their place, however, economically discriminatory practices continue to thrive with significant adverse racial and ethnic impacts. Most important is the widespread practice of *exclusionary zoning*. Through requiring large minimum lot sizes for homes or outright banning mobile home parks and multi-family apartments, local governments try to exclude low- and modest-income families from their communities. Jim Crow by income is replacing Jim Crow by race.

CHANGING THE RULES OF THE GAME: REGIONAL MIXED-INCOME HOUSING

The central issue of American metro areas is always "what gets built where for whose benefit." Anthony Downs summarizes the prevailing vision of metropolitan development as dominated by universal ownership of a single-family, detached house in a small, self-governing community distant from the workplace; universal car ownership; and a workplace in a low-rise, park-like setting with immediately adjacent parking.[13] It is a vision that, in many respects, has been substantially achieved.

- Since mid-century, home ownership has risen from 40 percent to over 65 percent.
- In 1950, 60 percent of the nation's metropolitan population resided in just 193 large central cities. By 2000, almost 70 percent of the residents of the same 168 major metropolitan regions lived in about 9,600 smaller suburban cities, villages, townships, and counties.
- By 2001, 91 percent of all households owned at least one vehicle; 20 percent owned three or more cars, trucks, and minivans.
- Suburban job locations: over 55 percent of all jobs are now located, separated from residential subdivisions, in suburbs outside central cities.

This vision of metropolitan development has always made no room for poor people. For decades the nation's acknowledged low-income housing policy was to concentrate the poor in massive public housing projects in the cities. The unacknowledged national low-income housing policy was to rely on systematic devaluation of older, "hand-me-down" housing in inner-city and many inner-suburban neighborhoods. Conforming to widespread exclusionary zoning, private, for-profit homebuilders concentrated first on middle-income housing (the postwar suburban boom) and, in more recent years, on higher-end housing. (What gets built where for whose benefit?)

Rolling back the racially skewed concentration of poverty requires changing the "rules of the game" in our regional housing markets. Two such rules are crucial: federal public housing policy and local exclusionary zoning policies.

HOPE VI: TRANSFORMING PUBLIC HOUSING

For several decades federal public housing policy was the greatest mechanism of economic segregation in America's metropolitan areas. Almost all census tracts with greater than 40 percent poverty rates had large federal public housing projects in or next to them or heavy concentrations of voucher-subsidized rentals. Typically, poor whites, using rent vouchers, were widely dispersed; poor blacks were heavily concentrated in large public housing projects in inner city ghettos.

In the 1990s HUD began to change the "rules of the game" for public housing. With HOPE VI grants, local housing authorities knock down the worst projects and replace them with attractive townhouses and garden apartments. However, the social changes are more important than the physical improvements, for these are mixed-income communities. Typically, only one-third to one-half of new residents are former project housing tenants; the others are working-class/middle-class renters and homeowners. HOPE VI is restoring economic diversity to many of the highest poverty neighborhoods.[14]

Where HOPE VI grants recast high-poverty projects as mixed-income communities, the 2000 Census revealed a remarkable reduction in the concentration of poverty in some central city neighborhoods. "We were the problem in many neighborhoods," one public housing authority official stated. And, indeed, thinning out the concentration of poverty has sparked a dramatic revival of private, market rate construction in places like Southeast Washington, D.C., and South-of-the-Loop Chicago.

FROM EXCLUSIONARY ZONING TO INCLUSIONARY ZONING

I mentioned earlier the widespread practice of *exclusionary zoning* that prevents low-income housing from being built in many suburban communities. In over 130 American communities (with almost 5 percent of the nation's population), local governments practice the reverse—*inclusionary zoning*. They require including a modest proportion of low- and moderate-income housing in new construction—typically 10 or 15 percent. A few, such as Montgomery County, Maryland, direct their public housing authorities to acquire a proportion of the affordable units.

Is such an inclusionary zoning law too modest to have an impact on the scale and intensity of poverty in declining urban neighborhoods? A little bit of everything built goes a long way. The six-county Chicago area, for example, is one of the United States' five most racially and economically segregated metropolitan areas. From 1970 to 1998, homebuilders built 1.8 million new homes and apartments. A Montgomery County-type, inclusionary zoning policy for all of the Chicago region's six counties and 265 municipalities would have produced 45,000 scattered site units owned by public housing authorities in low-poverty areas.

Owning 80 percent of the 45,000 new homes, the Chicago Housing Authority (CHA) could have torn down all 24,000 units in its notorious, high-rise projects like Robert Taylor Homes and Cabrini-Greene, replaced them with mixed-income townhouses and garden apartments with no more than 25 percent very low-income families as tenants, relocated 18,000 families into CHA-owned units scattered in low-poverty subdivisions throughout the region, and still had another 18,000 units to help reduce its long waiting list. In fact, using just half the 45,000 units could have brought the poverty rate below 40 percent in all of the region's 183 high-poverty census tracts!

Similarly, a regional inclusionary zoning policy would have lowered metro Atlanta's 103 or metro Charlotte's 40 poverty-impacted tracts below a 20 percent poverty rate. With a regional inclusionary zoning policy, no neighborhood in the Seattle, Portland, Minneapolis-St. Paul, or Washington, D.C. regions would have a poverty rate above 15 percent. Every neighborhood school would be majority middle-class!

Urban poverty appears so insurmountable (a) because of the high degree of concentration in inner city neighborhoods (and some older suburbs) and (b) because the broad, middle class, regional society exempts itself from being part of the solution. Yet just a modest proportion of new housing construction everywhere is all that is necessary to mainstream poor minorities in small proportions just as most poor whites are already mainstreamed.

Concentrated poverty exacts a high price—most cruelly through under-educating many poor children well below their potential. For thirty-five years American researchers have consistently found (1) that parents' income and educational attainment are the most powerful predictors of a child's success or failure in school and (2) that poor children's performance in school improves substantially when they attend middle-class schools—and preferably live in middle-class neighborhoods as well.

The issue is not how much money is spent; because of compensatory federal and state aid, many low-income schools often spend more per pupil than middle class schools. The difference is the influence of the child's classmates and playmates. With neighborhood schools, where you live largely shapes your educational opportunity. *Housing policy is school policy.*

Inclusionary zoning as practiced best by Montgomery County is the only housing policy I've found that guarantees that poor children will attend middle-class neighborhood schools. In the United States we may never eliminate poverty, but through inclusionary zoning we can eliminate *concentrated poverty.*

CHANGING THE RULES OF THE GAME:
REGIONAL LAND USE PLANNING

What gets built where for whose benefit? Suburbanization has occurred around all cities, but the movement began earlier and was more extensive in the United States. After World War II, underlying conditions made greater suburbanization inevitable in the United States as compared with Europe.

Pietro Nivola highlights four fundamental differences between America and Europe.[15] America has much more land, much faster population growth, and a more diverse population than European nations, as well as much more rapid mass diffusion of major technological changes, such as the automobile and air conditioning.

America's metropolitan development patterns are not the result of pure "free market" forces. "Actions of government, sometimes intentionally, often not, have supplied additional stimulus for the unbounded extension of suburbia," Nivola notes.[16]

Differences in the "laws of the landscape" that shape American and European cities go far beyond obvious differences in land use planning regimes. Among major public policy interventions Nivola highlights that shape European and American cities differently are

- America's self-financing, semi-autonomous, federal Highway Trust Fund that has led to 85 percent of all federal surface transportation monies being devoted to roads and highways (that support sprawling suburbs). In Europe, highway appropriations must compete with other fiscal needs, and rail and mass transit (which support denser cities) receive from 40 to 60 percent of all surface transportation funds.
- America's low gas prices promote much greater use of cars and hence facilitate lower-density development than do Europe's high gas prices. With the production cost averaging about $1 a gallon in both America and Europe, the difference is taxes. In 1996, U.S. taxes averaged 42 cents a gallon; in Europe, taxes ranged from $2.27 a gallon (Spain) to $3.54 a gallon (France).
- America's cut-rate furnace fuel and electricity costs promote large, detached homes and large home appliances (such as refrigerators and freezers that substitute for near-at-hand neighborhood shops in many European cities). European householders face home energy bills that average almost twice as high as their American counterparts—despite Europeans' smaller, less air-conditioned homes.
- In post-war America the federal government funneled money into the cities to build public housing for the poor and guaranteed the low-cost mortgages that fueled the building boom of middle-income suburban housing. Rebounding from wartime devastation, European governments financed much more "social housing" for a wider range of income groups, scattering such projects in outer areas as well as in cities.
- America primarily taxes income (at federal and state levels) and property (at local levels); Europe primarily taxes consumption of goods and

services. Such differences impact land use. European taxes that penalize using energy and buying large household appliances and automobiles promote space-saving life styles.[17] Conversely, American taxes that bear down on income and savings (that is, taxes on interest and dividends) but reward consumption (such as the mortgage interest deduction) promote buying roomy dwellings stuffed with household paraphernalia.

- Average European agricultural subsidies are a dozen times higher per acre than American agricultural subsidies. European farmers find growing crops more profitable than "growing houses."
- With restrictive anti-competition statutes and onerous labor mandates, European laws often favor small, family-run stores over American-style "superstores." Though American-style malls are making headway, Europe's protective regulatory regimes have slowed the process and helped sustain the small shops of older urban neighborhoods.

Many Americans would be very reluctant to embrace high gas prices, or higher fuel and electricity costs, or a ten-fold increase in farm subsidies, or added government regulations reducing retail choice and price competition. Yet changing some of America's "rules of the game" would curb the worst excesses of America's sprawling development patterns and produce much greater balance and equity in urban society.

FEDERAL RULES OF THE GAME: LAND DEVELOPMENT

To understand America's "rules of the game," one must first understand the structure of government in this continental nation.[18] American government is not a simple hierarchy of authority from national to state to local level. It is a federal system in which the federal (or continental) government has only the powers that are explicitly conferred upon it by the federal constitution as amended periodically (only 27 times in 215 years) or interpreted by the U.S. Supreme Court.[19] The American constitution is silent on the question of local government. Therefore, under the tenth amendment, all power over how local governments are organized and what they are authorized to do is reserved to state governments. Municipal and county governments (as well as independent public school boards, etc.) are literally "creatures" of state government.

Therefore, the federal government has no direct, formal jurisdiction over state and local land use planning and zoning powers. The United States Congress has no more formal role in land use planning with regard to state governments than the Parliament of the European Union or its other political bodies currently have with regard to European member states.

In reality, though, the federal government has had a huge impact on urban development through its capital expenditures, housing finance role, tax policies, and environmental regulations. All these are among the "rules of the game" and add up not to a national urban policy but to a national *suburban* policy. These have included

- Federally guaranteed, low-cost mortgages for homeowners and the federally-organized, secondary mortgage market, both of which, for several decades, explicitly favored new, owner-occupied, suburban housing even over older, owner-occupied, city-located housing. The federal government's housing finance policies now provide about forty times more support for owner-occupied housing (located primarily in suburbs) than for renter-occupied housing (located primarily in cities);
- Pro-homeowner tax policies: Through allowing deduction of mortgage interest and local property taxes against federal income tax liability, the federal government provides about eleven times more tax incentives for individual homeowners than it provides for apartment landlords.
- Massive highway subsidies: In building the Interstate Highway System, the federal government promoted a vast decentralization of America's urban centers. From 1956 onward, suburb-inducing highway subsidies were about eight times greater than city-supporting mass transit subsidies.
- Anti-city environmental protection laws: Federal money to build new sewage treatment plants subsidized suburban growth. Federal regulation of air pollution initially restricted regional industry growth (though it may now have some effect on reducing dependence on automobiles). Strict federal controls on abandoned factory sites ("brownfields") severely hampered cities' ability to compete with suburban "greenfield" sites as locations for new industries.

In short, the federal government may not have a land use planning agency, but federal "rules of the game" shape land development as surely as, if less visibly than, if our government were issuing European-style national planning directives.

STATE RULES OF THE GAME: LAND DEVELOPMENT

The State [i.e., state government] . . . at its pleasure may modify or withdraw all [city] powers, may take without compensation [city] property, hold it itself, or vest it in other agencies, expand or contract the territorial areas, unite the whole or a part of it with another municipality, repeal the charter and destroy the [municipal] corporation. All this may be done, conditionally or unconditionally, with or without the consent of the citizens, or even against their protest. In all these respects the State is supreme, and its legislative body, conforming its action to the state constitution, may do so as it will, unrestrained by any provision of the Constitution of the United States.

- U.S. Supreme Court decision in *Hunter v. City of Pittsburgh* (1907)

Ultimately, state governments—state legislatures, governors and executive agencies, state courts—control the "rules of the game" at both state government and local government levels. Thus, the United States, in theory, has fifty different land use policies among the fifty different states just as, at present, the European Union has twenty-five different land use policies among its twenty-five member states.

In reality, there are four broad categories into which state governments' impact on land development falls: (a) state planning and investment in roads, highways, and other public works; (b) annexation powers for local governments, (c) planning and zoning powers delegated to local governments by state laws, and (d) tax policies for local governments (discussed in the next section).

State transportation policy: State highway departments have been the federal government's partners in building the nation's road and highway system. In 1996, for example, state highway departments spent $57 billion from gasoline taxes—both their share *and* the federal government's that they received as federal grants-in-aid for highway construction. (Local governments spent about $37 billion on local roads and streets.) The broad outlines (and substantial details) of America's suburbanization were decided not by professional urban planners nor by local elected officials but by federal and state highway engineers. It was not until the Congress enacted the federal Intermodal Surface Transportation Efficiency Act of 1991 (called "ice tea") that local governments achieved real influence over major transportation planning.

State annexation laws: State annexation laws determined whether or not city governments would be able to defend themselves against the consequences of urban sprawl (in part, created by state highway departments) by expanding their boundaries to capture their share of the new development. In the Age of Sprawl, whether or not a city could annex new development— that is, could be "elastic" by expanding its boundaries—would have a crucial impact on its future social, economic, and fiscal health.

In general, during the past fifty years, annexation was impossible in New England, New York, New Jersey, and Pennsylvania. Northeastern states were entirely divided up into municipalities with no unincorporated land. Though having the constitutional power, their legislatures lacked the political will to merge municipalities or allow larger cities to annex parts of smaller municipalities. Annexation was difficult in Midwest states that were completely divided into townships. Annexation rarely happened in strong township states (e.g., Michigan), but generally occurred in weak township states (e.g., Indiana, Illinois). Annexation was relatively easy in Southern and Western states where municipalities were surrounded by unincorporated land.

However, by 2000, it is increasingly clear that the highway system is decentralizing urban areas so rapidly that even the most annexation-minded cities cannot keep pace. In the long run, it is better to control sprawl than for a city to try to simply capture its share through annexation. A city should annex what it can when it can. But without strong, regional, anti-sprawl, land use controls, central cities are competing in a game that they cannot win solely by annexation.

State municipal planning laws: Unlike some European governments, no American state government has enacted a statewide land use plan. (New Jersey's weak, voluntary plan does not qualify.) However, every state has enacted general laws authorizing local government to regulate land development. Most state municipal land use codes are remarkably similar. The typical state municipal planning code authorizes a municipality to "protect the public health, welfare, and safety" of its residents (the so-called "police powers") through regulating land use. Municipalities are to establish a general comprehensive plan and adopt a zoning map to implement the plan.[20] Typically, planning and zoning seek to segregate land uses—residential neighborhoods separated from retail stores as well as from office and industrial parks, single family homes separated from apartments, etc. Often this "Euclidean" zoning (named after the U.S. Supreme Court case, not the ancient Greek who was the "Father of Geometry") is further overlaid by standard street design codes, standard sidewalk design codes, etc. (These also are based on voluntary national model codes promulgated by private, national associations.[21])

The critical need is not to create new regulatory tools for local governments to use. Except in Dillon's Rule states (where all local government powers depend on explicit legislative delegation), most state laws endow local governments with a broad range of land use powers for use *within* their jurisdictional boundaries. The gap to be filled is that there are relatively few states that require collaborative planning *among* different local jurisdictions.

Forging joint land use plans has been less daunting in some Sun Belt regions with relatively few local governments and where "elastic" cities plan for and annex most new suburban development. In regions like Albuquerque, Charlotte, and Tallahassee, reaching bi-lateral agreement between city and county (covering unincorporated areas) is sufficient. But even for these examples (and for formally consolidated city-county governments like Indianapolis, Jacksonville, and Nashville) development has sprawled into adjacent counties in the 1990s, requiring core governments to pursue hard-to-achieve voluntary compacts with neighbors.

As a practical matter, forging binding, multi-governmental land use compacts is virtually impossible in the Northeast and Middle West where cities are surrounded by scores (even hundreds) of independent suburban cities, villages, towns, and townships. They must be required to collaborate. Without a multi-billion dollar federal land use planning grant-in-aid to which federal strings requiring multi-jurisdictional planning can be attached, only state legislatures (or state courts) can require local intergovernmental collaboration.Over the last three decades, twelve states have enacted statewide growth management laws.[22] They range from strong state mandates for local government, like Oregon's, to incentive-based systems for regional planning, like Maryland's. Even in these twelve states, state bureaucrats are not drawing up local land use plans. The state growth management laws simply require local governments to plan together.

REGIONAL LAND USE REFORM: SUMMING UP

In recent years, there has been a flurry of growth management legislation introduced in state legislatures. Maryland enacted its Smart Growth plan, Tennessee passed an Oregon-type land use law (without Oregon's more stringent state standards), and Georgia set up the Georgia Regional Transportation Authority for Greater Atlanta. The Utah legislature established a state study commission on sprawl. Anti-sprawl legislation has been introduced in the Ohio, Michigan, and Missouri (St. Louis only) legislatures. A much watered-down land use reform bill passed the Pennsylvania General Assembly. At the polls several California communities adopted strong, anti-sprawl initiatives.

Such regulatory approaches have been paralleled by approval of open space and farmland preservation bonds. New Jersey's $1 billion, ten-year plan is most notable. Voters across the country have approved over 70 percent of ballot measures, authorizing billions of tax dollars for land acquisition.

If there has not been a tidal wave of land use reform laws, there has been steady progress. To paraphrase the late Senator Everett Dirksen, "a state here and a state there and pretty soon you're talking about real reform."

CHANGING THE RULES OF THE GAME:
REGIONAL TAX BASE SHARING

What gets built where for whose benefit? Uneven commercial development and economically segregated housing patterns, not allegedly incompetent city bureaucrats and spendthrift politicians, are the roots of wide fiscal disparities among local governments. However, by contrast with Europe where

many national treasuries heavily subsidize local governments, American reliance on local taxation exacerbates fiscal disparities.[23]

About 77 percent of municipal government budgets in the United States
come from local taxes and fees; state governments provide 16 percent; and
the federal government provides just 7 percent (always for specified programs and purposes). However, in an important respect, American municipalities do not control 77 percent of their own fiscal destinies. The specific
taxes they can levy (and some times the fees they can charge for services)
depend on what state legislatures authorize municipalities to do.

A thorough study of eighty-six major American cities showed that they received only 10 percent of their revenues from income or payroll taxes; 17
percent from general sales taxes; 20 percent from a variety of miscellaneous
taxes; and 53 percent from property taxes.[24]

But the averages understated the importance of property taxes. All eighty-
six cities surveyed depended heavily on property taxes for from 23 percent
to 82 percent of tax revenues, and that has major implications for land development.

> With each of the myriad municipalities, towns, and counties in the typical U.S.
> metropolis largely forced to fend for itself, many resort to competitive strategies
> aimed at controlling the demand for services and bolstering the local economic
> base. Land use regulations that maintain low residential densities limit the num-
> ber of households requiring public services. By raising the per-unit cost of hous-
> ing, these regulations can also prevent the entry of low- and moderate-income
> households who typically contribute less in taxes than they cost in services. The
> exclusionary zoning renders any relocation of inner-city residents to the suburbs
> all the more difficult.
>
>   At the same time, localities often jockey for business investment, each seek-
> ing to beat their neighbors' base of taxable commercial property that in the
> long run is supposed to lighten the tax rate on homeowners. The competition
> can turn into something like a bidding war, as the parties tender "incentives"
> to attract the latest superstore, office park, or sports arena. In this contest, the
> central cities often find themselves at a disadvantage. Straining from the fiscal
> drain of their large, low-income enclaves, many can ill-afford the tax abate-
> ments, cheap land clearance, and other attractions that suburban counties and
> townships can offer developers.[25]

This is a perfect description of the property tax-dependence effects in "little boxes" regions. The effects are somewhat ameliorated in "Big Box"
regions where cities will annex most new development that occurs in unincorporated areas near their city limits.[26] (Many annexations occur before
new development as cities pledge to provide the utilities and other services
that make such development possible in the first place.) Newly annexed areas still remain under the county government's jurisdiction. County govern-

ment will still collect taxes, but will be relieved by the cities of providing many municipal-type services to the new sub-divisions, shopping centers, office and industrial parks.

Moving poor people to communities of opportunities through regional fair share housing is far more effective than trying to help them by moving more money into poverty-impacted communities. Sharing a modest portion of the growth in regional tax base merely ameliorates the fiscal burden that poverty-impacted jurisdictions must carry. More money does not change the destructive impact of concentrated poverty.

However, regional tax base sharing is an excellent issue around which to organize political coalitions since two-thirds to three-quarters of a region's localities will typically be net recipients of any tax base-sharing plan. And tax base-sharing can be the fiscal glue that helps bind local communities together in a region-wide land use plan. If all will benefit from wherever new development occurs, it is less painful to be designated a non-growth area. Earmarking a portion of the tax base-sharing funds can also finance buying up a portion of "fair share" housing for use by a region's poorest households.

Only state legislatures can create significant regional tax base-sharing plans. The nation's most extensive *voluntary* plan, the Dayton area's ED/GE program, results in only about $600,000 a year of shared revenues among the thirty local governments that signed on. That is about $1 per year per resident of the Dayton region. By contrast, the *mandatory* Twin Cities Fiscal Disparities Plan now shares about $175 per year per resident of the Twin Cities region.

CHANGING THE RULES OF THE GAME: BUILDING COALITIONS

To change the rules of the game, reformers' central challenge is not deciding what to do but how to do it. How can a broad-based coalition of interests be organized to secure new state laws to combat

- concentrated poverty and economic segregation through requiring regional fair share low- and moderate income housing;
- urban sprawl through requiring regional growth management; and
- fiscal disparities through requiring regional tax base sharing?

As I have argued, fair share housing would have the greatest impact. It is also the most daunting political challenge. By the calculus of pure political self-interest, tax base sharing might be easiest to achieve, but it has a minor impact on a region's core issues. I believe that securing state growth management laws is the most attainable reform target. (Every state growth management law I have reviewed has a fair-share housing goal on which to build later reforms.)

Anger and frustration over escalating traffic congestion in suburbia is fueling the nation's current anti-sprawl mood. Low density of people leads to high density of cars. The most common responses are to build even more highways and to restrict growth through allowing only large-lot new homes. Both "solutions" will compound the problems. And both will exacerbate social exclusion. "Social equity" is just beginning to edge onto the agenda of growth management advocates and is certainly not a widely shared concern.

Land use reformers, however, must find new allies to achieve the critical mass necessary. Environmental activists and farmland preservationists have traditionally championed growth management laws. (Farmers are ambivalent. Farm Bureau leaders say, "Save our farms." Many farmers say, "My land is *my* land. Don't mess with my right to 'grow houses' if I choose.")

New allies are emerging. They include

- business leaders and leadership groups like Chicago Metropolis 2020, the Silicon Valley Manufacturers Group, and the Greater Baltimore Committee;
- groups of declining suburbs like Ohio's First Suburbs Consortium; and
- some big city mayors, following the lead of Rochester's William Johnson and Grand Rapids' John Logie.[27] (Most mayors, however, are ambivalent, seeing regionalism as a potential infringement of their authority or dilution of their power base.)

However, faith-based groups, such as Northwest Indiana's Interfaith Federation, Metropolitan Communities United for St. Louis, MOSES in Detroit, and VOICE-Buffalo can play the decisive role.[28] The issues of social stewardship and environmental stewardship are inextricably interwoven. The connecting link is environmentally and socially destructive land development patterns. Winning today's civil right battles as well as today's environmental battles requires changing the same set of rules.

The faith community brings strengths the reform coalition often otherwise lacks: the ability to reach across racial, class, and jurisdictional boundaries; and energetic, innovative, often charismatic clerical and lay leaders who can effectively add the moral dimension to economic and environmental arguments.

But most importantly, faith-based coalitions bring the ability to mobilize large numbers of people. When constituents pour off church buses by the hundreds and thousands to pack city council hearings and legislative chambers, the politicians will act to change the "rules of the game."

The ultimate challenge of creating livable communities is: Will we live *together?*

NOTES

1. Michael Parkinson, *The Future of Urban Policy: The Search for Competitiveness, Cohesion, and Sustainability,* European Institute for Urban Affairs (Liverpool, U.K.: John Moores University, 2001).

2. Dirk H. Frieling in D. H. Frieling, L. Groenemeijer, and D. Rusk, "Inside Game/Outside Game: Segregation and Spatial Planning in Metropolitan Areas," published by ABF Strategie: Washington, D.C./Delft/Amsterdam (February 2001).

3. The advanced economies are considered to be the United States, Japan, and the other primarily European members of the Organization of Economic Cooperation and Development.

4. But not, I would note, by my European colleagues, Professors Frieling and Parkinson. Dirk Frieling is organizer and moving spirit behind Deltametropolis, an organization of the four metropolitan areas of the Randstad (Amsterdam, Rotterdam, Utrecht, and The Hague) into a super-regional body. Michael Parkinson is a staunch advocate of regionalism who has written that "the relationship between cities and regions is crucial—they cannot and must not be separated. There is a growing recognition that economic, social, and institutional links between cities and regions are becoming more complex. Just as urban regeneration cannot be confined to neighborhood initiatives but must connect to the wider city, the fate of urban areas cannot be considered outside their regional context," Parkinson, *The Future of Urban Policy.*

5. The only nine urbanized areas that gained density were Miami-Hialeah, Florida; Los Angeles-Long Beach, San Diego, San Jose, and Riverside-San Bernardino, California (all areas of major Hispanic immigration); Stamford and Norwalk, Connecticut (close to the suburbs of New York City); and two polar opposites, Atlantic City, New Jersey and Salt Lake City, Utah.

6. In 1950, twenty future central cities were either too small (e.g., Jonesboro and Rogers, Arkansas, or Myrtle Beach, South Carolina) for the census to report municipal area, or they did not yet exist (e.g., Paradise, Lancaster, Irvine, Palm Desert, and Temecula, California, and Port Saint Lucie, Florida).

7. For a full discussion of urban elasticity, see the author's *Cities without Suburbs,* 3rd ed. (Washington, D.C. and Baltimore, MD: Woodrow Wilson Center/Johns Hopkins University Press, 2003).

8. College towns like State College, Pennsylvania (Penn State); West Lafayette, Indiana (Purdue); and New Brunswick, New Jersey (Rutgers) have also grown in population.

9. In five of the most segregated regions (Providence, New York, Newark, Hartford, and Philadelphia), the largest Hispanic group was Puerto Rican—many of whom suffered a double whammy (Hispanic *and* black).

10. From 1970 to 1990, economic segregation increased in 45 of the 60 metro areas; economic segregation was stable in the Atlanta metro area and decreased in 14 fast growing, fast-desegregating Sun Belt regions. However, during the 1990s, economic segregation ticked downward slightly in 34 regions—probably primarily a reflection of the fact that the 2000 Census collected income and poverty data for 1999, the peak year of the nation's longest period of uninterrupted economic growth. In the wake of the 2000–2001 recession and a largely jobless recovery, this modest positive trend has probably reversed in many regions.

11. Racial deed covenants often did not seek to exclude only blacks, but often covered Hispanics, Jews, and other racial, ethnic, and religious groups. In 1966, we bought our first home in Washington, D.C. The irrevocable covenant of deed on our home (built in 1940), that we explicitly and formally disavowed, sought to exclude "descendents of residents of the former Ottoman Empire."

12. *Realtors* were always white; black real estate agents were required to be called *realtists*.

13. Anthony Downs, *New Visions for Metropolitan America* (Washington, D.C.: Brookings Institution, 1994).

14. For Fiscal Year 2004 the Bush Administration proposed zero funds for HOPE VI, allowing only projects in the pipeline from past years' appropriations to be completed.

15. Pietro S. Nivola, *Laws of the Landscape: How Policies Shape Cities in Europe and America* (Washington, D.C.: The Brookings Institution, 1999).

16. Despite all its philosophizing about "free markets," the National Association of Homebuilders (no fan of government regulation) has said it best: "Public policy *dictates* where development occurs [italics added]." NAHB, *Smart Growth: Building Better Places To Live, Work, and Play* (Washington, D.C., 2000), 8.

17. The sales tax on a new car in Denmark is thirty-seven times higher than in America.

18. This discussion also applies to the issues of inclusionary zoning and tax base sharing.

19. The U.S. Supreme Court also determines whether or not individual rights guaranteed to citizens of the nation have been violated by state or local government decisions. It was a federal court decision in *Village of Euclid (Ohio) v. Ambler Realty* that established the constitutionality of local government zoning powers as the "law of the land" in 1926.

20. Incredibly, some states, like Pennsylvania, explicitly say that the zoning code and map are *not* governed by the comprehensive plan. Pennsylvania's attitude seems to be that "planning is good as long as it doesn't mean anything." The dichotomy between planning and zoning was not resolved by a major reform of Pennsylvania's municipal planning code in 2000.

21. Ironically, under such "modern," "state-of-the-art," local regulations, many of the most aesthetically pleasing, resident-friendly, pre-Euclidian, city and village neighborhoods that many local residents most cherish could not be reproduced today. They would be against the law.

22. Hawaii, Vermont, Florida, Oregon, Georgia, Washington, Maryland, New Jersey, Maine, Rhode Island, Delaware, and Tennessee. Other states—most recently, Wisconsin and Pennsylvania—have improved incentives for voluntary collaboration and authorized new growth management tools but still do not require local governments to plan together within a region

23. See Chapter 7: "The Deficit Machine" in David Rusk, *Inside Game/Outside Game* (Washington, D.C.: The Brookings Institution, 1999) for fuller discussion.

24. Helen F. Ladd and John Yinger, *America's Ailing Cities: Fiscal Health and the Design of Urban Policy* (Baltimore, MD: Johns Hopkins University Press, 1991).

25. Nivola, *Laws of the Landscape*, 27.

26. "Little boxes" regions refer to metro areas that are divided into many small municipalities and multiple school districts (that is, "little boxes"). These are typically the

"township states" of the Northeast and Middle West that are totally divided into municipalities. "Big Box" regions are typically located in the South and West. They have large ("Big Box") cities that annex new development in unincorporated land around them and large, often countywide, ("Big Box") school districts. "Little boxes" regions tend to be much more divided by race and class, with significant fiscal disparities among the many jurisdictions. "Big Box" municipalities and school systems tend to be less racially and economically segregated, have broad tax bases, and are economically healthy. For an extensive analysis, see David Rusk, *Cities without Suburbs,* 3rd ed. (Washington, D.C., and Baltimore, MD: Woodrow Wilson Center/Johns Hopkins University Press, 2003).

27. Both mayors stepped down in 2003 after multiple—and successful—terms of office.

28. All are affiliated with the Chicago-based Gamaliel Foundation, a faith-based community organizing network.

3

From Industrialization to Globalization: Church and Social Ministry

Thomas J. Massaro

There is truly something special about metropolitan environments. They possess a unique power to touch the human spirit. Those who spend little time in metropolitan areas often report a rush of excitement as they cross the threshold of the city limits, perhaps as they steal an initial glimpse of the skyline looming on the horizon from their car or airplane. Regular city dwellers tend to take the excitement of city life for granted, but never grow completely immune to the breathless possibilities represented by the metropolis—our modern centers of culture, commerce, the arts and the entire drama of human life.

The metropolitan areas of contemporary America are filled with diverse populations, hope-filled individuals and groups, and challenges that ask much of all. How are we to share resources in a more equitable and mutually beneficial way? How are we to make communities vibrant places where all can live and work in safety and with the belief that each can make real contributions to the common good? While this book as a whole attempts to address those questions, this particular essay seeks to provide a framework to help us see the challenges in a broader context, namely that provided by the Catholic social tradition. Let us begin with a brief look at the historical context and explore the role of religious institutions.

RELIGION AND METROPOLITAN REGIONS

In the very center of most medieval cities in Europe lay the Cathedral, with its spires and bell towers reaching up toward heaven. The same geographical pattern characterizes the older cities of Latin America, where the centrally

located municipal plaza so often hosts the seats of both church and government. Because it is par excellence the land of religious pluralism, the United
States is full of cities that feature in their center entire rows of churches side
by side, with each of several denominations represented on a street often labeled "Church Street." This clustering of various churches is eloquent physical testimony to the American creed of separation of church and state,
reflecting our First Amendment prohibition against the legal establishment of
any one church as the officially sponsored religion of the citizenry.

But this American refusal to adopt an official religion of our land does not
mean that our cities are somehow stripped of religious influence. Just as we
share common elements of a national "civil religion" that mingles God,
homeland and patriotism in a creative and powerful mix of overlapping symbols and loyalties, so too does each American city and town display an aura
of religious sentiment and reverence. There is an undeniably religious flavor
to the civic rituals carried out in our cities, from parades marking civic holidays to mayoral inaugurations to the funerals of prominent citizens. The city
itself is a repository of shared memories, a concrete symbol of common beliefs in the shape of the universe and the meaning of the flow of historical
events.

For these reasons, we can say with confidence that cities benefit im-
mensely from the presence of religious institutions—churches, synagogues,
mosques, and the like. In our western culture, Christian churches in particular have always been public urban institutions that have opened their doors
generously and eagerly to the rich life of the city. Often this contribution is
one of hospitality, as churches play host, literally and figuratively, to the rituals of urban drama. In a broader sense, churches demonstrate their gen-
erosity by the simple daily act of adding beauty to their urban neighbors,
offering an antidote to the ugliness and alienation that can sour city life.

We can speak further of religious institutions as supplying cities with a
sense of right order, even of collective conscience in times of decision making and policy setting. Without this moral guidance, cities may fall unwit-
tingly into trouble. As one recent commentator put it, without the influence
of religious voices, cities may degenerate into Babel (the city of confusion),
Rameses (the Egyptian city of oppression where Israel was enslaved before
the Exodus) or Philistia (the city of ugliness, crass materialism and deprav-
ity).[1] Of course, merely having churches in a city is no guarantee of moral
rectitude, good government, or social justice. But if churches do have their
own house in order, they can serve as privileged places of public education,
serious moral dialogue, and civic spirit. They can play an important role
alongside government, business, universities, and other cultural institutions
as loci of public service and inspiration.

In short, churches at their best hold the promise of becoming permanent
sacraments within our cities and towns. In the programs and institutions they

sponsor, including hospitals, clinics, schools, food pantries, and shelters, they can be places of energetic service, of systematic charity, of advocacy for justice, and of sanctuary for the poor and homeless, the lonely and depressed. Through all their community outreach and their sheer presence in neighborhoods that many have abandoned, churches can be agencies of reconciliation and forgiveness and sources of wisdom, playing an indispensable role in calling our cities to be the best places they can be.

If it is true, then, that our cities need religious institutions, it is also true that our religious institutions need our cities. In order to be what they truly can be, churches are drawn to the city with an almost magnetic attraction. This has been the case ever since the earliest decades of the church, when the first Christians were quick to establish their presence in the major cities of the Roman Empire, gravitating almost instinctively to Antioch, Corinth, Carthage, Byzantium, and of course to Rome itself. Perhaps it is no coincidence that the Bible begins in a rural setting (the garden of Eden in the book of Genesis) and ends in a city (the heavenly Jerusalem as portrayed in the final chapters of the book of Revelation).[2] Along the way, of course, we encounter the story of Jesus, whose earthly ministry is portrayed as one long preparation for a final approach to the great metropolis of his homeland—Jerusalem, the political capital and seat of the Holy Temple.

From the very origins of Christianity, then, the city has been considered a place of fulfillment, an important destination for discovering our own religious identity and for encountering others. Curiously, among theologians the concept of "the city" has moved into the realm of metaphor, taking on even richer overtones than its literal meaning and coming to symbolize the common hopes of humankind for a better worldly order. The categories of "City of God" and "Earthly City" were central to the social theory of Saint Augustine, who is generally considered the most important theologian of Western Christianity in its first thousand years. His long and brilliant fifth-century work *City of God* is a classic treatment of key Christian theological themes, such as hope, sin, redemption, and the meaning of secular history. The strategy of comparing the perfect and imperfect social orders in terms of earthly and heavenly cities became a standard motif of subsequent Christian social thinkers, including utopian writings such as that of St. Thomas More.

CATHOLIC SOCIAL TEACHING RESPONDS TO CONTEMPORARY CHALLENGES

It is time to narrow our focus somewhat, to zero in on precisely how one particular church, the Catholic Church in the United States, may meet the challenges of social ministry in our new millennium. Two questions we might naturally ask are these: (1) What precisely is the task and mission facing our church in metropolitan areas? and (2) What resources can we bring to bear upon the challenges to accomplish our mission? In this small space, we are able to explore only partial answers, but even these may provide important directions for our subsequent investigations in this book.

The first question about the task facing the church today is a huge and open-ended one. Of course, the mission of the church is always framed in terms of evangelization, the sacred duty of spreading the gospel of Jesus Christ. What some people do not realize is the great diversity of forms that this sharing of the good news may take. While it certainly does include "churchy" activities such as preaching the Word of God and administering the sacraments, ministry must always involve care for the whole person, including attending to the physical as well as the spiritual needs of all the children of God. After all, news about God's infinite care for us and God's loving offer of eternal salvation is hardly credible to our brothers and sisters who are hungry, homeless, lonely, and depressed. Hence, Christian congregations have always been sponsors of the works of mercy: committed to feeding the hungry, clothing the naked, visiting the sick and imprisoned. In our day, this takes the form of participation in outreach programs, where churches become social service providers to insure that no one falls through the cracks into abject poverty and oblivion.

In recent decades, this traditional Christian orientation toward *charity* has been supplemented with an explicit orientation toward *justice* in the way the church understands its social mission. Besides providing the short-term "Band-Aids" of direct assistance to the needy, the Catholic Church now understands its task to include advocacy for permanent structural change in our society and economy. We speak now of making a "preferential option for the poor," a commitment which includes political advocacy for greater material equity among all people. Leaders of the church increasingly recognize the appropriateness, indeed the urgency, of becoming outspoken mobilizers of social responsibility, appealing to the powerful to adopt policies of greater social responsibility, so that the wealth of society benefits all our brothers and sisters created by God. This turn toward a justice orientation is not radically new for Christians, but does represent a refinement of the self-understanding of the church as it strives to become an agent of the common good and a source of reconciliation and renewal for all humankind. In a metropolitan context, reconciliation may include mediating between contending parties when conflicts (such as ethnic rivalries or labor unrest) arise, but it may also take the form of church advocacy for more equitable distribution of income and benefits, including a more just distribution across such political boundaries as "city" and "suburb."

The second question above asks about resources the church has at its disposal to accomplish this mission, especially in the metropolitan setting. Certainly, when we mention the term "resources," we usually think of the financial assets churches control, including their operating budgets, buildings and real estate, as well as less tangible items such as the good will of church members and neighbors, and the tremendous skills of the personnel engaged in church work. But we may also interpret the word "resources" to include the intellectual and theological heritages that have been passed down to today's churches, the rich fund of ideas that serve as tools church people use to engage the world of society. By making good use of such inherited ideas and approaches, churches can better understand current realities and respond to them in authentically Christian ways.

This is where Catholic social teaching comes in. Of all the resources the contemporary Catholic Church inherits, it is in its official social doctrines that the church has stored the wisdom that allows it to approach modern social realities, including the most pressing issues and concerns affecting urban environments. Modern Catholic social teaching, which began with Pope Leo XIII's encyclical *Rerum novarum*, represents the effort of church leaders over the past eleven decades to engage in a process best described as an attempt to "read the signs of the times," an important phrase that appears in the documents of the Second Vatican Council[3] as well as in the Gospels.[4] Although the agenda and priorities of the church are never simply a matter of responding to secular realities, the church's mission of evangelization can only be successful within the context of an ongoing dialogue with culture. Only by paying close attention to the economic, political, and social realities that affect all people can the church play a fully constructive role in humanizing the world and pursuing the core values of justice, peace, human dignity, and the common good.

How does the church fulfill this complex task? The actual process that serves as the basis of all Catholic social teaching is a simple three-step method that most people use almost instinctively every day. This is the process best summarized as see-judge-act.[5] Whenever we are confronted with a new situation, such as the challenge of new problems facing an urban area, the first necessary step is to take a careful look at the situation, aided by a series of questions. These are the usual questions that every reporter is trained to answer in the first lines of a newspaper story: who, what, where, when, how, why. After gathering reliable data, we move to the second step, where we make judgments about what we have observed and especially about what has caused a new situation or problem to arise. The project of probing into the complex causes of large-scale problems is often referred to as "conducting social analysis."

When the church embarks on this middle phase (the "judging" part) of the three-step process, it goes beyond mere social analysis to conduct theological reflection as well. This means that church members seek to view new social realities in the light of the gospel and to make sense of social phenomena in terms of theological categories (such as divine providence, sin, grace, hope, charity) that help us place present life experiences within the context of our beliefs about God's relationship with the secular world. Finally, the third step is the moment for action, when our investigation and reflection comes to fruition in the form of practical measures and action steps aimed at implementing our insights and desires for improvement. In church circles, the outcome is often called a "pastoral plan." This is a guideline for future action that is subject to alteration and improvement once we embark on another round of the see-judge-act circle and revise our plans and actions to better reflect our ever-sharper understanding of the social challenges we face.

The see-judge-act model is sometimes referred to by fancy names such as "the circle of praxis," the "pastoral circle," and even the "hermeneutical circle." Whatever name we use, the see-judge-act schema will surely continue to be a useful tool for conducting ministry in the future, as the church attempts constantly to update its understanding of the problems and possibilities of life in the cities and their environs, in both our nation and the world. In addition, knowing about the pastoral circle gives us tremendous insight into the development of Catholic social teaching over the past century. As popes, bishops, and other church leaders surveyed the world and felt moved to write and promulgate major documents of church teaching about social issues, they were engaged in nothing other than a high-level experience of the see-judge-act process.

What they left behind is a series of about a dozen Vatican documents[6] outlining the universal social teaching of the Catholic Church, a collection that is supplemented by many more documents that have been written by groups of bishops around the world to address more local or regional issues. Each of these documents represents an attempt by the leadership of the Catholic Church to engage in the pastoral circle—to offer accurate observations about contemporary problems of disorder and injustice, to engage in careful analysis of the social causes and theological significance of these concerns, and to propose constructive solutions and action plans to deal pastorally with the challenges of the age. A chart listing the twelve most important social teaching documents to come from the Vatican appears on page 47. The columns of the chart contain the essential information about these dozen documents: their Latin and English titles, their years of publication, their official authors, the major challenges each addressed, and the major new messages or ideas each introduced.

This documentary heritage should not be seen as merely a curious set of artifacts that bear witness to struggles that took place long ago and far away. Rather, each of the dozen social teaching documents (some are called encyclicals, others apostolic exhortations or letters from popes, councils, or synods of bishops) treats a range of issues that are still important today and will continue to have relevance into the foreseeable future. One reason for this is the simple fact that ten of these twelve Vatican documents were published since the year

Box 3.1 – Major Documents of Modern Catholic Social Teaching

Categories to correspond to the six lines of each entry below:
1) Latin title
2) English translation
3) Year of publication
4) Source
5) Major challenge it addressed
6) Major new message or idea

Rerum Novarum
The Condition of Labor
1891
Pope Leo XIII
Industrialization, urbanization, poverty
"Family Wage," workers' rights

Quadragesimo Anno
After Forty Years, or The Reconstruction of the Social Order
1931
Pope Pius XI
Great Depression, communist and fascist dictatorships
Subsidiarity as a guide to government interventions

Mater et Magistra
Christianity and Social Progress
1961
Pope John XXIII
Technological advances
Global justice between rich and poor nations

Pacem in Terris
Peace on Earth
1963
Pope John XXIII
Arms race, the threat of nuclear war
A philosophy of human rights and social responsibilities

Gaudium et Spes
Pastoral Constitution on the Church in the Modern World
1965
Second Vatican Council
Younger generations questioning traditional values
Church must scrutinize external "signs of the times"

(continued)

Box 3.1 – Major Documents of Modern Catholic Social Teaching *(continued)*

Populorum Progressio
The Development of Peoples
1967
Pope Paul VI
Widening gap between rich and poor nations
"Development is a new word for peace"

Octogesima Adveniens
A Call to Action on the 80th Anniversary of Rerum Novarum
1971
Pope Paul VI
Urbanization marginalizes vast multitudes
Lay Catholics must focus on political action to combat injustices

Justitia in Mundo
Justice in the World
1971
Synod of Bishops
Structural injustices and oppression inspire liberation movements
"Justice . . . is a constitutive dimension of the preaching of the gospel"

Evangelii Nuntiandi
Evangelization in the Modern World
1975
Pope Paul VI
Cultural problems of atheism, secularism, consumerism
The salvation promised by Jesus offers liberation from all oppression

Laborem Exercens
On Human Work
1981
Pope John Paul II
Capitalism and communism treat workers as mere instruments of production
Work is the key to "the social question" and to human dignity

Sollicitudo Rei Socialis
On Social Concern
1987
Pope John Paul II
Persistent under-development, division of world into blocs
"Structures of sin" are responsible for global injustices

(continued)

Box 3.1 – Major Documents of Modern Catholic Social Teaching *(continued)*

Centesimus Annus
On the Hundredth Anniversary of Rerum Novarum
1991
Pope John Paul II
Collapse of communism in Eastern Europe
Combat consumeristic greed in new "knowledge economy"

1961, and so the vast majority are still quite recent. But even the first of this genre of modern papal social encyclicals, *Rerum novarum* published by Pope Leo XIII in 1891, contains words of wisdom about labor and industry that have timeless relevance and appeal. A brief glance back to the social conditions that prevailed in the latter decades of the nineteenth century will help illustrate the remarkable character of the Catholic Church's response to the struggles and aspirations of workers in that age and every age.

In the most advanced industrialized nations of Europe and North America, the decades from 1830 to 1890 witnessed the rise of a phenomenon often called "social Catholicism." Great pioneers of church-based social concern began to argue for (and even began themselves to enact) greater involvement of Catholics in meeting the needs of the poor and reshaping social and economic structures for the achievement of greater social justice. Many of the efforts of social Catholicism were focused on the distinctive concerns of city life, including urban poverty and industrial labor relations. The ranks of such activists included bishops (such as Cardinal Henry Edward Manning in England and Archbishop Wilhelm Emmanuel von Ketteler of Germany), priests (such as John Ryan and Isaac Hecker in the United States) and lay people (such as the Frenchmen Charles de Montalembert and Frederick Ozanam who founded the Saint Vincent de Paul Society). The social involvement undertaken by such Catholic luminaries as these paved the way for the growth of official Catholic social teaching, encouraging popes and other church officials to take bold measures to focus the attention of the worldwide church upon issues of social justice.

When *Rerum novarum* made its appearance on May 15, 1891, many observers did not know what to make of it. There were no precedents for this first "social encyclical." It marked the birth of a completely new genre of church writing, for popes had not previously addressed such controversial political and economic issues as the right of workers to strike, to organize for collective bargaining, and to earn a salary sufficient to support a family. Some perhaps found it disconcerting that a pope would get involved in such seemingly minute details of working conditions as the length of the work day, the frequency of holidays, and the prohibition of child labor. Many observers were surprised that a pope, even while strongly upholding the capitalist principle of the right to own private property, would adopt many of the same arguments that Marxists, "scientific socialists," and the labor movement of the age had advocated. The most cynical voices saw *Rerum novarum* as primarily a last-ditch effort to prevent the church from "losing the working classes of Europe" to various schools of philosophy (such as socialism) that were contending for the loyalty of the masses.

It would be dishonest to deny that there is a grain of truth in this last observation. The church at the end of the nineteenth century was indeed in danger of forfeiting the allegiance of formerly staunch Catholics if church leaders had remained deaf to the cries of the downtrodden workers of the rapidly industrializing lands of Europe. If the church continued to be perceived as offering exclusively otherworldly comforts to heavily burdened people in desperate economic straits, its credibility would likely have rapidly deteriorated. But it would be a serious mistake to interpret the message of *Rerum novarum* as solely a strategic response to a political challenge facing the Vatican. Rather, we can readily find in the words of Leo XIII's sincere concern about the plight of workers and their families and a prophetic call for social justice. This 1891 encyclical may be interpreted as a principled appropriation in its era of the constant religious messages about charity, mercy, and justice that echo through the words of innumerable preachers, theologians, and even back to the scriptures, in the words of the prophets and of Jesus Christ as well. *Rerum novarum* was at once an innovation and a document remarkably faithful to a long tradition of social concern on the part of believers.

One of the labels often applied to *Rerum novarum* is "Christian classic," a term coined by theologian David Tracy.[7] This phrase suggests something similar to what we mean when we call a book, poem, or play a literary classic—that it contains a surplus of meaning such that readers in any age can appreciate its message and drama. Like Shakespeare's *Romeo and Juliet* or Homer's *Odyssey*, *Rerum novarum* and its successor encyclicals observe truths about human affairs that transcend the passing tastes or preferences of a given age. These Vatican documents address the nature and conditions of justice and peace in ways that allow them to make a permanent contribution to our reflections on how we ought to live together in society in ethically responsible ways. While some aspects of a given encyclical may appear to be time-bound (for example, when *Pacem in terris* addresses the realities of the Cold War of the early 1960s), these documents repeatedly and courageously address perennial threats to human values (such as recurring episodes of arms races which threaten life and rob resources from the poor). So even though the precise conditions which alarmed Leo XIII when he wrote *Rerum novarum* may be no longer a serious issue for most people in the world, that classic encyclical remains eminently relevant in its call for broad categories of worker justice.

The social teaching documents treat many issues: human rights, economic development, the dignity of labor, property ownership, the need for peace and disarmament, rampant consumerism, and so on. In fact, only one of the twelve documents deals at any length specifically with the problems of cities and urban ministry. Pope Paul VI's 1971 apostolic letter *Octogesima adveniens* contains several pages[8] dealing with the reality of urbanization and the challenges facing Christian communities in the world's cities. He portrays modern people as facing a new type of loneliness as a result of the anonymity, poverty, indifference, and individualistic consumerism often found in cities. Perhaps Pope Paul was more aware of these problems than his predecessors, since he was the first pope in modern times to travel widely while in office. In the decade before he published *Octogesima adveniens*, he had concluded ambitious trips to many of the world's largest cities, including a visit to the United Nations in New York, as well as journeys to several of the major cities of Europe, Latin America, and the Indian subcontinent.[9]

Although it may seem that urban realities and concerns have been generally overlooked in the documents of Catholic social teaching during the eighty years before *Octogesima adveniens* and in the thirty years since its publication, there is another way of viewing this paucity of explicit treatment of cities in these Vatican writings. I would argue that, in a real sense, the encyclical tradition is tied inextricably to the reality of the modern urban setting. Indeed, there would be no tradition of modern Catholic social teaching if it were not for urbanization. Without the great cities, no social encyclicals. After all, the church had gone along for centuries without explicitly addressing political and economic questions in great detail through major social teaching documents. It is more than mere coincidence that the explosion of such documents in the past eleven decades was preceded by the greatest influx of population into metropolitan areas in the history of the world during the nineteenth and twentieth centuries.

The exponential growth of cities, accompanied as it was by an unprecedented level of technological innovation, meant the growth of an industrial base and the factory-based system of mass production. Urbanization and industrialization spelled the end of the simpler way of life that had characterized the ancient and medieval settings the church had previously encountered. Whereas life in an agrarian society was relatively easy to organize and allowed for clear lines of authority, the urban revolution of the last two centuries has generated a need for more ethical guidance about political and economic life. In a world where property relations are more complex than ever and where the demarcations of the political and social order are much less clear than they were for our grandparents, Catholic social teaching has stepped in to offer its wisdom and moral analysis of contemporary issues. This in no way means that these documents overlook the specific challenges facing people in non-urban contexts; the U.S. Bishops, for example, speak out frequently on the distinctive concerns of rural life, such as the health and viability of the agricultural sector and specifically of the family farm.[10] Nevertheless, it is important to recognize that so many of today's most pressing issues have arisen precisely because of the trends and developments which account for the new phenomenon of the modern metropolis.

READING THE "SIGNS OF THE TIMES" IN TODAY'S WORLD

Of course, every generation (and probably every decade or even every year!) has its own distinctive challenges and problems to face. It would be a great simplification to claim that every document of Catholic social teaching over the past eleven decades was prompted by the same urban realities. But it is no exaggeration to say that the whole complex of social issues that arose together in the course of the nineteenth and early twentieth centuries sparked a continuous effort at serious soul-searching on the part of Christians around the world.

The questions that naturally arise for us today include the following: How is the church at the present moment continuing the efforts of the social Catholicism of decades past? Are we merely satisfied that our church has "gone on record" with impressive documents about social justice? What bold steps and initiatives are we forging to meet the challenges of our metropolitan environments and the many desperate needs of our world?

The answers to these questions will surely be clearer after surveying the materials in the remainder of this book. One observation that will become obvious is that remarkable efforts are underway at all levels of activity, as social justice initiatives proceed as projects of isolated individuals; of parishes; of dioceses; of national organizations such as Catholic Charities USA, the Catholic Campaign for Human Development, and the Catholic Healthcare Association; and even of worldwide church-based organizations such as Caritas International and the Jesuit Refugee Service. Much of the work of concerned Christians at all these levels looks quite routine and is devoted to the maintenance of ongoing programs that meet human needs for material and institutional support. Some contributors to the work of social justice live lives of remarkable drama indeed, while the heroism of others is partially obscured by their generous preoccupation with humble and repetitive tasks that serve others in mundane but indispensable ways.

One shining example of this generous service is the work of Mother Teresa of Calcutta, now being carried on by her religious order, the Missionaries of Charity. The work of caring for the indigent ill can be at once dramatic and quite routine; in the absence of media coverage, the life of Mother Teresa would have been one of the quiet outpouring of gentle love as is lived out by thousands of missionaries, teachers, and nurses working through and for the church. One of the most interesting aspects of the ministry of Mother Teresa and her colleagues is how it sprang up as both a spontaneous response to the needy and as the fruit of a conscious social analysis. After a process of seeing, judging, and some tentative "acting," a deliberate choice was made to serve the desperate and dying through this ministry of direct presence and material assistance. Meanwhile, many others have been confronted with the same dire conditions of people dying on the streets and, with equal integrity and single-heartedness, they have chosen to assist their neighbors in a more indirect way, through the form of advocacy to change the social structures that contribute to their destitution. This "justice path," in contrast to the "charity path," is trod by people who, however much they feel the urgent pull of direct service, nevertheless decide to focus their energies on the long-range goal of improving the larger systems that influence the root causes of social problems such as poverty.

There is certainly room in the church for both approaches. In fact, it seems that each complements the other, so that our response as Christians would not be complete unless we somehow combine the paths of charity and justice, of direct service and structural change. What is indispensable in both paths is the imperative to be ever vigilant about "reading the signs of the times." Without constant attention to the ever-changing data of our metropolitan areas and to the wider world of human culture and our natural environment, our responses as a church to the needs of our age would be doomed to irrelevance and certain failure. This insight is confirmed by even a cursory study of the history of Catholic social teaching and the movement of social Catholicism over the past two centuries. We find that development and growth did not progress because the church underwent a process of introspection and then went forth to look for problems to solve; rather, social problems regularly arose and continually confronted the church from the outside. Crucial to the church's ability to respond to the needs of the world is its commitment to look beyond its own walls and to notice (and even to anticipate) ways that people of faith can make a difference in improving the conditions of human life.

It is always perilous to play the role of the prophet and attempt to predict the future. Yet it may be useful (and not all that risky!) to anticipate a few themes that will likely become increasingly prominent in future Catholic social teaching as it attempts to "read the signs of the times" in this new millennium. In fact, anyone who regularly reads a newspaper or follows current events could predict several new directions the church might take in addressing pressing social concerns in the coming years. Here I will mention just three areas where renewed church attention might be focused. The first is on the complex phenomenon of globalization of the economy. As manufacturing and trade increasingly cross national and cultural borders, how will the church respond in its efforts to advocate for those who are exploited or left behind? How might church leaders interpret the gospel's call for all to live in dignity in a world where unprecedented prosperity for some is accompanied by utter destitution for so many? Second, the issue of equitable treatment of women remains unresolved in many sectors of life. While Vatican social teaching documents occasionally make reference to the aspirations of women for "equal rights to participate in cultural, economic, social and political life,"[11] there is still the widespread hope that future church teachings might pay more adequate attention to the concerns of women for gender equality. The third area of likely development of Catholic social teaching regards the natural environment. Except for a few scattered passages,[12] the major Vatican social encyclicals largely ignore the ecological crisis. As environmental awareness grows, it is not hard to predict that church social teaching will reflect these urgent concerns as it attempts to discern "the signs of the times" in the contemporary world.

As each of us charts out our own paths of justice and charity, it is enormously helpful to have exemplars upon whose efforts we might model our own. The church has recognized many saints in each century whose lives reflect the very concerns we have treated above. These include men and women, residents of cities and rural districts alike, who have dedicated their lives to the service of the poor in whatever ways they could find to make a difference. If the examples of the great saints known for their works of charity and justice—St. Vincent de Paul (a seventeenth-century Frenchman), St. Francis of Assisi (a thirteenth-century Italian), or Saint Elizabeth Ann Seton (a nineteenth-century American)—seem too distant, consider the example of Dorothy Day. Many people, especially among lay Catholics, discover in the life of this founder of the Catholic Worker a most approachable witness to values that include peace-making and social concern for the least fortunate.

In fact, near the end of her life just a generation ago, Dorothy Day quipped that it was her preference not to be considered a saint precisely because she did not want to risk being placed on a pedestal of any sort. All of Dorothy's efforts—from editing a newspaper that exposed injustices to running houses of hospitality to participating in acts of civil disobedience as a witness against militarism—were a wonderful blend of advocacy and direct service that truly made justice real to those whose lives she touched. Perhaps the most impressive aspect of Dorothy Day's dramatic life was the constant attitude of confidence in God's love and mercy, which she maintained even in the face of tremendous adversity. She did not worry about whether her pet projects became popular or grew in size because, as she often quipped, "God calls us to be faithful, not successful." This principle of the priority of fidelity to our call over any inordinate preoccupation with success (measured in worldly terms) is a fine point of orientation for anyone involved in urban ministry.

Yet, despite this pearl of wisdom shared by Dorothy Day, we know that we would be foolish to avoid the hard task of planning for the future and providing for the continuation of worthwhile projects in which we are engaged. There is simply no substitute for the "brass tacks" of organizational management that turn our ideas and intentions into reality. Assisting the sick is almost impossible today unless your efforts are supported by an efficient and well-funded hospital system; helping the poor is a lot easier when your base of operations is a recognized social service provider; the task of contributing to the well-being of children is best carried out within the confines of a well-run school or licensed day-care center. Institutions such as these are the very places where social ministry happens, where resources and people intersect, and where our commitments to see, judge, and act to benefit the most vulnerable come to fruition. We may sometimes need to put aside our impatience with the bureaucracy and unwieldiness of large-scale institutions in order to accept their indispensability in the struggle for social justice.

When the Catholic Church does muster its energies to address social concerns, it is not difficult to detect a distinctive style of engagement with the world, a feature that makes Catholic social action different from secular efforts or even from endeavors undertaken by other religious groups. An important feature of Catholicism is its commitment to a view of the world that is best described by the word "incarnational." This distinctive style of viewing reality includes the Catholic emphasis on embodiment, which takes seriously the material world and recognizes the importance of the physical conditions that can either frustrate or greatly enhance human flourishing. While it is accurate to say that a Catholic approach to life is ever mindful that human destiny is tied ultimately to the Kingdom of God, it also never forgets that Jesus (in the parable of the Good Samaritan and elsewhere) calls us to be concerned about the bodily needs of our neighbors. Ours is not an otherworldly religion that seeks to escape the bonds of the physical world, but a life-affirming faith that finds its mission in God's call ever to renew the earth.

The Catholic affirmation of this theological principle of incarnationalism is linked to many features of church life. It helps us to understand the Catholic emphasis on the sacraments as visible signs of God's grace and presence, and many of our doctrines such as the Resurrection of the Body and the mystery of the Incarnation itself, in which we attribute to God's overflowing love for humankind the decision to send Christ into the world in fully human form. On a more mundane level, an incarnational stance also explains all those fund-raising letters we receive from Catholic Charities recounting the thousands of people fed, clothed, housed, and medically treated as a result of ongoing church-based efforts. Offering physical assistance to neighbors in need is an imperative for Catholics. Yet, being guided by incarnational principles influences not only "what" we do, but also "how" we do it. All our efforts for justice and charity are shaped by a care that seeks to mirror the love of God for humans and all of creation.

A final point to note about an authentically Catholic approach to reading "the signs of the times" is especially important for the work of urban ministry. It is the same insight that generations of missionaries have rediscovered over and over as they sought to evangelize more and more of the world. As much as we value the work of contributing to the lives of the economically disadvantaged and of those deprived of the riches of the Gospel, we must never succumb to the illusion that we are bringing God for the first time into any place or to any people. An incarnational view will not allow us to adopt this mistaken notion, for it reminds us that wherever we venture, God has already preceded us there. As the One who creates and redeems the world, God is absent nowhere. No place or people, rural or urban, have been abandoned or left as orphans by God. Our job is not to import God, but to reveal God's presence already at work in the lives of the people we serve.

Social ministry makes a vital contribution to the life and energy of the church in today's complex and rapidly changing world. It is indeed an indispensable context in which the church scrutinizes the signs of the times and explores new ways to serve the world. What does this service look like today? We find a partial description in these encouraging words from the most recent of the great papal social teachings, the 1991 encyclical *Centesimus annus* of John Paul II:

> As far as the church is concerned, the social message of the Gospel must not be considered a theory, but above all else a basis and a motivation for action. . . . Christ's words, "as you did it to one of the least of these my brethren, you did it to me" (Matt. 25:40) were not intended to remain a pious wish, but were meant to become a concrete life commitment.
>
> Today more than ever, the church is aware that her social message will gain credibility more immediately from the witness of actions than as a result of its internal logic and consistency. This awareness is also a source of her preferential option for the poor, which is never exclusive or discriminatory toward other groups. This option is not limited to material poverty, since it is well known that there are many other forms of poverty, especially in modern society—not only economic but also cultural and spiritual poverty as well. The church's love for the poor, which is essential for her and a part of her constant tradition, impels her to give attention to a world in which poverty is threatening to assume massive proportions in spite of technological and economic progress. . . .
>
> Love for others, and in the first place love for the poor, in whom the church sees Christ Himself, is made concrete in the promotion of justice. Justice will never be fully attained unless people see in the poor person, who is asking for help in order to survive, not an annoyance or a burden, but an opportunity for showing kindness and a chance for greater enrichment.[13]

NOTES

1. M. Francis Mannion, "The Church and the City," *First Things* 100 (February 2000): 31-36.

2. See especially Rev. 21:2-4, which reads in part: "I . . . saw a new Jerusalem, the holy city, coming down out of Heaven from God, beautiful as a bride prepared to meet her husband. I heard a loud voice from the throne cry out: 'This is God's dwelling among the people. They shall dwell with him and they shall be His people and He shall be their God who is always with them. He shall wipe every tear from their eyes, and there shall be no more death or mourning, crying out or pain, for the former world has passed away.'"

3. See, inter alia, Vatican II's "Pastoral Constitution on the Church in the Modern World," also known by the Latin name, *Gaudium et spes*, 4

4. See Matthew 16:3.

5. See Pope John XXIII's encyclical letter *Mater et magistra,* 236-41 for a succinct description of this process.

6. The full texts of twelve Vatican social teaching documents (along with two important pastoral letters on social issues from the U.S. Catholic Bishops) are found in David J. O'Brien and Thomas A. Shannon, eds., *Catholic Social Thought: The Documentary Heritage* (Maryknoll, NY: Orbis Books, 1992).

7. See chapters 3-5 of David Tracy, *The Analogical Imagination: Christian Theology and the Culture of Pluralism* (New York: Crossroad, 1981), 100-229.

8. See especially *Octogesima adveniens*, 8-12, which fall under the two headings "Urbanization" and "Christians in the City."

9. Paul VI makes explicit reference to these travels as one wellspring of his social concern in his 1967 encyclical *Populorum progressio*, 4.

10. See the U.S. Bishops' 1986 pastoral letter on the economy, "Economic Justice for All," especially paragraphs 216-50. The full text appears in Shannon and O'Brien (as above), 572-680.

11. This phrase appears in *Octogesima adveniens*, 13. See also *Gaudium et spes*, 60 and *Laborem exercens,*19.

12. See most notably *Gaudium et spes*, 34; *Octogesima adveniens*, 21; *Sollicitudo rei socialis*, 26 and 34; *Centesimus annus*, 37 and 38.

13. Pope John Paul II, *Centesimus annus*, 57-58.

4

Catholic Social Teaching: Starting with the Common Good

Todd David Whitmore

One of the key obstacles to both conveying and practicing Catholic social teaching is the fact that the genre of the social encyclical—the primary means through which the tradition is articulated—is a difficult one to penetrate.[1] My effort is to provide a coherent overview of modern Catholic social teaching. The chapter proceeds in four parts. First, I will indicate why the best place to begin a synthesis is with the concept of the common good. In the second and third sections, I will unpack the content of the concept of the common good. Finally, I will elaborate on concepts related to this core of Catholic social teaching, ones that are often listed as key themes—such as rights, the option for the poor, private property, subsidiarity, and peace—in summaries of the official documents.

BEGINNING WITH THE COMMON GOOD

Most commentaries on Catholic social teaching begin with the idea of the dignity of the human person. This idea is important to affirm, but it is not the best place to begin when presenting the teaching. The common good is better. This is because of the repeated claim in the teaching that human beings are fundamentally social. Leo XIII's *Rerum novarum*, the 1891 encyclical which inaugurated modern Catholic social teaching, refers to "the natural propensity of man to live in society." He elaborates in *Immortale dei*: "[H]e cannot, if dwelling apart, provide himself with the necessary requirements of life, nor procure the means of developing his mental and moral faculties. Hence it is divinely ordained that he should live his life—be it family or civil—with his fellow man." Forty years later, Pius XI confirms both the basic claim and the theological basis. People are "endowed with a social nature." Indeed, "God has destined" them for civil society.[2]

Later documents develop both the claim regarding our social nature and the theological underpinnings for it. They use the term *inter*dependence to accent the social nature of human beings in large part because they find our reliance upon each other intensifying. John XXIII's 1961 encyclical, *Mater et magistra*, written on the seventieth anniversary of *Rerum novarum*, states, "As the mutual relations of peoples increase, they each become daily more dependent upon the other." He elaborates, "One of the principal characteristics of our time is the multiplication of social relationships, that is, daily more complex interdependence of citizens, introducing into their lives and activities many and varied forms of association." Most recently, John Paul II, in his 1991 encyclical, *Centesimus annus*, observes, "It is in interrelationships on many levels that a person lives, and that society becomes more 'personalized.'" He therefore goes on to state, "Today, the church's social doctrine focuses especially on man as he is involved in a complex network of relationships within modern societies."[3]

Official Catholic documents have not only increasingly accented interdependence in the last sixty years, they have provided a deeper theological underpinning. While it is often said that people have dignity because they are created "in the image of God," the social documents stress that the *imago Dei* ("image of God") doctrine is precisely about our imaging of the *triune*—that is, interrelational—God. There is no human dignity apart from the dignity we all have in relation to each other. John Paul II also stresses this point in the 1987 encyclical *Sollicitudo rei socialis*, when he says that persons in society are in "the *living image* of God the Father, redeemed by the blood of Jesus Christ and placed under the permanent action of the Holy Spirit. . . . This supreme *model of unity*, which is a reflection of the intimate life of God, one God in three Persons, is what we Christians mean by the word *communion*" (italics in original).[4]

So thoroughgoing is this emphasis on the theological basis for the social nature of persons that Catholic social teaching affirms that even human salvation is social. The Second Vatican Council (1962–1965) is emphatic on this point: "God did not create man for life in isolation, but for the formation of social unity. So also 'it has pleased God to make men holy and save them not merely as individuals, without any mutual bonds, but by making them into a single people.' . . . So from the beginning of salvation history he has chosen men not just as individuals but as members of a certain community. Revealing his mind to them, God called these chosen ones 'His People' (Exod. 3:7–12)."[5]

The emphasis on the social nature of persons distinguishes Catholic teaching from much of Western political and economic thought, particularly classical and neo-classical liberalism—not to be confused with what is today commonly referred to as liberalism when people have Senator Ted Kennedy in mind. Classical liberalism is premised on the autonomous individual for its social theory: individuals in a state of nature freely—that is, without encumbrance or coercion—form "contracts" to associate with each other because it is in each of their best interests. Both contemporary conservatives (for instance, Ronald Reagan and George W. Bush) and liberals (Kennedy) are indebted to this tradition. Thomas Hobbes (1588-1679) gives what is perhaps the most severe form of classical liberal social theory. The state of nature is a war "of every man against every man," where the only right is that of self-preservation. Individuals transfer their natural right to self-preservation to a sovereign in exchange for a maintained social order.[6] John Locke (1632-1704) does not similarly reduce self-interest to base self-preservation. In his state of nature, people can accumulate property, so that the primary rights are "life, liberty, and property." Still, they are *individual* rights, and persons join together in both economic and political society because and only because it serves their self-interest.[7] More recently, John Rawls, in his *A Theory of Justice* (1971), the *locus classicus* of contemporary Anglo-American political thought, begins by placing the individual in a hypothetical state of nature—what he calls "the original position"—and then argues that all individuals would agree to—that is, contract into—the society that he later describes. There is no robust common good, but, at best (and even this has been debated), what is called a "thin theory of the good."[8]

To begin a treatment of Catholic social teaching with "the dignity of the human person" makes the teaching look more like classical liberal social thought than is warranted.[9] To be sure, such treatments usually say soon thereafter that such dignity can only be "realized in society." But this ordering of presentation is not far different from Hobbes, who argues that we have the right to self-preservation, but, given the dangerous nature of the state of nature, this right can only be realized in society. It is also worth noting that treatments of Catholic social teaching that start with the dignity of the individual human person also cite the *imago Dei* doctrine but do not mention the fact that the God in whose image we are created is a triune God. This robs the claim concerning the social nature of the person of its theological push and further reinforces any tendency toward individualism.

THE MORAL CONTENT OF THE COMMON GOOD

Fulfillment

The claim that the person is social in Catholic social teaching is not simply an empirical observation, but also involves moral obligation. It is at once both the way things in fact are at their most fundamental level, and the way that they ought to be. For Pius XI, social harmony, a reflection of the divine harmony, is both a gift and a "work on earth." When John XXIII tells us that "the interdependence of national economies has grown deeper;" he goes on to say, "Given these conditions, it is obvious that individual countries cannot rightly seek their own interests and develop themselves in isolation from the rest." The Second Vatican Council likewise links observation with obligation, the way things are and the way things ought to be. "Today the bonds of mutual dependence become increasingly close between all citizens and all peoples. The universal common good needs to be intelligently pursued and more effectively achieved."[10]

We can get at the moral content of the concept of the common good by unpacking the definition given in the documents. While the earlier documents use the term as if we already know what it means, beginning with John XXIII's *Mater et magistra* in 1961 there is a concerted effort to offer a precise definition of the common good. That definition, with some variation, describes the common good as "the sum of those conditions of social life which allows social groups and their individual members relatively thorough and ready access to their own fulfillment." The two questions that arise are "What is meant by *fulfillment?*" and "What are the *conditions* of this fulfillment?"[11] In this section I will address the first question and in the section following I will take up the second.

We have already seen indications that fulfillment is a social phenomenon. Therefore, when the definition of the common good refers to groups' and persons' "own fulfillment," this should not be taken as supporting a kind of individualism. Salvation—the highest form of fulfillment—itself is social, an ultimate communion with God and neighbor that images the communion between the persons of the trinity. There are also more proximate and earthly forms of fulfillment, and Catholic social teaching bridges these two dimensions of fulfillment—ultimate and penultimate, supernatural and natural—through means of the analogous terms of *harmony, order, balance, and solidarity*. The documents bring these terms to bear on the complete range of the kinds of social relationships—for instance, those of employer and worker, church and state, state and economy, economy and family, rich and poor, agriculture and industry, individual and society. The ubiquity and range of the application of these terms are evidence of their role as articulating the governing norm that gives the concept of the common good its fundamental substance. The basic idea is not new. Pius XI refers, for instance, to Thomas Aquinas, in making the point: "Order, as the Angelic Doctor well defines, is unity arising from the apt arrangement of a plurality of objects; hence, true and genuine social order demands various members of society, joined together by a common bond."[12]

In *Immortale dei*, Leo XIII draws upon the norm of harmony as read off of God's created nature to make the case for a cooperative relationship between church and state. "Even in physical things . . . the Almighty has so

combined the forces and springs of nature with tempered action and won-
drous harmony that no one of them clashes with any other, and all of them
most fitly and aptly work together for the great purpose of the universe.
There must, accordingly, exist between these two powers [of church and
state] a certain orderly connection, which may be compared to the union of
the soul and body in man." Analogies between harmony in the cosmos, the
social order, and the person, such as Leo makes here, run throughout
Catholic social teaching. This multifaceted use of the norm of harmony allows the documents to apply it to the full range of social relationships.
Therefore, Leo does not need to take any additional steps in his argument in
order to bring the idea of harmony to bear on the relationship between employer and worker, this time using the analogy with the human body.[13]

Pius XII develops the theological context for the norm of harmony more
thoroughly in his 1957 Christmas Address, itself titled, "The Divine Law of
Harmony." The idea of harmony guides consideration of the common good.
Without the former, the latter, at least in its more proximate forms, is in peril.
"For the sake of the common good, the chief basis of action, not only of
Christians but of all men of good will, should be order and divine harmony
of the world. Their preservation and development should be the supreme
law which ought to govern the important meetings among men. If humanity today should fail to agree on the supremacy of this law, that is, on
absolute respect for universal order and harmony in the world, it would be
difficult to foresee what would be the proximate destiny of nations." So central is the language of divine harmony for Pius that he finds musical terms
the most apt for describing the universe. It is "a wonderful symphony, composed by the spirit of God."[14] The task of humanity, its "work on earth," is
to embody the harmony of God and God's creation. Humanity is not a pas-
sive audience—its being in the image of God does not place it in the front
row orchestra as a patron in the hall of creation—rather, it is "a performer
of the divine symphony."[15]

While Pius sometimes moves freely between the term "harmony" and that
of "order," John XXIII's *Pacem in terris* accents almost exclusively the latter,
drawing on the metaphor of God's law rather than the more aesthetic one
of God's symphonic spirit. Still, the basic claim is the same: there is a unity
that structures the plurality of the created order. This unity in plurality is
found in microcosm in the human person, who is created in the image of
the triune God. Its presence in the person as well as the cosmos allows its
application as the normative pattern to the full range of social relationships.
Thus *Pacem in terris* begins with the claim that there can be peace on earth
"only if the order laid down by God be dutifully observed." In line with Pius
XII, John argues that God's order suffuses the created universe. "Both in living things and in the forces of nature, an astonishing order reigns." There is
plurality in unity. The majesty of God's name "fills all the earth," and yet

there is remarkable "diversity." Such order "witnesses to the greatness of God."[16]

The Second Vatican Council's *Gaudium et spes* retrieves the language of harmony and balance. God creates an original harmony, and humanity is to play its role in restoring it. *Gaudium et spes* concurs with *Pacem in terris* that the proximate result of human participation in God's will for creation is peace on earth. "Peace results from that harmony built into human society by its divine Founder, and actualized by men as they thirst after ever greater justice." To achieve this peace, there must be a mutual harmonization between persons and society. On the one hand, persons must make their actions consonant with the common good. "Hence, the norm of human activity is this: that in accord with the divine plan and will, it should harmonize with the genuine good of the human race." On the other hand, society should be so ordered as to foster concord within persons. In the midst of various tensions, "human culture must evolve today in such a way that it can develop the whole person harmoniously." *Gaudium et spes* addresses these tensions in terms of "imbalances," which once again refer to the full range of the types of societal relations.[17]

Essayists on modern Catholic social teaching comment frequently on the shift of philosophical underpinnings from natural law theory to "personalism." Evidence of a change in emphasis is present in the development of the term "solidarity" as the new analogue to harmony, balance, and order. Pius XII is the first to use the term,[18] and Paul VI continues its usage as a way of linking empirical observation and moral obligation: "The reality of human solidarity which is a benefit for us, also imposes a duty."[19] Solidarity, like harmony, is at once both the way the world, at its most profound level, *is*, and the way it *should be* in all human affairs.

John Paul II is the pope who develops the idea of solidarity most fully, and he does so in *Sollicitudo rei socialis*. He begins by retracing the move from interpretation of reality to normative ideal. "In a world divided and beset by every type of conflict, the conviction is growing of a radical interdependence and consequently of the need for a solidarity which will take up interdependence and transfer it to the moral plane." However, John Paul goes further to develop the idea of solidarity as a virtue that is the practical link between solidarity as interpretation of reality and solidarity as normative vision. It is the *practice* of solidarity that allows one to move from interpretation to normative vision. "[Solidarity] is above all a question of interdependence, sensed as a system determining relationships in the contemporary world, in its economic, cultural, political, and religious elements, and accepted as a moral category. When interdependence becomes recognized in this way, the correlative response as a moral and social attitude, as a 'virtue,' is solidarity. This then is not a feeling of vague compassion or shallow distress at the misfortunes of so many peoples, both near and far.

On the contrary, it is a firm and persevering determination to commit one-self to the common good."[20]

In keeping with Catholic social teaching, John Paul II develops the idea of solidarity by providing a theological backing for it in terms of the triune God. In the light of faith, another person is "not only a human being with his or her own rights and a fundamental equality with everyone else, but becomes a living image of God the Father, redeemed by the blood of Jesus Christ and placed under the permanent action of the Holy Spirit." This view generates a different perspective on society. "Beyond human and natural bonds, already so close and strong, there is discerned in the light of faith a new model of the unity of the human race, which must ultimately inspire our solidarity. This supreme model of unity, which is a reflection of the intimate life of God, one God in three persons, is what we Christians mean by the word communion. . . . Solidarity therefore must play its part in the realization of this divine plan. . . ."[21]

The Conditions of Fulfillment

What we have seen so far is that the theological social theory in Catholic social doctrine begins with the empirical observation that all persons are social. This empirical observation implies a moral obligation to order society such that the patterns of interdependence—the unity of all the pluralities—allow and even foster the flourishing of all groups and persons. Such a society can be described as exhibiting harmony, balance, order, and solidarity. The next question, however, is this: what, more precisely, leads to this harmony, balance, order, or solidarity? What, in other words, are the *conditions* of fulfillment?

We can get at answering this question by noting two more observations made in Catholic social teaching. The first is that people relate to each other in a variety of social spheres—economic, familial, religious, cultural, as well as political. For instance, in *Redemptor hominis*, John Paul II writes, "Man in the full truth of his existence, of his personal being—in the sphere of his own family, in the sphere of society and very diverse contexts, in the sphere of his own nation or people, and in the sphere of the whole mankind—this man is the primary route that the Church must travel in fulfilling her mission."[22] The pope is saying that in order to understand persons at all, we must understand them in their social contexts. Moreover, he is saying that persons are not just social generically; they are social in particular ways, for instance, by being a parent, a business owner, a soccer coach, or a Eucharistic minister. The language of social "spheres" runs throughout the teaching.[23] In relating to each other, such spheres are what social theorists call "semi-autonomous." That is to say, to a large extent they have their own proper logic—for instance, the market and the parent-child relationship have their own dynamics. However, they are not utterly autonomous in that they overlap and affect each other—for instance the state of the market affects family life and vice versa—and, from a normative standpoint, they are all to be oriented toward the common good. In *Centesimus annus*, therefore, John Paul II articulates a concern: "People lose sight of the fact that life in society has neither the market nor the state as its final purpose, since life itself has a unique value which the state and the market must serve."[24]

Classical liberal political theory—with its move from the autonomous individual in the state of nature to contracting with others to form a state—tends to ignore the other forms of association through which persons relate to one another.[25] The role of the state is to protect individuals in their "private" zones of activity. As we saw with John Locke's delineation of fundamental rights in terms of "life, liberty, and property," the primary zone of protection is economic activity. Classical liberal *political* theory combines with classical liberal *economic* theory—the chief classical source of the latter being Adam Smith. While there are debates about whether Locke's natural-law limits on the acquisition and use of private property have any real force, Smith leaves no doubt concerning the absolute freedom a person has with regard to private property. Such a right gives a person, "the sole claim to a subject, exclusive of all others, but can use it himself as he thinks fit, and if he pleases abuse it or destroy it."[26] In other words, when the purer forms of classical liberal political and economic thought join together, the only discussion of the spheres of social life regard how the state is to protect the material things we produce and acquire. This is why immediately after John Paul II says that it is "in interelationships on many levels that a person lives and that society becomes more 'personalized,'" he goes on to observe, "The individual today is often suffocated between two poles represented by the state and the marketplace. At times it seems as though he exists only as a producer and consumer of goods or as an object of state administration." It is also why we need what John Paul II and the rest of Catholic social teaching call "intermediate communities," multiple forms of living in society that foster our flourishing in large part because they help to keep us from being sucked up into either the market or the state. Such intermediate groups, "in their turn, should not selfishly insist on their particular interests, but respect the interests of others."[27]

The second observation that Catholic social teaching makes that helps us get clearer on the conditions of fulfillment in the definition of the common good is that not all persons are fully involved in the various social spheres. For a variety of reasons—some complex and others quite simple and brutal—many persons are excluded. The state of society as it *is* is not the common good as it *ought to be*. The question then is how to include in the web of social relationships those persons who are excluded. It is in answering this question that Catholic social teaching in the last century has undergone its most profound change. There are a number of specific areas in which the social teaching has developed—for instance, with regard to the right to private property and the right of religious freedom—but the most fundamental change (it underpins the developments on both property and religious freedom) is from a hierarchical to a relatively egalitarian ordering of society as the primary condition of fulfillment.

Over the course of modern Catholic social teaching, the understanding of what kind of social arrangements produce the unified diversity in fulfillment undergoes a basic shift, particularly in the political and economic spheres. We have, to continue the musical metaphor, a modulation in the harmony. The earlier documents stress the importance of the hierarchical structuring of society across the full range of social spheres. One must relate properly "higher" and "lower" orders, groups, or persons, or else risk disorder. The documents speak of the participation *of* the "higher" element *in* the "lower"; that is to say, the lower groups have value insofar as they have the patronage of the higher. Those who would otherwise be totally excluded are integrated into the lower levels of society.

Gradually and selectively, Catholic social teaching has shifted to relative egalitarianism: the presupposition that equality best facilitates harmony and therefore that it is inequality that must be explained.[28] While the earlier documents speak of the participation of the higher in the lower, the later documents speak of *all* groups and persons' participation *in*—as opposed to their marginalization *from*—the full range of social spheres. Coupled with this shift in prudential judgment regarding what best facilitates harmony is a change in the degree to which the vision of an egalitarian eschatological community is allowed to impact the shaping of temporal society. The more the spiritual and temporal dimensions of salvation history intertwine, the more egalitarian the social theory.

This much said, it is important to make some clarifications before proceeding with the analysis. What occurs is a gradual shift in presumption in a limited range of social spheres. This means, first of all, that neither before nor after the shift does Catholic social teaching understand either hierarchical order or equality to be disharmonious *per se*. The change is in which ordering, once the general guidelines are set out, enjoys the benefit of presumption and which bears the primary burden of explanation. A presumption in favor of equality does not entail, for instance, that good reasons cannot be given for hierarchical structures within a business corporation, though it would mean greater alertness to the abuses of the latter organizational pattern. Secondly, the shift is a gradual one. However much the Second Vatican Council might have been a watershed event—and in my assessment it indeed was—the developments that are the focus of this section begin to take place early on in modern Catholic social teaching and continue to unfold in the writings of Paul VI and John Paul II. Thirdly, the shift in presumption does not take place to the same degree or even in the same way in all of the social spheres. In this chapter, I will focus on the political and economic spheres, where the change has been greatest.[29]

In Leo XIII's writings, the hierarchical language of "higher" and "lower" extends across the various social spheres. In each case, the one in the "higher" position is to command, legislate, judge, and punish for the sake of the common good; the one in the "lower" position is to obey—to carry out the order—also for the common good. Therefore, even in the economic sphere, where Leo decries excessive inequality and calls for a just wage that allows workers to acquire some private property, he does not, as his successors do, recommend worker ownership of the means of production or participation in workplace decision making.[30] Similarly, while he follows Aquinas in stating that there is no one legitimate form of government exclusive of others, his political theory is strongly anti-democratic. The *imperita multitudo* (variously translated "illiterate masses" and "untutored multitude") is incapable of self-rule.[31] In each case, only through the participation *of* the "higher" *in* the "lower" is the latter an active agent.[32]

The shift toward greater equality in the economic sphere begins with Pius XI's *Quadragesimo anno*. Central to this shift is Pius' extension of the distinction—made, but not emphasized by Leo—between the right to private property and the use of that property. Individuals may have the former, but considerations of the common good dictate the latter. As a result, the right to private property changes from being virtually absolute to being, however "natural," more of an instrumental right that must be exercised for the common good. When Pius applies this public understanding of the role of property to the workplace, his recommendations move beyond that of the just wage in language that speaks of everyone's participation or sharing *in* the activity rather than the participation *of* the higher in the lower. "[W]e deem it advisable that the wage contract should, when possible, be modified somewhat by a contract of partnership, as is already being tried in various ways with significant advantage to both wage earners and employers. For thus workers become sharers in the ownership or management, or else participate in some way in the profits." At play in the shift is the judgment that the gap between rich and poor, both in terms of material well-being and agency, is a threat to harmony. "[S]o vast and unfair a distinction in the distribution of goods" is not "in harmony with the designs of an all-wise Creator." After detailing its recommendations, the document insists that "unless efforts are made with all energy and without delay to put them into practice, let no one persuade himself that public order and the peace and tranquility of human society can be defended effectively against agitators of revolution."[33]

Pius XII continues this trend in the economic sphere—"Solidarity demands that outrageous and provoking inequalities in living standards among different groups in a nation be eliminated"[34]—and extends it to the political order.

The emphasis is on the agency of the full populace. The key distinction is that between the "people"—who display "the consciousness of their own responsibility, the true instinct for the common good"—and the "masses"— who, because they "wait for the impulse from outside," are "the capital enemy of true democracy and of its ideal of liberty and equality." Like Pius XI, Pius XII is not a strict egalitarian. His opposition to inequalities refers to only those based "on whim." Also like Pius XI, however, Pius XII shifts the burden of explanation to hierarchy. Indeed, for Pius XII, the primary question is which form of democracy best contributes to harmony.[35]

The shift to relative egalitarianism in the economic and political spheres becomes so thorough in the writings from John XXIII to John Paul II that not only do they no longer give the presumption to hierarchy, they focus on the "gap" between the rich and the poor, the powerful and the weak, as a problem of particular concern, not only in economic life, but in all spheres of society. John XXIII warns that "the wealth and conspicuous consumption of a few stand out, and are in open and bold contrast with the lot of the needy." When the inequalities are so dramatic, "human rights are rendered totally ineffective and the fulfillment of duties is compromised." The Second Vatican Council concurs that "Luxury and misery rub shoulders," in such a way that those who lack economic means "live under such personal servitude that almost every opportunity for acting on their own initiative and responsibility is denied to them, and all advancement in human culture and all sharing in social and political life are ruled out." Such a situation is "to the scandal of humanity." Paul VI warns that "the imbalance is on the increase," involving "the scandal of glaring inequalities not merely in the enjoyment of possessions but even more in the exercise of power."

In *Dives in misericordia*, John Paul II also emphasizes both the fact and the moral importance of the widening gap. "This fact is universally known. The state of inequality between individuals and between nations not only still exists; it is increasing. It still happens that side by side with those who are wealthy and living in plenty there exist those living in want, suffering misery. . . . This is why moral uneasiness is destined to become more acute." He elaborates on the issue at several points in *Sollicitudo rei socialis*, and comments, "The word *gap* returns spontaneously to mind" (emphasis in text). In *Centesimus annus*, John Paul expands the concern to include the gap in education and training that contributes to economic inequality.[36]

The primary problem with inequality is that it denies groups and persons the ability to participate in the life of the institutions that constitute civil society. The repeated call in the social teaching for society to be so shaped that groups and persons can indeed "participate in," "share in," or "take part in" its activities is so frequent that participation itself becomes the new norm guiding assessment of the health of the common good—that is, of whether groups and persons in fact have access to the conditions of fulfillment.[37] The oppositional term is "marginalization."[38] The link between equality and participation is so tight that the documents in this span often couple the terms, such as when Paul VI, in *Octogesima adveniens*, refers to "the aspiration to equality and the aspiration to participation" as the "two forms of man's dignity and freedom."[39]

As modern Catholic social teaching develops, then, it becomes increasingly clear that relative equality rather than hierarchy is the primary condition for the harmonious flourishing that characterizes the common good. Moral agency through participation in the various associations and institutions of society constitutes the main form of that flourishing because it also is how groups and persons participate in the life of God. While formal equality has gained the presumption over formal hierarchy, it alone, although necessary, is not a sufficient condition for flourishing. Indeed, the practice of equality without the practice of the virtue of solidarity does not yield harmony at all, but rather an individualism at the expense of the common good.

SIGNIFICANT THEMES FLOWING FROM THE COMMON GOOD

We have seen so far that any synthesis of Catholic social teaching best begins with the concept of the common good. The official documents define the common good as the conditions for fulfillment. Fulfillment itself is a quality of unity in plurality in society where each person's flourishing depends on and contributes to the flourishing of others, a quality articulated by the terms order, balance, harmony, and solidarity. The understanding of the primary condition of that solidarity has shifted from a more hierarchical to a more egalitarian presumption. In the remainder of this chapter, I will detail five specific themes that flow from this concept of the common good. Our work up to this point will allow me to do so without simply presenting a loose list of items because it will be clear how each of the themes follows from and relates to the core constellation of ideas that make up the common good and Catholic social teaching. The five themes are: human rights and duties, the option for the poor, private property and consumer society, subsidiarity, and peace.

Rights and Duties

The first theme regards the understanding of rights and their corresponding duties. Classical liberal social thought begins with the autonomy of the individual. Therefore, rights are simply protections of that individual against interference from others. Traditionally understood, such rights require little in the way of positive action on the part of others, and thus are often called "negative rights." They include those rights generally summed up under the heading of "civil and political rights," such as the right to be secure in one's person or property, to assembly and speech, and to religious freedom. Civil and political rights are often contrasted with those rights—called "social and economic rights"—that require more in the way of positive action on the part of others. Included in the latter, for instance, are the rights to work, food, clothing, housing, and health care. Classical liberal social thought, because it does not provide an adequate account of positive obligation toward other persons, rejects the idea of economic rights. Persons may have a *need* for food, housing, and clothing, for instance, but, the theory holds, these needs are best met if we simply protect private property; the general production of wealth in a market economy will serve everyone's self-interest in meeting these needs.

Because Catholic social teaching begins with an understanding of persons as from the beginning and always interrelated with each other, its presentation of rights, both in concept and content, is quite different from that of liberal political thought. In concept, Catholic social teaching provides a more communitarian basis for rights. Rather than being simply negative protections of isolated individuals against incursions from other isolated individuals, rights in Catholic social thought are, in the phrase of the American Catholic bishops, "the minimum conditions for life in community."[40] If the test of a society is whether persons are participating in rather than being marginalized from various spheres of communal life, then rights are best understood as the minimum conditions for that participation. Such an understanding makes sense: if, for instance, a person does not have the ability (the right) to vote, it is hard to have any significant form of participation in the political sphere; if a person does not have a job (the right to work), it is virtually impossible to participate in the economic sphere.

Moreover, the content of the Catholic approach to rights is different than that of classical liberalism because given that Catholic teaching begins with the understanding of persons as interrelated, there is no inherent exclusion of those rights—the economic and social rights—that require positive action on the part of others in order to be fulfilled. Indeed, Catholic doctrine strongly supports economic rights. In *Centesimus annus*, John Paul II writes that "the material goods which sustain life, satisfy people's needs," are "an object of their rights." His 1999 World Day of Peace Message goes even further, insisting on the "universality and indivisibility of human rights." In other words, economic as well as political rights apply to everyone and to everywhere. The pope elaborates, "Human rights are traditionally grouped into two broad categories, including on the one hand civil and political rights and on the other economic, social, and cultural rights." He continues, "All human rights are in fact closely connected" such that the "integral promotion of every category of human rights is the true guarantee of full respect of any individual right."[41] Thus, when they reject economic rights—together with rejecting the moral significance of the rich–poor gap and other aspects of official Catholic social doctrine—those who are commonly called Catholic neo-conservatives resemble (in an odd reversal of terms) classical and neo-liberal thought rather than the thought of the popes.[42]

Given that Catholic social teaching not only allows but calls for positive obligation toward others, it understands even civil and political rights to entail corresponding duties. This moral and legal point also has the support of an empirical insight: civil and political rights, traditionally understood as calling only for negative protections against incursion, actually require much more in the way of positive social arrangements in order to be realized. For instance, as we all witnessed with the 2000 presidential election, for the right to vote to be adequately realized requires from the state the significant positive action of providing reliable voting mechanisms, from machinery to personnel and even to transportation. In the Catholic view—as distinct from the classical liberal view—all rights, including political and civil rights, involve corresponding duties beyond simply that of not interfering with others. Catholic teaching summarizes these duties—to be carried out in all of the social spheres—under the general obligation to act out of the "duty of solidarity," but, as we see with the case of the right to vote, in particular instances these duties will take specific shape.[43]

Option for the Poor

An understanding of rights which accents the active participation in society of those persons previously excluded leads to the second theme that follows from the concept of the common good. In the last thirty years, beginning with Latin American liberation theology, the term "option for the poor" has developed, come into increased usage, and even been adopted by papal encyclicals.[44] This term has two interrelated meanings. The first involves a kind of priority of attention from society. If our understanding of the common good emphasizes all persons participating in the life of society, then the first question a society concerned with justice ought to ask is: who are the marginalized? The second meaning of option for the poor takes the idea of participation further to insist that the common good requires not only that those marginalized be included in society, but that their voices also be heard. The earlier social documents, those which favored a more hierarchically ordered society, articulated a version of the first meaning of option for the poor. Leo XIII insisted that their basic needs be met. Absent the second meaning, however, this is more simply (though importantly) a *concern* for the poor than an *option* for the poor.[45] The primary moral and social agents are those who are well off.

Later documents emphasize that including those previously marginalized from society involves their participation in a fuller sense: they have social agency of a kind that includes a say in the shaping of society. We have seen that while Leo XIII referred to the poor as the "illiterate masses" and counseled them to be patient, Pius XI extended economic justice to include not only a living wage, but also worker cooperatives, and Pius XII urged that we not remain "inert" as "the masses," but rather become a "people" acting in freedom and with responsibility. John XXIII writes in *Pacem in terris*, "that the men of our time are becoming increasingly conscious of their dignity as human persons. This awareness prompts them to claim a share in the public administration of their country." In *Centesimus annus*, John Paul II accents the economic sphere. "It is not merely a matter of 'giving from one's surplus,' but of helping entire peoples which are presently excluded or marginalized to enter into the sphere of economic and human development." Once in that sphere, those previously excluded can organize into "unions and other workers' organizations," which "enable workers to participate more fully and honorably in the life of their nation," and form an integral part of "a society of free work."[46]

Catholic social teaching and some versions of liberation theology differ on the amount of weight to be given to the voice of the marginalized. Official teaching insists that the option for the poor means only that all persons have equal voice, that the concept, in John Paul II's words, "is never exclusive or discriminatory toward other groups." In contrast, some instances of liberation theology press the point that the poor have a special and perhaps unique ability to interpret both the Gospel message and empirical reality. Therefore, the voice of those who are on the periphery of society ought to be given more weight than that of others. In either case, the participation of those persons previously marginalized from society will involve and require changes in the patterns of society itself in ways unanticipated by those persons who have been longstanding participants.

Private Property and Consumer Society

One area in which I think Catholic social teaching can improve is in addressing more frequently and in more detail the kinds of sacrifices that the well off will have to make in order to have the degree of participation for all people that the teaching itself calls for. At times, it appears that the inclusion of those who are now marginalized will involve simply an expansion of the pattern of activity that is already going on. There are, however, a number of notable passages that indicate otherwise. I cited above Paul VI's insistence that the option for the poor means that "the more fortunate should renounce some of their rights so as to place their goods more generously at the service of others," and that without this kind of action, "even equality before the law can serve as an alibi for flagrant discrimination, continued exploitation, and actual contempt," creating a society where "each one claims his own rights without being answerable to the common good."

John Paul II picks up this emphasis on the necessity of sacrifice in *Centes-imus annus*. Creating the conditions of fulfillment for all "involves sacrific-ing the positions of income and of power enjoyed by the more developed economies." To make good on the option for the poor, "it is not enough to draw on the surplus goods which in fact our world abundantly produces; it requires above all a change of lifestyles, of models of production and con-sumption, and of the established structures of power which today govern so-cieties."[47]

The primary lifestyle and model of production and consumption that needs to change is an understanding of private property that culminates in what John Paul II calls "consumer society," the third theme of Catholic social teaching that follows from the concept of the common good. The Pope writes in *Sollicitudo rei socialis* that private property is "under 'social mort-gage,' which means that it has an intrinsically social function, based upon and justified precisely by the principle of the universal destination of goods." A society driven by the quest for wealth such that all people do not share in the goods of the earth is a consumer society. John Paul II notes in *Redemp-tor hominis*, "Indeed, everyone is familiar with the picture of the consumer civilization, which consists in a certain surplus of goods necessary for man and for entire societies—and we are now dealing with the rich highly devel-oped societies—while the remaining societies—at least broad sectors of them—are suffering from hunger, with many people dying each day of star-vation and malnutrition."[48]

According to Catholic social teaching, the created goods of the earth are intended for everyone. Therefore, although there is a right to private prop-erty, from Leo XIII forward all of the popes have insisted, as indicated ear-lier, that there is a limit to the accumulation of wealth for one's own use. Leo states, "Man should not consider his outward possessions his own, but as common to all," and goes on to insist that "it is one thing to have a right to a possession of money, and another to have a right to use money as one pleases." Pius XI continues this line of thinking, and the Second Vatican Council cites Thomas Aquinas to take it even further. If the "universal desti-nation of created goods" means that material goods at the level of basic need are indeed rights, then what appears to be theft from the rich by the desti-tute is actually legitimate. "If a person is in extreme necessity, he has the right to take from the riches of others what he himself needs." Paul VI clarifies this point by quoting the early church father, Ambrose, who insists that such ac-tions are not theft because the goods were properly the poor person's in the first place. Therefore, when the well off give to the poor, Paul VI tells the for-mer, "You are not making a gift of your possessions to the poor person. You are handing over to him what is his. For what has been given in common for the use of all, you have arrogated to yourself." Put another way, "you" are the thief.[49]

Catholic social teaching's emphasis on the universal destination of goods, therefore, sets what I have elsewhere called a "maximum living wage."[50] One can earn as much as one wishes and even be worth as much financially as one can possibly be. There are limits, however, on how much of that income and wealth one uses for one's own living; the rest belongs to the common good. Such giving is not necessarily to the state and for the state to manage. Following the principle of subsidiarity, which I will discuss below, using one's wealth for the common good can be carried out, for instance, through mediating institutions like charities or through ownership of private businesses that turn profits not into exorbitant officer salaries but into the payment of living wages to workers or the creation of more jobs. When the consumerist doubter objects, "But I have earned this money," the reply from Catholic social teaching can be summarized, "Indeed you have. Our question is, 'Earned it for whom?' And our answer is, 'For yourself, yes, but also for the common good and for yourself only insofar as you are part of—that is, in harmony with and not disproportionate to—that larger good.'"

It is important to recognize that the gap between rich and poor in consumer society affects the well off as well as the poor, albeit in different ways. This follows from the starting point of the social theory in Catholic social teaching: we are social, and no one of us flourishes fully unless all of us are flourishing. This point can be easy to dismiss because it may seem that the well off materially are also doing well in other respects. However, Catholic social teaching is quite emphatic in its point that the well off in consumer society are in deep moral and spiritual peril, and not simply in relation to the afterlife. Consumer society is "contrary to what is good and true to happiness" not only because it consists of "the excessive availability of every kind of material good for the benefit of certain social groups," but, according to John Paul II, also because those privileged groups themselves often experience "a radical dissatisfaction" where "the more one possesses the more one wants, while deeper aspirations remain unsatisfied and perhaps even stifled."[51]

Subsidiarity

Accent both on giving the poor a voice and on recognition that the well off have their own moral liabilities indicates that Catholic social teaching inclines toward beginning with people where they are. The empirical claim that is the starting point of the teaching—that persons are social, are so through a variety of associations, and first of all through associations that are small and even intimate—here becomes a moral principle, that of "subsidiarity." This is the fourth theme that follows from Catholic social teaching's understanding of the common good.

Subsidiarity is a regulative principle; that is, it regulates how the various persons, associations, and institutions in society are to interact with each other in their exercise of solidarity. Present as an idea from the start but first articulated as a principle of Catholic social teaching in *Quadragesimo anno*, the basic insight of subsidiarity is that those persons, associations, and institutions most proximate to a problem situation are the best able to respond because they are most likely to have a fine-grained sense of the texture of the problem.[52] The actions of more remote institutions, however well-intentioned, can often lead to the opposite effects of those intended precisely because of that remoteness.

In the context of what we have said thus far, we can see that subsidiarity, with its emphasis on localness or proximity, also facilitates the active participation of persons. It is important to note, however, that the role of the larger and more remote institutions is not to abandon the persons and associations that are most proximate, but is rather to support them in their efforts. (The Latin root for subsidiarity, *subsidere*, means to "support.") Public education in the United States is an excellent example: while the primary role and responsibility in the education of children is that of the parents, the state "supports" this process by providing a primary and secondary school system. Situations *in extremis*—when the closer and more intimate groups fail—allow for direct intervention by the more remote institutions, but this is not intended as a permanent remedy. Excessive direct involvement leads to the atrophy of the intermediate associations. Foster care in the United States has the right idea, even if it is sometimes poorly executed: the presumption is that parents best care for their own children; in extreme situations, the state can intervene directly, but even here it is with the intention of ultimately returning the children to their parents. Permanent removal and alternative placement is a last resort. It should be added that the concern with subsidiarity is not simply over state intervention in other spheres of life and activity, but also over (a) the excessive intervention of any sphere in another (for example, economics into politics through lobbying and Political Action Committees) and (b) the excessive intervention of large and remote institutions *within* a particular sphere (for instance, when a large chain store with low overhead drives out small businesses which are already meeting the needs of the community).

I noted earlier how classical liberalism, with the idea that autonomous individuals "contract" into political society, tends to overlook those forms of association that form the matrix of most of human life and provide a mediating buffer between the person and the state. Strip away these mediating institutions and we can see why both present day conservatives and liberals are wedded to classical liberal thought. The strong emphasis is first on *no* state involvement except for the negative protection of civil and political rights. There is at best only thin rationale for positive "support" from the state.[53] Here is contemporary conservatism in its purest form. However, when there is call for state involvement, because there is insufficient emphasis on intermediate associations, that involvement tends to be excessive with regard to both its intensity and its duration. Here is contemporary liberalism in its purest form. Both stem from over-reliance on classical liberalism.

Peace

The September 11, 2001 attacks on the World Trade Center towers and the Pentagon have brought home a truth for those living in the United States that has already been a stark reality for many people throughout the world: the question of peace is not first of all a remote one. This theme of peace and armed conflict is the fifth and final one that I will discuss, and it follows from all that we have said above regarding the emphasis on the common good that grows out of an empirical observation that people and the associations which they form and inhabit—including states—are deeply interrelated; they are social.

In a social theory that begins with the observation that people are deeply interrelated with each other, peace is not simply the negative absence of overt conflict; it is the positive concept of "right relation with God and neighbor," and the documents variously describe peace as either the *result* of that right relation—that order, harmony, balance, and solidarity—or the right relation itself. The Second Vatican Council's *Gaudium et spes*, for instance, draws on the language of "harmony" to articulate the point clearly. "Peace is not merely the absence of war. Nor can it be reduced solely to the balance of power between enemies. Nor is it brought about by dictatorship. Instead, it is rightly and appropriately called an 'enterprise of justice' (Isa. 32:7). Peace results from that harmony built into human society by its divine Founder, and actualized by men as they thirst after ever greater justice."[54]

The American Catholic bishops, in their 1983 pastoral letter, *The Challenge of Peace*, continue the theme of peace as right relation with neighbor, as harmony or order. In the first major section of the document, the bishops elaborate on the scriptural understanding of peace to which they are indebted. The "individual's personal peace is not greatly stressed. The well-being and freedom from fear which result from God's love are viewed primarily as they pertain to the community and its unity and harmony. Furthermore, this unity and harmony extend to all of creation; true peace implied a restoration of the right order not just among peoples, but within all of creation." In the Bible, this right order is promised and sealed in a covenant that required people to act on behalf of their neighbor. "Living in covenantal fidelity with God had ramifications in the lives of the people. It was part of fidelity to care for the needy and the helpless; a society living with fidelity was one marked by justice and integrity."[55]

The positive conception of peace as a certain kind of relationship with God and neighbor described as order or harmony leads to a particular understanding of the just war tradition. This latter tradition is often described simply in terms of its summary principles: just cause, right intention, legitimate authority, last resort, reasonable chance of success, proportionality, and discrimination (also called non-combatant immunity). The just war tradition produces these principles, but to understand the tradition rightly, it is best to begin with its positive conception of peace as right relation with neighbor. When war is simply the absence of overt conflict, then war and peace are on the same moral plane; they are just two ways to carry out policy. This view is conveyed in the quote from Karl von Clausewitz's *On War:* "War is but a continuation of politics by other means." However, if peace is right relation with neighbor, then war is an aberration, not a continuation of the usual. As a result, there is at the heart of the just war tradition, both historically and normatively, a strong presumption against war. The burden of proof that a war has moral purpose and will be fought with moral restraint is on those who would use lethal force. The just war theory, therefore, is a theory about exceptions, and the principles are best understood as the strict conditions (arrived at over centuries of reflection) that must be met if war is ever to have as its purpose the return to and furtherance of peace.

The proposals and recommendations that are perhaps the most directly relevant to the United States after September 11, 2001, are those which take up the last two sections—one hundred twenty-nine paragraphs—of *The Challenge of Peace.* The bishops begin this portion of the document by taking up the scriptural theme of peace as a positive concept. "In a world which is not yet the fulfillment of God's Kingdom, a world where both personal actions and social forces manifest the continuing influence of sin and disorder among us, consistent attention must be paid to preventing and limiting the violence of war. But this task . . . does not exhaust Catholic teaching on war and peace. A complementary theme, reflected in the Scriptures and the theology of the Church and significantly developed in the papal teaching of this century, is the building of peace as the way to prevent war. This traditional theme was vividly reasserted by Pope John Paul II in his homily at Conventry Cathedral: 'Peace is not just the absence of war. It involves the mutual respect and confidence between peoples and nations. It involves collaborations and binding agreements. Like a cathedral, peace must be constructed patiently and with unshakable faith.'"[56] The rest of the document makes recommendations not only on the national policy level, but also, in recognition of the various spheres of life in which people live, to various vocations: priests, educators, parents, youth, the military, science, and media, as well as political figures. If one's understanding of peace is simply that of the absence of overt conflict, then these last one hundred twenty-nine paragraphs are irrelevant.

Yet, post-September 11, they may be the most relevant. No doubt, a document indebted to Catholic social teaching as I have described it and written in response to recent events would have to include analysis regarding the use of force. Moreover, even though it is arguable that, legally speaking, the acts of the terrorists fit under the category of criminal activity rather than "war" perpetrated by a nation-state, the just war tradition as a tradition in the restraint of the use of force is, as Tobias Winright has shown, still illuminating when what is in question is a kind of police activity rather than war in the technical sense.[57] However, given that the terrorist "cells" are transnational non-governmental organizations, it appears that much if not most of the focus ought to be at this level, and the positive conception of peace that extends to our relations with all persons and groups coupled with the principle of subsidiarity's local focus takes us right there.

When looking at models regarding peace, particularly after September 11, it is perhaps best to begin with intermediate associations like the Community of Sant'Egidio, Catholic Relief Services, and the Catholic Campaign for Human Development. The Community of Sant'Egidio is a Catholic lay association that began in Rome in 1968. It now has more than forty thousand members in sixty countries. Joined by a life of prayer and an ecumenical outlook, the community joins work on behalf of the poor with "peacebuilding." In their words, "Friendship with poor people led Sant'Egidio to understand better that war is the mother of poverty. In this way, love for poor people in many situations became work for peace, protecting it whenever it is jeopardized, helping to rebuild it, facilitating dialogue where it has been lost."[58] Members of the Community of Sant'Egidio have not only provided humanitarian relief to war-torn countries, but have also served as mediators in, for instance, Mozambique and Guatemala when otherwise the opposing parties would not have come together.

Catholic Relief Services, a relief and development agency of the United States Conference of Catholic Bishops since 1943 and presently serving eighty countries and territories, has also recently undertaken the explicit role of fostering peacebuilding in the form of (1) education, training, and workshops; (2) prevention and early warning; (3) peace and justice commissions; (4) interreligious dialogue; (5) citizen diplomacy; (6) mediation; (7) trauma healing and psychosocial work; and (8) post-conflict reconstruction as well as economic relief and development.[59] The CRS "Guiding Principles" are explicitly informed by Catholic social teaching. Recall the definition of the common good as the conditions for flourishing in all spheres of society. The CRS principles include the statement, "We believe that the development of economic, social, political, material, spiritual, and cultural conditions are necessary for all people to flourish and reach their full human potential and we accept our responsibility to promote the common good of the larger society."[60]

It is precisely in carrying out their efforts on behalf of the common good that the Community of Sant'Egidio and the CRS staff have come to recognize that economic relief and development require also the activities described under peacebuilding and that the building of peace requires forms of activity in all spheres and on all levels of social life. In other words, empirical field experience backs the moral point: peace and the pursuit of justice in all social spheres are closely interrelated.

Such empirical observations are also found in the official documents of the church. The Second Vatican Council's *Gaudium et spes* states, "If peace is to be established, the primary requisite is to eradicate the causes of dissension among men. Wars thrive on these, especially on injustice." Paul VI warns without advocating, "When whole populations destitute of necessities live in a state of dependence barring them from all initiative and responsibility, and all opportunity to share in social and political life, recourse to violence, as a means to right these wrongs to human dignity, is a grave temptation." He adds, "Excessive economic, social, and cultural inequalities among peoples arouse tensions and conflicts, and are a danger to peace." John Paul II makes clear that this point has transnational relevance when he says, "In fact, if the social question has acquired a worldwide dimension, this is because the demand for justice can only be satisfied on that level. To ignore this demand could encourage the temptation among victims of injustice to respond with violence, as happens at the origins of many wars. People excluded from the fair distribution of goods originally destined for all could ask themselves: why not respond with violence to those who treat us first with violence?"[61]

In short, Catholic social teaching does not support the actions of the terrorists, and may even back the use of armed force as part of a response; indeed, right relationship with neighbor may require the use of armed force. However, understanding people, groups, and nations as all deeply interrelated first and foremost presses the teaching to raise the question of what sort of relationships tend to foster violence. The September 11 terrorists gave into the temptation of violence and must be held accountable for doing so. The social teaching points in addition to the fact that there are conditions that persist that make that temptation palpable, and it is prudent in the deepest sense of an act of moral wisdom to attend to those conditions of social life that are hindering fulfillment for millions of people. The just war tradition, as a theory of exceptions, may allow force in response in this case, but Catholic social teaching urges us to look at and respond in a consistent manner to the day-to-day conditions that are all too common and that feed the temptation to violence. From the perspective of Catholic social teaching, only if groups and states follow this approach can recourse to violent responses to violence indeed become the exception.

It might be assumed that because the Catholic Campaign for Human Development focuses on the United States that any relation with peace is at best tangential, but such an assumption would be both thematically and empirically incorrect. Such an assumption might be based on an understanding of peace as pertaining to the absence of overt conflict between nation-states. However, from a thematic standpoint, an understanding of peace as right relation with neighbor coupled with subsidiarity's accent on local communities puts the activity of CCHD squarely in the concern of peace. Moreover, from an empirical standpoint, it is now evident that most of the violence in the world is indeed local violence, and any presupposition that the United States is exempt runs the danger of a shock similar to that following the Trade Center bombings.

CCHD, established by the National Conference of Catholic Bishops in 1969, has funded over four thousand projects developed by grassroots groups for poor persons. The mission is in keeping with all that we have said regarding the participatory nature of the common good: "By helping the poor to participate in the decisions and actions that affect their lives, CCHD empowers them to move beyond poverty."[62] In doing so, CCHD has reduced the incidence of violence in these communities by reducing the force of this "grave temptation." Again, the pope notes, "People excluded from the fair distribution of goods originally destined for all could ask themselves: why not respond with violence to those who treat us first with violence?" CCHD in conjunction with the groups it helps fund provides concrete reasons why not and concrete means for participation in a society where solidarity, order, balance, and harmony—in short, the common good—are manifested.

NOTES

1. This is a point made by Monika Hellwig in the Foreword to this volume.

2. Leo XIII, *Rerum novarum*, 38; *Immortale dei*, 3; *Libertas*, 21; Pius XI, *Quadragesimo anno*, 118; *Divini redemptoris*, 29.

3. John XXIII, *Mater et magistra*, 49 and 59; *Pacem in terris*, 130; Second Vatican Counsel, *Gaudium et spes*, 6 (cf. also 23, 25–26, 33, 75, and 84); John Paul II, *Centesimus annus*, 49 and 54.

4. Pius XII, "Christmas Address of 1942: The Internal Order of States and People," in *The Major Addresses of Pope Pius XII, Volume II: Christmas Addresses*, ed. Vincent A. Yzermans (St. Paul, MN: The North Central Publishing Company, 1961), 54; Second Vatican Council, *Gaudium et spes*, 24; John Paul II, *Sollicitudo rei socialis*, 40.

5. Pius XI, "Christmas Address of 1957: The Divine Law of Harmony," in Yzermans, 231; Second Vatican Council, *Gaudium et spes*, 32, quoting Second Vatican Council, *Lumen gentium*, chap. II, art. 9.

6. Thomas Hobbes, *Leviathan*, ed. C.B. MacPherson (Harmondsworth, England: Penguin, 1986), 185 and 189.

7. John Locke, *Second Treatise of Government*, ed. Peter Laslett (Cambridge, U.K.: Cambridge University Press, 1960), secs. 128–30.

8. John Rawls, *A Theory of Justice,* rev. ed. (Cambridge, MA: Belknap Press of Harvard University, 1999); for debates over whether Rawls' "thin theory of the good" is really a sustainable theory of the good, see Norman Daniels, ed., *Reading Rawls: Critical Studies on Rawls' "A Theory of Justice"* (Palo Alto, CA: Stanford University Press, 1989).

9. The two most influential treatments of Catholic social teaching that begin with the dignity of the human person are Cardinal Joseph Bernardin's "consistent ethic of life" and David Hollenbach's early book, *Claims in Conflict*. See Joseph Cardinal Bernardin, *Consistent Ethic of Life*, ed. Thomas Fuechtmann (Kansas City: Sheed & Ward, 1988); and David Hollenbach, *Claims in Conflict: Retrieving and Renewing the Catholic Human Rights Tradition* (New York: Paulist Press, 1979). John Coleman has criticized *Claims in Conflict* for its classical liberal bias in "Catholic Human Rights Theory: Four Challenges to an Intellectual Tradition," *Journal of Law and Religion* 2, no. 2 (1984): 343–366. It might be countered that, as his subtitle suggests, Hollenbach was only trying to get at the Catholic rights tradition. Others, however, have taken the dignity of the human person to ground the teaching as a whole. Moreover, it can still be asked whether the dignity of the human person is adequate to ground even the rights aspect of the social teaching. Hollenbach's more recent work itself attempts to ground rights in a more overtly social way, and his more recent thought, including a book in progress, focuses on the common good. See Hollenbach, "The Common Good Revisited," *Theological Studies* 50 (March 1989): 70–94.

10. Pius XI, "Christmas Address of 1957: The Divine Law of Harmony," 235–38; John XXIII, *Pacem in terris*, 131; Second Vatican Council, *Gaudium et spes*, 84.

11. Second Vatican Council, *Gaudium et spes*, 26. See also 74. Also, John XXIII, *Mater et magistra*, 65, and *Pacem in terris*, 58; Second Vatican Council, *Dignitatis humanae*, 6; Paul VI, *Populorum progressio*, 42; John Paul II, *Sollicitudo rei socialis*, 38.

12. Pius XI, *Quadragesimo anno*, 84; citing Thomas Aquinas, *Summa Contra Gentiles*, 3, 71, and *Summa Theologiae I*, Q. 65, A. 2, C.C.

13. Leo XIII, *Immortale Dei*, 14; and *Rerum novarum*, 15–16, and 21.

14. Pius XII, "Christmas Address of 1957: The Divine Law of Harmony," 244–45, 235, 241, and 237.

15. Pius XII, "Christmas Address of 1957," 238 (cf. also 239 and 240), 237, and 242.

16. John XXIII, *Pacem in terris*, 1–5.

17. Second Vatican Council, *Gaudium et spes*, 78, 35, 56, 8, and 10.

18. Pius XII, "Christmas Address of 1952: The Rights of Man," 160, 163, and 165–66. To my knowledge, Pius is the first of the modern popes to retrieve the patristic idea of solidarity. Cf. "Christmas Address of 1942: The Internal Order of States and People," 62; "Christmas Address of 1944: True and False Democracy," 87; "Christmas Address of 1950: Hope for the Future," 145 and 146.

19. Paul VI, *Populorum progressio*, 17.

20. John Paul II, *Sollicitudo rei socialis*, 38.

21. John Paul II, *Sollicitudo rei socialis*, 26, 38, and 40.

22. John Paul II, *Redemptor hominis*, 14.

23. Sometimes the term social "power," "domain," or "sector" is used as well as that of "sphere." See, for instance, Leo XIII, *Immortale dei*, 13–14; Pius XI, *Quadragesimo anno*, 42, 84, 103, and 108; *Divini redemptoris*, 23 and 34; Pius XII, "Christmas Address of 1942: The Internal Order of States and People," 54–55, and 59; John XXIII, *Mater et magistra*, 79; *Pacem in terris*, 18, 40, 98; Paul VI, *Octogesima adveniens*, 46–48; John Paul II, *Laborem exercens*, 5, 7, 10, and 18; *Centesimus annus*, 4, 19, and 44–45. The Second Vatican Council divides the entire second half of its document, *Gaudium et spes*, into sections on the different social spheres: family, culture, economics, politics, and international relations.

24. John Paul II, *Centesimus annus*, 49.

25. On this point, see Susan Moller Okin, *Justice, Gender, and the Family* (New York: Basic Books, 1991).

26. Adam Smith, *Lectures on Jurisprudence*, eds. R. L. Meek, D. D. Raphael, and P. G. Stein (Oxford: Oxford University Press, 1978): (A), vol. 1, 9–10. Two sets of students' notes of Smith's *Lectures on Jurisprudence* are extant. In the literature on Smith, they are abbreviated /LJ/ (a) (notes dated 1762–63) and /LJ/ (b) (notes dated 1766).

27. John Paul II, *Centesimus annus*, 49, and *Sollicitudo rei socialis*, 39. For other references to intermediate associations, see Leo XIII, *Rerum novarum*, 36–40; Pius XI, *Quadragesimo anno*, 78–87, 91–96; *Divini redemptoris*, 64–69; Pius XII, "Christmas Address of 1952: The Rights of Man," 163; John XXIII, *Mater et magsitra*, 65, 82–89, and 120; *Pacem in terris*, 23–24 and 64; Second Vatican Council, *Gaudium et spes*, 25, 52, and 65; Paul VI, *Octogesima adveniens*, 11–12, 25; John Paul II, *Laborem exercens*, 14; *Centesimus annus*, 13, and 48–49.

28. While my analysis differs in some key respects from his, particularly regarding the dating of the shift from justified inequality to relative equality, I have benefited much from Drew Christiansen's work in this area. See his "On Relative Equality: Catholic Egalitarianism after Vatican II," *Theological Studies* 45 (1984): 651–75.

29. For a treatment of the domestic sphere, and of women in domestic and other spheres in Catholic teaching, see Todd David Whitmore, "Cairo, Beijing, and Beyond: A Problematic Aspect of Catholic Teaching on Gender," in *The Challenge of Global Stewardship: Roman Catholic Responses*, eds. Maura A. Ryan and Todd David Whitmore (Notre Dame, IN: University of Notre Dame Press, 1997): 253–306, especially 264–300.

30. Cf. Leo XIII, *Rerum novarum*, 1–2, 16–17, and 35.

31. Leo XIII, *Immortale dei*, 3–4 (cf. also 17–20); *Libertas*, 23 (cf. also 24–25).

32. Leo XIII, *Rerum novarum*, 28; *Libertas*, 8.

33. Pius XI, *Quadragesimo anno*, 45–49, 56–57, 62, 5, and 64–65.

34. Pius XII, "Christmas Address of 1952," 165.

35. Pius XII, "Christmas Address of 1944," 81 and 80.

36. John XXIII, *Mater et magistra*, 69; *Pacem in terris*, 63; Second Vatican Council, *Gaudium et spes*, 63, 71, and 88; Paul VI, *Populorum progressio*, 8 and 9; John Paul II, *Dives in misericordia*, 11; *Sollicitudo rei socialis*, 14; and *Centesimus annus*, 33. See also from John Paul II, *Laborem exercens*, 17; *Sollicitudo rei socialis*, 9, 12–16, 28, 39, 42, and 44–45.

37. For the language of "participate in," "take part in," and "share in," cf., for instance, John XXIII, *Mater et magistra*, 49, 61, 65, 75–77, and 91–92; *Pacem in terris*, 26, 40–41, 56, 73–74, 79, 145–147, and 150; Second Vatican Council, *Gaudium et spes*, 9, 31, 60, 65, and 71; Paul VI, *Populorum progressio*, 1, 6, 27–28, and 30; *Octogesima adveniens*, 13, 22–23, 41, and 47; Synod of Bishops, *Justice in the World*, 6, 9, 18, 28, 42, 46, 53, 55, 65, and 67; John Paul II, *Redemptor hominis*, 17; *Laborem exercens*, 14, 22; *Sollicitudo rei socialis*, 15, 17, 33, 39, 44–45; *Centesimus annus*, 35, 43, and 46.

38. Cf., for instance, Synod of Bishops, *Justice in the World*, 10 and 16; *Evangelii nuntiandi*, 30; John Paul II, *Centesimus annus*, 33 and 42.

39. Paul VI, *Octogesima adveniens*, 22.

40. National Conference of Catholic Bishops, *Economic Justice for All* (Washington, D.C., 1986), 79ff.

41. John Paul II, *Centesimus annus*, 31; and "Message of His Holiness Pope John Paul II for the Celebration of the World Day of Peace," http://www.vatican. va/holy_father/john_paul_ii/messages/peace/documents/hf_jp-ii_mes_14121998_ xxxii-world-day-for-peace_en.html (January 1, 1999), 3.

42. On the many differences between neo-conservative thinking and Catholic social teaching, see Todd David Whitmore, "John Paul II, Michael Novak, and the Differences Between Them," *The Annual of the Society of Christian Ethics* 21 (2001): 215–232.

43. For reference to the "duty of solidarity," see, for instance, Paul VI, *Populorum progressio*.

44. See, for instance, John Paul II, *Centesimus annus*, 11, 57, and 58.

45. For the distinction between option for the poor and concern for the poor, see Donal Dorr, *Option for the Poor: A Hundred Years of Vatican Social Teaching* (Maryknoll, New York: Orbis, 1983). Dorr holds that there is less of "option" for the poor in later Catholic social teaching than I do.

46. John XXIII, *Pacem in terris*, 79; John Paul II, *Centesimus annus*, 57 and 35.

47. John Paul II, *Centesimus annus*, 57 and 35.

48. John Paul II, *Sollicitudo rei socialis*, 42; *Redemptor hominis*, 16.

49. Leo XIII, *Rerum novarum*, 19; Pius XI, *Quadragesimo anno*, 45–49 and 56; Second Vatican Council, *Gaudium et spes*, 69; and Paul VI, *Populorum progressio*, 23.

50. Todd David Whitmore, "The Maximum Living Wage, I," and "The Maximum Living Wage, II," at www.nd.edu/~cstprog (click on "Observer Columns" and find title).

51. John Paul II, *Sollicitudo rei socialis*, 28.

52. Early intimations of the principle of subsidiarity are in Leo XIII, *Rerum novarum*, 11, 28–29, and 41. The first use of the term is in Pius XI, *Quadragesimo anno*, 79–87. For later uses, see John XXIII, *Mater et magistra*, 53, 117, and 152; Second Vatican Council, *Gaudium et spes*, 86; Paul VI, *Populorum progressio*, 33; *Octogesima adveniens*, 46; John Paul II, *Centesimus annus*, 48. The passages which use the concepts of subsidiarity but do not name the principle are too many to mention.

53. Originally, the call for a public school system in the United States was the result of a concern for the establishment of moral—read Protestant—virtues, and it was religious and other associations that were the principal respondents to children in need who were without adequate family support.

54. Second Vatican Council, *Gaudium et spes*, 78. For the same point, but using the analogue term "order," see John XXIII, *Pacem in terris*, 167.

55. National Conference of Catholic Bishops, *The Challenge of Peace: God's Promise and Our Response* (Washington, D.C.: United States Catholic Conference, 1983), 32 and 34.

56. National Conference of Catholic Bishops, *The Challenge of Peace: God's Promise and Our Response* (Washington, D.C.: United States Catholic Conference, 1983), 200; quoting John Paul II, "Homily at Bagington Airport," Conventry, #2, *Origins* 12 (1982): 55.

57. Tobias Winright, "The Challenge of Policing: An Analysis in Christian Social Ethics" (PhD diss., University of Notre Dame, 2002).

58. The Community of Sant'Egidio, http://www.santegidio.org/en/contatto/cosa_ e_6.html.

59. Catholic Relief Services, *Peacebuilding Activities* (Baltimore: Catholic Relief Services). The Joan B. Kroc Institute for International Studies now hosts an annual summer in-service on peacebuilding for CRS field staff to aid in the reflection on peacebuilding and the development of the necessary skills.

60. Catholic Relief Services, "Catholic Relief Services Guiding Principles," at http://www.catholicrelief.org/about_us/what_we_believe/index.cfm.

61. Second Vatican Council, *Gaudium et spes*, 83; Paul VI, *Populorum progressio*, 30 and 76; John Paul II, *Sollicitudo rei socialis*, 10.

62. See http://www.nccbuscc.org/cchd/inbrief.htm.

II

CASE STUDIES

5

Introduction to Case Studies

Rev. Robert J. Vitillo

This collection of case studies is a timely and much-needed "roadmap" that guides the readers through various ways of putting Catholic social teaching into action in a practical and participatory manner. Regrettably, many students are not familiar with the concept or practice of Catholic social teaching. This fact was made painfully clear to me recently when, in the first class of a graduate level course on this topic, I asked my students why they had registered for the course. One student replied that she liked the sound of the words "Catholic Social Thought" and that the course hours were scheduled conveniently. She—and several other students in the classroom—acknowledged no prior knowledge or interest in the rich body of Church teaching that has its roots in the prophets of Israel, that was modeled on the life and deeds of Jesus Christ, that has been practiced for centuries by Christian communities throughout the world, and that has been articulated so clearly and persistently by our present-day pope and bishops.

As he has done so often during his pontificate, Pope John Paul II placed special emphasis on the Church's social mission when he closed the Great Jubilee Year 2000 and opened the Third Christian Millennium. Challenging the Church to center its attention on the plight of those living in poverty, he spoke of our world's great "economic, cultural and technological progress," which offers "immense possibilities to a fortunate few," while leaving millions of others not only marginalized but in living conditions "far below the minimum demanded by human dignity." He asks: "How can it be that even today there are still people dying of hunger? Condemned to illiteracy? Lacking the most basic medical care? Without a roof over their heads?" (*Novo millennio ineunte,* 50)

The pope did not pose these as mere rhetorical questions. He forcefully pledged the resources of the Church community and encouraged the commitment of individual Catholic believers to address the underlying causes responsible for the plight of poor people in the United States and throughout the world. Thus he offered the following guidelines to tackle poverty and injustice in this world:

> Christians must learn to make their act of faith in Christ by discerning his voice in the cry for help that rises from this world of poverty. . . . Now is the time for a new "creativity" in charity, not only by ensuring that help is effective but also by "getting close" to those who suffer, so that the hand that helps is seen not as a humiliating handout but as a sharing between brothers and sisters (*Novo millennio ineunte*, 50).

The community efforts described in this "case study" section represent a new "creativity" in social development and charity that facilitates "getting close" to those who suffer. They offer a "hand up" to people living in poverty by recognizing and refining the God-given talents and skills already possessed by people living in poverty and by promoting community-based action to end poverty, not just for a day, but for a lifetime. Of happy note to me personally is the fact that most of the community projects mentioned in this book have received start-up and ongoing funding from the Catholic Campaign for Human Development (CCHD). Founded in 1969 by the Catholic bishops of the United States, the Campaign was given a mandate to support community-based, self-help efforts at community change that are initiated and led by people living in poverty. In addition, the CCHD promotes "transformative" education among Catholics and others—an education that leads to conversion of individuals, families, and entire communities from self-centered concerns to a focus on the common good.

The case studies in this book generate a strong and vibrant sense of hope and power. They demonstrate what can be done when people gather together in community-based organizations that are committed to secure a "place at the table" of social-policymakers and elected officials and thus to rebuild the social fabric of our modern-day world. Whether focused on social planning or community organizing or advocacy on behalf of exploited workers in far-away lands, the protagonists in these various projects are shining examples and living proof that Catholic social teaching need not collect dust on bookshelves but can be put into action, that we can make a difference in our own lives and in the lives of countless others in our local communities. In the mantra of farm-workers for more than thirty years, *Si, se puede!* (Yes, we can!)

Now a roadmap for the reader. The following eight case studies take us on an extensive tour to very different communities and regions in this country. Our first stop is the South Bronx in New York where we meet young people with a vision and working plan for community revitalization and environmental renewal of their neighborhood. From New York, we head west to Chicago where we learn about The Resurrection Project and its work to build affordable housing, to promote home ownership, employment opportunities, and day care, and to nurture the community's cultural heritage. Traveling further north we visit the Twin Cities of St. Paul/Minneapolis, where we hear about the Neighborhood Development Center and its work to equip immigrant entrepreneurs with the skills they need to succeed. St. Anthony's parish and a PICO (Pacific Institute for Community Organization) local organizing committee is next as we reach the west coast in Oakland, California. Then on to San Antonio, home of the Alamo, where we see the work of COPS (Communities Organized for Public Service) to improve the quality of life for all San Antonians and to equip young people for quality jobs. Further east in agricultural Florida, we witness the struggles of today's farm workers to claim their human dignity. Next we circle back north to Baltimore, where we meet the leaders of BUILD (Baltimoreans United in Leadership Development). We learn about their landmark effort to achieve a living wage for city-contracted workers.

The last case study is unique. "Students against Sweatshops" explores the work of students on seven different college campuses throughout the country to respond to the issue of sweatshops, an issue with clear global and local dimensions. These students were concerned that some university apparel was produced in factories that operated under sweatshop conditions overseas, and they worked in various ways to respond to this concern.

Enjoy your learning tour!

6

Young Visionaries in the South Bronx

Alexia K. Kelley

In the South Bronx, New York City, Alexie Torres-Fleming and her young colleagues came together to found Youth Ministries for Peace and Justice (YMPJ) to make a difference in their community. The poverty of their area, with its loss of manufacturing jobs and concomitant creation of lower-paying service jobs, is striking. Mr. Rusk's discussion of "concentrated poverty" comes to mind here. How does the South Bronx compare to the national trends Rusk outlined? What are the opportunities for local residents to change their situation?

Given the poverty and the very real environmental and health problems associated with the sewage outflows into the river, along with high concentrations of diesel and car traffic, the group decided to focus its initial efforts on the restoration of the Bronx River. How does the "see-judge-act" process Professor Massaro described apply to this decision? One concern in applying it is the dearth of material in the Catholic social tradition on the environment. As Massaro notes, there are just a "few scattered passages." Why do you think this is the case? How do you think the tradition can develop in this area? In the meantime, what resources do you think the tradition does have to offer groups like the YMPJ?

That many of the key decisions for the South Bronx are obviously being made elsewhere raises the issue of "subsidiarity" that both Professors Massaro and Whitmore discuss. Who should have a say in decisions that affect the South Bronx? How might that work? Clearly related are the issues Mr. Rusk discusses on how policies affect local communities. One example is the Sheridan Expressway. Where is this decision being made? Who benefits and who loses with that decision? What skills and/or resources do the different actors bring to bear on that decision?

Facing the reality of environmental and health problems, Ms. Torres-Fleming is determined to stay and continue working: "I don't want to have to move to the suburbs to have clean air. People should be able to have clean air in their home community," she argues. Mr. Rusk urged that the "real city" is the whole metro area. What does Catholic social teaching offer in terms of the urban–suburban–metro links? What do you see happening in your own community?

Finally, in reflecting on the work her group does, Ms. Torres-Fleming asks, "How do we connect ourselves to the people around us and create the conditions of our common existence?" It's a large question. How would you answer it in light of the Catholic social tradition?

INTRODUCTION

Alexie Torres-Fleming believed that the young people in her South Bronx neighborhood could become visionaries and together create a new kind of future for their community. In 1992, she and a group of young people in the neighborhood founded Youth Ministries for Peace and Justice (YMPJ), a faith-based center for urban ministry dedicated to community organizing and youth development. Youth Ministries is located in the Bronx River and Soundview/Bruckner neighborhoods of the South Bronx. A focal point of YMPJ's vision is the restoration of the Bronx River. YMPJ members described the Bronx River in terms similar to their community—rich in diversity and assets, but neglected over time.

The Bronx River is twenty-three miles long and stretches from Westchester county in the north to the South Bronx. While it is beautiful and fully accessible to wealthier communities north of the Bronx Zoo, it is highly industrialized, dumped upon, and inaccessible in YMPJ's South Bronx neighborhood (YMPJ proposal to CCHD, Jan. 31, 2000). When there is a heavy rain, up to four million gallons of raw sewage are dumped into the river along the South Bronx neighborhood. This occurs because the South Bronx riverfront contains all five sewage outflows, and heavy rains cause the sewage to overflow through the rain pipes and into the river. In addition, childhood asthma rates in the South Bronx are among the highest in the country, triggered in part by air pollution and particulate matter from high concentrations of diesel and car traffic.

When neighborhoods experience environmental and health problems as serious as those of the South Bronx, success is often defined by the ability to escape from home and perhaps "give back" in charity to those left behind. This is just the message that Alexie and other YMPJ members, including David Shuffler Jr. and Carmine Kalil, heard growing up. Alexie herself succeeded on those terms by going to business school and getting a high-paying job as a corporate communications executive in Manhattan. But it is a message that YMPJ turned around when they created a complementary after-school and summer education program to engage young people as leaders and visionaries in their own South Bronx community.

Youth Ministries engages neighborhood young people in a four-phase process that promotes consciousness raising and critical thinking about their community and the world around them. This educational process helps young YMPJ members to take action in their community. Because of Bronx River pollution, limited park and green space, and disproportionately high asthma rates among residents, YMPJ zeroed in on environmental justice as its key focus. Since its founding, YMPJ has addressed Bronx River restoration, transportation, air quality, and issues of park and open space.

THE BRONX RIVER COMMUNITY—HISTORY AND CHALLENGES

As working-class Italians and Irish left the Bronx in the 1950s and 1960s, zoning and transportation policies changed, and the waterfront was industrialized. In those same years, city and state policies resulted in the Bronx being surrounded by four expressways—the Cross Bronx, the Bruckner, the Sheridan, and the Bronx River Parkway. The Cross Bronx Expressway sliced the peninsula in half and created a new neighborhood—the South Bronx on the southern peninsula. In constructing the Sheridan expressway, engineers rechanneled the Bronx River, effectively destroying farmland and displacing thousands of families.

Because the South Bronx lies right between Manhattan and the suburbs of New Jersey, Westchester County, and Connecticut, this "peninsula" was a convenient place for city officials to put subways and highways that allow people from these outlying neighborhoods to come through as quickly as possible. Every day more than 220,000 vehicles and diesel buses come through the South Bronx. This high concentration of diesel and car traffic contributes to disproportionately high rates of childhood asthma. The community has a 15.6 percent hospitalization rate for asthma, compared to 9 percent citywide (Keeping Track of New York City's Children, 1999).

In addition to asthma, particulate matter may also contribute to kidney diseases, and YMPJ is working with New York University Medical School to study the environmental impact on respiratory and kidney health in the community. Alexie herself has developed asthma, as have many of the YMPJ members. She carries an inhaler with her wherever she goes and has used diet along with breathing and relaxation techniques to control her symptoms.

The YMPJ target neighborhoods (Bronx River and Soundview/Bruckner) are two of the most impoverished neighborhoods in the South Bronx

Congressional District, one of the poorest congressional districts in the country. Within the congressional district, the poverty rate is 35 percent. The poverty rate is much greater—50 percent—for all the children living in YMPJ's target area. Sixty-five percent of children in the district are born into poor families, 40 percent of children live in families on public assistance, and over 90 percent of public school students receive free lunches.

The South Bronx, along with Harlem, has been designated as a New York City Empowerment Zone community. The socioeconomic distress in these two Empowerment Zone communities is due primarily to the region's economic shift from a manufacturing center to a center of information exchange, finance, and administration. The city lost more than 500,000 manufacturing jobs between 1970 and the early 1990s. Although almost 400,000 new jobs were created in the 1980s, they were primarily in services, including financial, real estate, business, legal, and health care. A substantial proportion of Zone residents do not have the education and training that the new industries demand and cannot compete for jobs in the newly structured labor market. This, in addition to the fact that a large number of service sector jobs pay minimum wages, keeps many South Bronx residents in poverty. (Bronx County Empowerment Zone/Proposal www.ezec.gov/ezec/NY/ny.html)

ORIGINS OF YOUTH MINISTRIES

In interviews at the YMPJ offices, David, Alexie, and Carmine all talked about getting the strong message either from parents or coaches that success meant getting as far away as possible from poverty and their poor neighborhood. As a teenager attending a Catholic Franciscan parish, Alexie was introduced to Catholic social teaching through the parish's community action, which planted other seeds.

Alexie points to a powerful faith experience that called her back to her community while working in corporate communications uptown. She began volunteering and doing some work in her childhood parish. When she helped organize a neighborhood prayer rally against drugs, local drug dealers responded by torching a local parish, making death threats against the priest, and burning the sanctuary, breaking stained glass windows and statues. Twelve hundred people attended a prayer march, offering forgiveness and reconciliation to the arsonists. Ultimately, Alexie quit her job in midtown Manhattan and returned to her community, living on savings and unemployment as she organized YMPJ. In a neighborhood of fifteen thousand young people, there had never been a youth-serving organization.

Alexie described traditional youth programs as "warehousing youth," keeping them away from negative influences and off the streets. She noted that the YMPJ young founders had a different vision, asking themselves,

"How do we design a program . . . that still encourages young people to do well in school, encourages higher education, but then challenges young people to stay in the neighborhood to use the skills they have gained, not just for charitable giving back, but to see yourself as one with the community?"

YMPJ founders began to build a community of young people "who see their success tied up" in the community of people, rather than being driven by an exclusive concern for their own individual success. Alexie talked about how a sense of solidarity can emerge very naturally. "It is very different for me to struggle for a clean river or better education from afar; it is much more compelling if my own children will be a part of that education system. The whole idea of solidarity becomes important. . . . Our children will be in the education system or have or not have the opportunity to play in the river. This builds a sense of solidarity in a natural, organic way."

Alexie described this "individual hero" mentality as a strong emphasis on individual financial and career success and the strong message to escape and get something better for your children. She pointed out that Catholic social teaching challenges this message:

> There's a principle of Catholic social teaching that says we have a responsibility to family and community, that we see the community as our larger family. Sure it's great that your kids have trees and get to go to good schools, but the problem with that is that all the gifts that God has given you are being used to protect just two or three people. I think the call to family and community is to share and use our gifts to protect other people and to live a life of generosity. This is a different level than wanting only to "take care of your own."

YMPJ'S YOUTH DEVELOPMENT PROGRAM

YMPJ's youth development program teaches young people about the role of faith in repairing the community, with a specific emphasis on Catholic social teaching. It culminates with young people leading community-organizing projects that seek to directly impact and improve their neighborhood. The program is a membership-based model that consists of four distinct educational phases: (1) Arts for Activism, (2) Education for Liberation, (3) Assessment and Training, and (4) Community Organizing. In the first phase, Arts for Activism, young members are introduced to concepts of social justice and activism through dance, mural painting, music, and drama. Young members learn to tell their stories and visions of the world and their community, and they learn the power of the arts in self-awareness and social change.

In Education for Liberation, young people participate in education and wellness activities and focus on a curriculum of peace and justice, indigenous

Latino and African American history, and current events. The youth-developed curriculum introduces them to leaders, movements, and social justice history, while improving analytical reasoning, basic math ability, literacy, and academic skills. Young participants explore community health issues such as asthma and AIDS, as well as their connection to environmental and social inequities.

In Assessment and Training, young people prepare themselves for community action through mentoring and training in community organizing activities and through community mapping and assessment, critical print and video journalism, and through prayer and reflection. In the final phase, Community Organizing, young people step into action, based on St. Thomas Aquinas' "See, Judge, and Act" principles. In the "See" stage, members gather information, attend meetings, and conduct meetings with peers, residents, and leaders. In the "Judge" stage, young people critically engage what they discovered in the prior stage, through power analyses and strategy development. In the "Act" stage, the members implement an organizing strategy.

A FIVE-POINT PLAN

David Shuffler Jr., twenty-one years old and a graduate of St. Raymond's Catholic High School in the South Bronx, was a founding member of Youth Ministries. He got involved just after eighth grade when he was fifteen, with a little push from his mom. Today, David is on the staff and is co-coordinator of the RIVER Team, as well as a New York City certified tree pruner.

RIVER Team, short for "Reaching and Including Youth Voices for Environmental Rights," is YMPJ's youth-led environmental project. The RIVER Team emerged from a community needs assessment. David coordinated a group of fifteen young people, ages thirteen to eighteen, to map the assets and needs of the community. The mapping was part of the third phase of the youth program, Assessment and Training, during which the young people noted every single asset of the community, for example, the number of stores, parks, and vacant lots. David described the results:

> Some things that came up were: housing, policing, open space/environment, schools, employment. . . . These were from oral surveys; we had a chart when we talked to people. How do you feel about the community? People would say: "Okay, but there aren't parks for my kids to play in; or the policing or the housing is awful; or my kids have asthma."

With these five general areas, the team decided to tackle the issues of environment and open space. "We sat down and strategized. How do we tackle this big issue? We decided: Let's go to every park in our community (there are only four or five) and assess what they have. We knew most parks in the community were cement parks; they have some swings and fields, but really no space to just relax and be with your family, because our community did not have this kind of space."

RIVER Team's findings were significant. As noted above, the Soundview–Bruckner/Bronx River community is criss-crossed by four highways, and the Bronx River, which runs through it, is not accessible. Although there are more than fifteen thousand young people living in one square mile of the neighborhood, there are more parking lots and vacant lots than there are parks. The national standard proposes 6 acres of parkland per 1,000 people, but the district has only 1.7 acres per 1,000 people. The community is 144 acres deficient in parkland, with only .3 percent of the land used as open space for outdoor recreation.

According to David, the RIVER Team was particularly interested in Starlight Park, which had been abandoned for twelve years due to inaccessibility and poor lighting. The park is bordered by the river on one side, and by a highway and highway ramps on another side. RIVER Team noticed that there were other issues related to the park and that a comprehensive plan was needed. The RIVER Team thus developed a five-point environmental organizing effort, Project ROW (Reclaiming our Waterfront), which consists of the following five strategies:

1. *Renovation of Starlight Park*: a campaign to have the New York City Department of Parks and Recreation and the New York State Department of Transportation finance the redevelopment of the park, including river access, row boating, lighting, and a riverfront amphitheater.
2. *Restoration of the Bronx River and Greenway Development*: restoration of the portion of the Bronx River bordered on the north by the Cross Bronx Expressway and on the south by the Bruckner Expressway. Development of an extended Bronx River Greenway connecting the communities along the Bronx River.
3. *Decommissioning of the Sheridan Expressway*: this plan would create twenty-eight acres of parkland to replace the Sheridan Expressway. The Sheridan Expressway was planned to run north–south through the Bronx, linking all the other Bronx Expressways and the New England Thruway. However, the northern segment was never built, and a disorganized interchange causes perpetual traffic jams—with related pollution contributing to asthma and other health concerns.
4. *Edgewater Road*: designate an abandoned cement plant on Edgewater Road in the community a "brownfield site" (an abandoned, potential toxic industrial site), and, following cleanup, develop parkland, a community arts gallery, and other small business ventures. ROW is seeking

to designate a one-hundred-year-old abandoned train depot, designed
by architect Cass Gilbert, as a historic landmark.

5. *Increase use of mass transit and decrease diesel bus use*: YMPJ advocates increased city and state spending on public transportation, without increasing diesel bus use in the Bronx (diesel-produced particulate
matter is a known trigger for asthma).

MAKING CHANGE: TACKLING THE ISSUES, POLICIES, AND THE PROCESS

Significant state funds of $420 million are already appropriated right now to
double-deck and expand all three highways that border YMPJ's neighborhood: the Sheridan, the Bronx River Parkway, and the Bruckner Expressway.
YMPJ sees these appropriations as a major threat to the health of the community, and they work on many levels to address the interrelated issues.
YMPJ is addressing relevant laws that include neighborhood zoning, federal
clean air and water acts, dumping laws, and basic enforcement regulations
for all of the above. YMPJ members take their concerns for more clean and
accessible transportation (including natural gas buses instead of more diesel
buses) to the city, the State Transportation Department, the mayor's office,
and the state assembly.

State policies do not support public transportation expansion, nor do they
support increasing its accessibility to all people. These policies also often
create the need for more car travel by expanding highways. Alexie describes
a misperception on the part of the Burrough president, who sees more highways as links to jobs and economic development. In reality, most people in
YMPJ's neighborhood and in surrounding neighborhoods do not use highways to get to their jobs: only 20 percent of South Bronx residents own cars.

David described the state and local agencies and officials not as enemies,
but as sometimes "opponents." He noted that in their work, YMPJ has opponents sometimes because we "have different points of entry." For example, with the State Department of Transportation, "their job *is* transportation,
mass transit, buses, highways." And for elected officials, "often they have
certain things they want to accomplish in their own lives; a lot of politics get
involved."

Zoning laws often disproportionately place industrial facilities along wa-
terfronts in poor neighborhoods, or they place a higher concentration of
waste-transfer stations in lower income areas. For example, the South Bronx
handles 80 percent of waste for the entire city of New York. YMPJ works with
other community organizations (such as La Puente, Hunts Point Community
Development Corporation) to challenge the policies that place these facilities. The State Department of Environmental Conservation, the City Depart-

ment of Environmental Protection, and the Federal Environmental Protection Agency (EPA) are among agencies that permit these facilities. Only the city regulates zoning laws. For example, the South Bronx waterfront is zoned for placement of a waste station or industrial site, while the waterfront in upper Manhattan is zoned residential.

Enforcement is also a problem in lower income communities like the South Bronx. "There is very little enforcement of the Federal Clean Air and Water Acts in poor neighborhoods," Alexie observed. According to Alexie, in wealthier communities there is strong enforcement against illegal dumping, including protective fencing and cameras. But in the South Bronx there are no signs posting the fines or cameras to monitor illegal dumping.

Recently the RIVER team, with help from the National Guard, pulled forty-eight cars from the two mile stretch of the Bronx River in their neighborhood. The effort received a lot of press, and the governor came to talk about the cleanup. YMPJ had adopted their neighborhood section of the river through a public/private parks partnership. The YMPJ members wrote a letter to ask the National Guard for help and did intensive preparatory work for the cleanup. They mapped out the width and depth of the river and the distance between the cars. They also mapped each tree along the riverbanks and constructed tree guards to protect them. RIVER Team members checked for turtles and fish to protect their habitats and cleared out weeds for the National Guard.

POLICE RELATIONS

Relations with police are also a top concern of YMPJ, and it hits very close to home for the young members. Amadou Diallo, a young immigrant to the Bronx, was shot over forty times by city police officers five blocks from YMPJ offices in February 1999. He was shot in the doorway of his apartment building as he reached for his identification. Officers thought he was reaching for a gun and had confused him with another man. David noted the importance of living in the community in relation to working on this issue: "As a young man living in the community, these are my problems that I live and see every day. Police brutality is not a long-distance issue. . . . These issues affect me."

Alexie described the threat of violence by police that the young people feel all the time and the especially high tensions during the trial. YMPJ has been concerned about changing the tone of anger and hatred. Alexie referred to the dignity of the human person, that even if you are in "total disagreement with the mayor on something, behind all that is the person. We are called to stand for what is right and to struggle for what is just; but we are called also to be rooted in love. You don't put out a fire by adding more fire. Nothing in nature gets better by adding the same thing; you have to do something different to make it grow." In this spirit, YMPJ seeks to "work responsibly on our community policing projects with young people."

COMMUNITY EMPOWERMENT— OPPORTUNITIES AND OBSTACLES

In their work, both Alexie and David talked about the central importance of empowerment and ownership by the community. "Just as important as not having a highway is the process of empowerment that we go through to get to this place." They noted that it may take longer because they may not all have relevant training, but "we can't have a missionary mentality." "Something happens psychologically when there is no ownership for change. People will continue to believe that somebody from outside will come in and save us. Sometimes the enemy is ourselves and our reliance on the pastor or somebody to do it for us."

Creating a sense of ownership is key. Alexie observed that social change happens with "enabling people in the community to run the process, to develop strategies, and it happens nonviolently." David noted how important it is for the community to feel a sense of ownership: "To feel as they cleaned this river, that is everything. . . . Once you have a sense of ownership you don't litter. I have that same ownership of my community as I do of my parents' house because they own it. I am inclined to clean up my community, because this is where I plan to live the rest of my life. I plan on raising my kids here."

Some of the obstacles and challenges that YMPJ faces relate to both how the community perceives itself and how it is perceived by outsiders. Alexie described the problem: people don't believe that "poor people in a community can be organized to do anything. . . . Sometimes there are assumptions made and the community is not respected." For example, sometimes YMPJ is not invited to an event around which it is has played a major role. Other times officials may use language and expertise in a way that excludes community members from participating in the process. David described the challenge of convincing the community about the importance of what "we can do." It is a challenge to change people's mind-set about needing to escape from the community. In addition, Alexie noted that sometimes the community is not connected to the importance of nature. For example, she described how sometimes residents cement over rare green space in yards.

"Making sure that we are getting to the root causes of things" is also a big challenge, according to David. In responding to the community's needs for employment, YMPJ has to be careful not to turn into a direct service organization. When they are trying to organize around an issue, "it is sometimes hard to get people to come work with us, because they have so many other needs." YMPJ tries to respond to those needs by supporting young people with internship stipends and offering day care at meetings. It is a challenge to stay focused on "changing the systems that are in place."

Also, issues are often complex and deep. Even if YMPJ achieves a goal, the road ahead is often complicated. For example, the brownfield site was given to Parks and Land, and now YMPJ is raising money for assessment and cleanup. However, on that same property there is private land with tires and an unused road, so YMPJ is required to explore the private ownership. Even victory can be complicated.

CATHOLIC SOCIAL TEACHING

Reflecting on Catholic social teaching more directly, Alexie noted that "a great thing about Catholic social teaching is that it's all written in the affirmative. It doesn't say 'you should not do this.' Rather it affirms things: the dignity of human life, the dignity of work, solidarity." This provides a great reservoir of energy for YMPJ's work. She concluded, "We are constantly acting in the affirmative, as opposed to fighting against oppression (although this is inherent), but the main thing that pushes you is the positive force and vision."

She noted that the preferential option for the poor is very important, especially because "when the world teaches the preferential option for the wealthy, God chose to be made flesh amongst us. This gives great dignity to people, when they can really embrace this and understand this. . . ." The dignity of work is also important, and YMPJ sees this value expressed especially when they stipend the young people involved in the program. "They have a responsibility and work to do; people are counting on them, looking to them; that's what dignity of work is about: To make a contribution in work, and to be honored for what I do in my own community." Alexie also noted that there will be "lots and lots of jobs created on this waterfront." YMPJ wants to make sure that the people in the neighborhood have an opportunity to work in those jobs.

Carmine Kalil, who coordinates YMPJ's elementary school program for six- to eleven-year-olds, said that he "learned the deeper meaning of church and Catholic social teaching" at YMPJ. "It is responsibility not only to ourselves, but to others, to the community." A lot of the social teachings are "things we already do, and I just didn't know it—that makes me feel good."

Alexie elaborated on the call to family and community:

It's a beautiful thing really to see yourself as called to family and community, not just to your primary family. How do we connect ourselves to the people around us and create the conditions of our common existence? Not just my own personal existence, not hiding away. . . . How do you disconnect yourself from all the things that divide you from your community and keep you blind to the reality that the community is your family?

VISIONS FOR THE FUTURE

David's hopes for the immediate future in the South Bronx include practical successes such as restoration of the Bronx River, decommissioning of the Sheridan Expressway, and, in the long run, the fulfillment of the RIVER Team's five strategies. Alexie envisions a renewed South Bronx neighborhood: "I want my kids to be able to swim and play in the water and my Dad to be able to fish. I don't want to have to move to the suburbs to have clean air. People should be able to have clean air in their home community." She spoke of the importance of nature in her own life: "I live here, and sometimes I can go out on the river and see the swans and egrets and camarats and all sorts of fish and turtles—this gives me peace and a break that I need; it renews me in my work."

Alexie pointed to Martin Luther King Jr.'s understanding of a dream versus a fantasy: a dream is grounded somewhere in reality. She noted that at YMPJ's beginnings, many people thought she was crazy, but so many of the young people's dreams have been realized:

> While to many people our dreams might seem crazy, they are grounded in reality, and we have young people who have become visionaries . . . who can close their eyes and draw a picture of the world as it should be, and the Bronx River as it will be. This does something beyond social change; this does something to young people that adults have been trying to figure out for a long time. How do you get a kid to care enough about themselves to not hurt themselves, get pregnant, or hurt someone else? Give them a bigger project, bigger than themselves, they can be part of, connect to, have a vision and picture in their mind, something to make them want to get up in the morning.

7

The Resurrection Project

William P. Bolan

Chicago is home to some three million people in a tapestry of racial, ethnic, and class groupings. In the lower west side are three low-income neighborhoods, Pilsen, Back of the Yards, and Little Village, which are home to mostly Hispanics, African Americans, and immigrant families. It is here that "The Resurrection Project" (TRP) was created to meet the needs of the diverse communities struggling with such issues as poverty, crime, lack of jobs, and affordable housing. Six parishes joined to form TRP in the hopes of addressing those major issues. This effort brings to mind the discussion of Professor Massaro on religion and metropolitan regions. Neighborhood housing became the focus of their work, and issues of "gentrification" or "progress" were encountered. How does Mr. Rusk's discussion of racial and economic segregation as well as his analysis of housing issues relate to this?

An enormous challenge TRP faced was the initial reluctance of the skeptical residents to get involved in the political process. Professor Weigert noted this reluctance in the body politic in general. And as Professor Whitmore pointed out in discussing the conditions of fulfillment in the definition of the common good, "not all persons are fully involved in the various social spheres." Why is it important that they be involved? What did TRP deem as necessary steps to change this situation in its communities?

Throughout the story of TRP, the concept of subsidiarity is evident. One example: the Archdiocese of Chicago closed St. Vitus Church, a loss for the community, but the late Joseph Cardinal Bernardin eventually agreed to sell the church complex to TRP for one dollar. To determine what use to make of the complex, TRP went to the people to see what they deemed crucial. With decisions often being made at higher levels, what role should be played by more grass roots groups, as well as authorities in the political arena?

One of the central frames for the work of TRP is voiced by Fr. Dahm: "We're committed to the poor—the poorest of the poor." How does the discussion of Professors Massaro and Whitmore on the (preferential) "option for the poor" relate to this aspect of TRP's approach? How do you think it plays out in your own community?

INTRODUCTION

How much difference can a community organization make? The neighborhoods of southwest Chicago are commonly the location of economic inequality, racism, gang violence, and widespread drug use. Many would think that a community couldn't fight for social change against such endemic conditions. But in 1990 a small coalition of southwest-side parishes set out to prove that real change can come by challenging people to draw on their faith and form organized community relationships. Their success has been striking.

The Resurrection Project (TRP) achieved its dreams by organizing to improve housing, supporting the community's marginalized women and children, promoting its residents' opportunities for employment, encouraging community businesses, and nurturing its cultural heritage. Above all, it has supported the formation of lasting networks and institutions through which its people may effectively advocate for their community vision.

Among its successes, TRP has seen the construction of over 110 homes for low- and moderate-income families. Through successful lobbying, over two million dollars has been secured from the city of Chicago for this project. In addition to building new homes, the organization has helped close over two hundred new home, conventional, and home improvement loans. TRP has also developed a $1.2 million community center that provides day care for 208 children, an after-school program, and a community arts center. It has begun a supportive housing and social services program for homeless women and children. The unemployed and underemployed are assisted through a community employment center. And neighborhood businesses receive support through a cooperative, which assists contractors in getting bids and provides a loan fund, which gives them the necessary funds. Finally, networked community block clubs and TRP's participation in a larger city-wide effort to shape policy enables its members not only to voice their opinions but also to become involved and powerful agents for change.

THE AREA

Chicago is the largest city in the Midwest, with a population of nearly three million. Like most major American cities, Chicago is strongly divided along ethnic, cultural, and class lines. Also like most major cities, neighborhoods whose residents have been the victims of discrimination tend to fare the worst in levels of income, employment, housing, health care, crime, and gang activity. This is the case in the lower west side neighborhoods where TRP has initiated its efforts to build healthier communities—Pilsen, Back of the Yards, and Little Village.

Pilsen is a well-defined neighborhood that had, in the late 1990s, a population of approximately 46,000 residents, 88 percent of whom were Hispanic. Of these, about 90 percent were Mexican American. Back of the Yards had a population of 53,000 and was also predominantly Latino. While Little Village was more diverse, it was still constituted by a majority of people of color: Latinos comprised 38 percent of its residents, and African Americans 41 percent. These neighborhoods were largely working poor immigrant families, with over 50 percent of residents having been born outside the United States.

Starting over twenty years ago, these neighborhoods witnessed a dramatic decrease in levels of employment and adequate housing while the population level soared. As of the time of this study, almost 30 percent of Pilsen residents and 32 percent of Back of the Yards residents are below the poverty level, compared to a citywide average of 21 percent. Median family income is $23,000 in Little Village, $22,000 in Pilsen, and $20,800 in Back of the Yards, but the overcrowding that characterizes Latino communities (23 percent of Pilsen residents live in overcrowded conditions, compared to 8 percent citywide) drops the per capita income to approximately $8,000—one of the lowest rates in the city. By comparison, in 1990 the median income for a family of four in Chicago was $43,000. Only 22 percent of Pilsen's housing units are owner-occupied, as opposed to a rate of nearly 50 percent throughout the city. Local gangs and the presence of drugs have also reduced the level of safety and quality of life. Pilsen, for example, has one of the highest violent crime rates in the city. Despite all of these factors, though, Latino immigrants keep coming to Chicago, while the overall population of Chicago continues to go down. The higher standard of living available in America continues to draw impoverished families out of Mexico and other Latin American nations.

HOW IT HAPPENED: THE CHALLENGE OF ORGANIZING

When TRP was conceived in 1990, its initial focus was to organize the people of Pilsen and to help them take action on the issues that most affected their struggling community. Like many grassroots organizations, however, TRP was not experienced in organizing their people and motivating them for community action. It was also unclear which issues the residents of Pilsen most wanted to address. The leadership of the six founding parishes, therefore, committed $30,000 for the hiring of a community organizer, Michael

Lofton. Lofton asked for a list of community leaders and conducted personal one-on-one visits with each of them. The purpose was to identify and clarify the pressing concerns of the community, to gain their commitment to TRP, and to identify possible leadership for the project. The six founding parishes also prepared reflections for the block clubs. These reflections contained passages from scripture and were intended in part to help elicit reflection upon community members' hopes and dreams for the barrio. In the end, several core issues emerged, among which were cleanliness, safety, housing, jobs, education, and youth.

The project initially attempted to reduce crime by appealing to local police. However, it soon became clear that they lacked the power and organization to move the police effectively. Furthermore, the scope of the problem was enormous. The project changed tacks and focused instead on issues of neighborhood housing. TRP saw the attainment of decent and affordable housing as a task that they could address realistically. TRP thought that local residents could best strengthen their community by first buying land and improving existing properties. Improving housing was seen as a way to build up the community and address problems such as crime at the root.

The project worked to secure low-interest loans for home improvements and to purchase existing housing stock. The project pursued these goals by working with Neighborhood Housing Services (NHS), a nonprofit agency. They also made active use of the major opportunity provided by Mayor Richard M. Daley's "New Homes for Chicago" program. This program sold vacant lots to residents for the construction of new homes. Lots were sold for ten dollars, and grants of up to $20,000 were given toward construction costs. TRP partnerships with ten institutions provided low-income mortgages with no points and no application fee. To encourage participation in the program, The Resurrection Project conducted workshops to educate residents in the home-buying process. Over 110 homes were built by this initiative, making TRP the largest not-for-profit participant in the "New Homes for Chicago" project.

The Resurrection Project also worked to provide more affordable rental units for neighborhood residents, including seniors. TRP now owns and manages six redeveloped low-rent buildings with a total of fifty-five apartments that house over two hundred people. Federal corporate tax credits for affordable rental units helped make these projects possible. When its rental units and commercial developments are combined, TRP has secured the management of over $40 million in development projects.

How were these feats achieved? The leaders of TRP realized they needed to develop and forge institutional and political partnerships to meet their goals. TRP knew that theirs would be a relatively short-lived effort if they did not receive their life and direction from their members. Thus, Lofton worked to make community members actively and visibly involved in the building of their neighborhoods. Also, community businesses and city leaders had to be convinced that the community was behind their efforts. As Raul Hernandez, current president of TRP's board of directors, put it, TRP "had to convince the politicians that the community was behind the ideas we had." However, getting Pilsen residents involved in political processes was not as easy as the leadership might have wished. Based on past experiences at home, Mexican immigrants in particular viewed the political process as inherently corrupt and pointless. Furthermore, in a community where roughly 50 percent of the residents are undocumented, political participation was seen as a possible threat to resident status. As Fr. Chuck Dahm, a member of the board of directors, noted, the "biggest wake-up call" in his organizing efforts was coming to grips with locals' resistance to politics.

These obstacles notwithstanding, TRP persisted and succeeded in securing the involvement and organization of the community. At the inaugural meeting in 1990, TRP members were asked to commit not only to improving housing, but also to voting and participating in the census. Workshops were held in TRP parishes to inform residents of their eligibility for the "New Homes for Chicago" program and to educate them in the home-buying process. More importantly, the existing base communities, represented by the local block clubs, were strengthened and expanded as vehicles for voicing community concerns, for establishing and maintaining partnerships with the institutions vital to their survival (e.g., local banks, businesses, area police, and local and city government), and moreover for building the social fabric of the community. In tandem with the churches, these clubs came to form a backbone of TRP initiatives and advocacy.

TRP realized that further expansion of its partnerships and initiatives was vital to overall community health. To this end, TRP expanded into the neighborhoods of Little Village and Back of the Yards, broadening its membership from six member parishes in 1990 to fourteen today. It was also the key factor leading to its participation in United Power for Action and Justice, a citywide organizing effort that focuses on issues of housing, healthcare, and community life. Only by joining forces in a metropolis-wide organization did TRP feel that it could act to institute the structural changes necessary for the permanent improvement of their neighborhoods. Likewise, TRP's leadership regularly participates in Industrial Areas Foundation (IAF) training programs. Through these partnerships and the continued cultivation of its relationship with city and regional power structures, TRP strives to become more than just a surface-scratching solution to the problems of southwest Chicago. TRP believes that social change occurs to a limited extent at the neighborhood level. In the future, they hope to help bridge the gap between the local, regional, and national issues that affect their communities.

These organizational steps have given TRP the ability to leverage additional financial and political support. Once the early involvement and successes of the community were witnessed by the mayor, aldermen, and local financial and civic institutions, it soon became clear that they, in turn, needed TRP support and business. For example, TRP had to carefully cultivate its early relationship with Mayor Richard M. Daley. While his initial response was positive. It was only when TRP became a substantial organization in its own right, however, that the city awarded the lion's share of the two million dollars that provided the linchpin of TRP's new home construction program in 1993. Similarly, banks and other financial institutions that initially had to be persuaded to grant high-risk mortgages now actively seek TRP business. Fr. Dahm's goal to "convince authorities that we need[ed] to be taken into consideration" was met through the project's initial organizing achievements. These, in turn, led to the housing successes that captivated the attention of the community and the city at large.

SUCCESS BREEDS SUCCESS

These successes paved the way for the other achievements that came to represent TRP. Moving beyond its focus on housing, TRP recognized that much more than physical infrastructure was necessary to achieve its goal of building a healthy community. New initiatives were born out of both "opportunity and necessity," and likewise by the passions and drives of its members. For example, when the Archdiocese of Chicago closed St. Vitus Church in 1990, this setback was turned into a triumph when Cardinal Bernardin eventually agreed to sell the church complex to TRP for one dollar. Polling its membership, the project decided that day care and after-school programs were some of the most pressing concerns of the community. Thus the Guadalupano Family Center was born. TRP used the old St.Vitus Church complex for a $1.2 million project that opened in 1995. This community facility houses a day care center that provides care for 208 children and an after-school program. It also houses a community arts center with resident Latino theater, music, and dance troupes. This center has been a dynamic vehicle for nurturing the vibrant cultural heritage of the TRP neighborhoods. *Centro Familiar Guadalupano* also houses the administrative offices of TRP.

Membership concerns also drove TRP initiatives when a local woman religious made the TRP board of directors aware of the urgent need for shelter and counseling for homeless women and their children. To help those of its members in such crisis situations, TRP began a supportive housing program (1996) to provide shelter, support, and counseling. This comprehensive program of social services tries to make single-parent families self-sufficient in one to two years. It has a particular focus on Latino women with a history of domestic violence. In a related initiative, in 1998 TRP started project *Esperanza Familiar* (Family Hope) to help build strong families by helping mothers and fathers improve communication and parenting skills. This program is important to families who have just relocated from Mexico and are dealing with cultural readjustment issues, especially intergenerational ones. Slowly but steadily TRP has grown from a community organizer focused on housing to also become a provider of comprehensive services.

Another issue that TRP has recently taken up is how to promote its residents' employment opportunities. The Resurrection Employment Center was initiated in 2000 to provide job-skills assessment and employment counseling. In addition, it offers access to computers, photocopiers, voice mail, and fax machines. TRP has also encouraged entrepreneurship through the formation of a coalition of local construction businesses. The Resurrection Construction Cooperative currently helps thirty-two local contractors get contracts, estimate bids, and establish accounting procedures. It also makes loans available to both new and established contractors. The Resurrection Loan Fund provides short-term loans ranging from $30,000 to $90,000 for new construction and rehab projects managed by TRP.

Of course, TRP's emerging success brought new challenges of its own. As soon as TRP became a real player in Pilsen, at least one community-organizing effort opposed it, seeing it as a threat to its own city funding. Likewise, in recent years some aldermen and residents have opposed TRP initiatives to renovate buildings for use as rental units. Rental development, it is alleged, contributes to the overcrowding problem in Pilsen. Some TRP members have also seen racism as an element of this opposition. Since quality low-income housing attracts not just Hispanics, but also African Americans and members of other racial groups, opponents have characterized TRP's work as one of "integrating" the community. In meeting these challenges, TRP has had no hesitation about fighting for justice and all its members' rights. As a general rule, however, TRP has tried to avoid acrid confrontations, striving instead to settle disputes by trying to build partnerships and by opening minds wherever possible. TRP has focused on changing community attitudes in order to be the most effective instrument for social change.

CHALLENGES FOR THE FUTURE

From the beginning, TRP has worried about a threat of gentrification posed by its own efforts. By improving the quality of life and property values in their neighborhoods, TRP risked contributing to the displacement of the very people they wanted to help: the working poor families of Pilsen, Little Village, and Back of the Yards, and those who want to move there and find a better way of life. Fr. Dahm observed that the challenge is to find a way "to make all boats rise and yet avoid gentrification." Property values and property taxes have indeed risen in the TRP neighborhoods. Fr. Dahm is encouraged, however, that "all the [housing] that we've built has been affordable." Further, he adds, "we have recruited people from the area—we have not brought in people from outside the neighborhood" to live in TRP's developments. In the final analysis, he says, TRP made the decision to improve the neighborhood knowing the risks involved. He notes that "you can't build a real nice new home and clean up the whole street and then say, 'Well, its value is still the same as it was ten years ago.'" He insists, however, that "that's part of progress . . . that's not gentrification."

Some members worry that TRP might move away from its grassroots character as a community organizing effort, especially because it provides a great number and variety of services. The organizing role, in their opinion, forms the core identity of TRP and has made it successful. By becoming more of a comprehensive service provider, they fear TRP will be unable to concentrate on involving residents in their community. As one staffer said, TRP must continue to challenge and educate its citizens "to act for change." Insofar as TRP functions as a service provider, it is harder to ask this of their residents—to get them to see that TRP is about more than the meeting of immediate needs. Others do not agree that the dual goals of providing services and organizing are causing problems for TRP. But as one TRP pastor noted,

> the biggest challenge is forming people and [their] critical consciousness....When we serve somebody, we want that person to be involved. And we have to have the structure for the involvement, we have to have a formation so they understand [what we're about] and get committed. . . . If they just come for a basket of food and they get the basket and they go away—what difference have we made?

A related problem that TRP workers mentioned is the question of how to continue to be led by the concerns and desires of the community itself. As one former organizer says, "The challenge is always to stay connected with the community." Another worker notes, "This is what has kept us on track." TRP still recognizes that the core of its mission is to empower its residents to be able to effect change themselves. Lead organizer Juan Salgado believes that real social change requires the "transformation of people, [and] not necessarily of institutions. You could transform the Chicago Board of Education and have it fall apart tomorrow. When you transform people . . . you change things forever." For this reason Salgado says, "We need to make others change makers." The biggest resource that he and other leaders of TRP see in their communities is their capacity to "keep hope alive" and to maintain the vision that change is possible. The biggest enemy is apathy. Raul Hernandez, president of the board of directors, noted that TRP's driving force is its belief that "We all have the chance to be the controller of our destiny." The best hope for TRP, he says, lies in cultivating a new generation to inherit this message.

Recent initiatives include increasing TRP's block club organization, creating one hundred units of affordable housing, launching an innovative community-based college dormitory, developing a new health clinic, and expanding its employment centers. Above and beyond these, Susana Vasquez, until recently the deputy director of TRP, states that the "last issue" is community safety. The crime rate on the southwest side continues to stunt the growth of Pilsen, Little Village, and Back of the Yards. While TRP's initiatives have substantially improved the quality of life in these areas, the problem still remains largely intractable. TRP hopes, however, that the efforts to restructure their neighborhoods will eventually dismantle this final foe.

CATHOLIC SOCIAL TEACHING AND TRP

Fr. Dahm insists that "one of the major problems of community organizations in the United States is they are only superficially connected to the churches; they are not infused with the spirit of Catholic social teaching." This is not the case with TRP. As one staffer says, "we *live* Catholic social teaching." From its conception, the leadership of TRP saw the message of the social encyclicals as an embodiment of their mission statement: "to build relationships and challenge people to act on their faith and values to create healthy communities through organizing, education, and community development." The key, Fr. Dahm says, is to make people aware that there is not a distinction "between the Church and action and the community."

Raul Raymundo, the executive director of TRP, stresses that Christianity is much more than what goes on in houses of worship. "We *are* our brother's keeper," he insists. Faith is "not just about praying—it's really more about acting." This vision of faith is about providing services, building relationships, and establishing structures that can effect real social change in the community. TRP, he states, has "issued a challenge to the community . . . to develop a vehicle to address issues of social justice." This social justice is not about isolated acts of charity directed toward individuals, but establishing patterns of change for the community. This is what he sees as the role of TRP. "It's part of our faith that we lead by example," Raymundo proclaims.

The leadership of TRP is consciously committed to the core values of Catholic social teaching. "The role of the church . . . is to assure justice and equality and lack of discrimination," Fr. Dahm says. This commitment is articulated in various ways. One way TRP speaks of their mission is by exercising a preferential option for the poor. "We're committed to the poor—the poorest of the poor," Fr. Dahm stresses. TRP believes that the principle of the preferential option for the poor distinguishes itself from many other community organizations. For example, TRP does not target the population at large. Fr. Dahm notes, "We're not here to help the better off people. That's not what we're about. If we're going to do that we could be any kind of development corporation." For this reason TRP has seen to it that all of its housing has been affordable. TRP has helped make it possible "that people making even minimum wage . . . could buy a home," Fr. Dahm observes.

Raymundo speaks of another way TRP understands its mission. Faith, he says, is about "building the kingdom [of God] on earth." This kingdom, he insists, is not just spiritual. It's about justice in and for the community. Echoing Raymundo, Fr. Dahm sees the concept of the kingdom as the central kernel of Catholic social teaching. Fr. Dahm stresses that "the Church's job is to promote the kingdom of God, and the kingdom of God is not just religious. It's economic, it's political, it's social. . . ." Jesus' example of caring for the conditions of his time, Fr. Dahm says, forms the paradigm for Christians today. "Jesus was concerned about [building] the reign of God and *we're* concerned about building the reign of God. That's the role of the Church." This understanding of the Church's mission guides all of TRP's activities. Fr. Dahm emphasizes that "we're trying to establish a society where [the values of] equality, justice, and preferential option for the poor are being lived and celebrated."

In the organizational meetings of the base communities and in the training of staffers, TRP members meditate on biblical passages from which the social encyclicals are derived. "The gospels form the basis of Catholic social teaching," one worker notes. The primary passage used is Luke 4:18–19: "The Spirit of the Lord is upon me, because he has anointed me to bring glad tidings to the poor. He has sent me to proclaim liberty to captive and recovery of sight to the blind, to let the oppressed go free, and to proclaim a year acceptable to the Lord."

The meaning of this passage and the struggle to implement it is the prism through which TRP sees the community and the world around it. Ultimately, they say, the saving work of TRP is born out of reflection on their faith.

8

The Neighborhood Development Center

Steven M. Rodenborn

In 1993, Mihailo Temali founded the Neighborhood Development Center (NDC), a not-for-profit organization that assists small business entrepreneurs in twelve low-income neighborhoods in St. Paul and Minneapolis, Minnesota. As Rusk discussed, the growth in population for the United States in the 1990s was largely due to increased immigration, including illegal immigration, and this is borne out in the story of the NDC and the Twin Cities. How does your community compare?

Mr. Temali himself grew up in St. Paul in an immigrant family, and the Serbian Orthodox Church offered critical support to his family and to many of the immigrants. There are special challenges involved when not all immigrants are legally documented. What is the role of the NDC? What can/should the Church do in such a situation?

Professor Massaro talked about the "charity path" and the "justice path." The approach of NDC, centered as it is on development of skills that will enable people to start and/or carry on their businesses, seems to exemplify the latter. Can we (must we?) combine both "paths" somehow? How does the work of NDC compare/contrast with that, for example, of the YMPG in the South Bronx?

People are inspired to do their work for different reasons, as seen by the articulated motivations of several NDC staff and people served by it. Mr. Temali, on the one hand, is clearly motivated by his Christian faith and sees NDC as a contemporary equivalent of the Church of his youth in supporting newcomers. So, too, with one of the people served by NDC; he, like Mr. Temali, draws strength from his faith. Two staff members, on the other hand, while recognizing the significant role the Catholic Church has played in their commitment to justice, no longer practice their faith. Yet clearly *many of the themes of the Catholic social tradition take on life in the NDC work, from affirming the call to community and participation, to working in solidarity with others, to opting to help those most vulnerable in our society. How important is it that the CST be explicitly articulated in this work? What kind of challenges do different motivations present to the common work of NDC?*

INTRODUCTION

The Neighborhood Development Center (NDC) was founded in 1993 to serve St. Paul/Minneapolis residents as a response to the challenges faced by a community development corporation known as Western Initiatives for Neighborhood Development (WIND), a subsidiary of Western Bank in St. Paul. WIND successfully employed the methods utilized at the South Shore Bank in Chicago by making available financial capital in low-income urban neighborhoods for revitalization. WIND found, however, that it was exceedingly difficult to attract businesses into these neighborhoods. WIND learned about the underground entrepreneurs active in these neighborhoods and set up NDC as a nonprofit organization to develop their talents for the purpose of neighborhood development.

THE COMMUNITY

Minneapolis and St. Paul lie directly next to each other on the Mississippi River in southeastern Minnesota and are often referred to as the Twin Cities. With a total metropolitan area population of nearly three million people, St. Paul is the state capital while Minneapolis is the larger of the two cities and sees itself as the cultural capital of the state. The close proximity and unique characteristics of each city create plenty of friendly competition. Important industries in the area include education, technology, insurance, and agriculture. According to the 2000 census, the per capita personal income for the area is $26,347. The unemployment rate sits below 3 percent. It is a prosperous and successful economic hub in the upper Midwest.

Yet, there are certainly those who have not been included in the economic success of the region. There is a family poverty rate of 4.3 percent and a child poverty rate of 8.3 percent. The Twin Cities have experienced a dramatic demographic change in the last twenty years, from almost entirely white to larger percentages of immigrants and people of color, including Latinos, Native Americans, Hmong, and Somalians. The population is 5.5 percent African American, 4.3 percent Asian American, 3.4 percent Hispanic and under 1 percent Native American. Metro Trend Watch 2001 (Wilder Research

Center, August 2001) documents the following. The Minneapolis school district is 71 percent minority (versus 50 percent in 1990), and the St. Paul public school district is 65 percent minority (versus 42 percent in 1990), which contrasts with any suburban district in this area (which are 95 percent white). Second, in St. Paul, 37 percent of all public school students do not speak English at home. Third, lower-income students in the Minneapolis and St. Paul public school districts have risen from approximately 45 percent in 1990 to approximately 62 percent in 2000. It is within this context and these challenges that NDC attempted to serve the community.

THE MISSION

The Neighborhood Development Center offered training, lending, and technical assistance to emerging small business entrepreneurs in twelve low-income neighborhoods throughout the Twin Cities, attempting to address the unique concerns faced by these neighborhoods. A 1988 study, undertaken in one of the neighborhoods in which NDC now operates, discovered that 11 percent of the residents operated home-based businesses, creating a literal underground economy.[1] An underground economy fosters businesses that rarely employ more than the entrepreneur, fail to revitalize local vacant business corridors, and do not allow for the formation of local leaders and a corresponding sense of community pride. NDC attempted to bring these entrepreneurs into the mainstream economy, which in turn would create employment opportunities, encourage the redevelopment of aging commercial space, and form new leaders living and working within their neighborhoods.

The neighborhoods in which NDC offered its services were facing daunting challenges at the time of the organization's conception. In 1992, the family poverty rate in the targeted neighborhoods reached 30 percent, while the child poverty rate stood at 45 percent.[2] The main business corridors were facing abandonment due to a deteriorating infrastructure and rising crime. Those who had the means to escape these blighted areas moved to the new neighborhoods of the suburbs or into gentrified regions of the city, leaving behind vacant homes and commercial buildings. In return, waves of immigrants and many of the urban poor moved into these areas. Of course, these individuals had many of the same dreams as their predecessors. The new residents wanted to support their neighborhoods and families, and, for many, the possibility of accomplishing this as business owners was appealing. Most of the new residents, however, were lacking the education and experience necessary to successfully operate a small business. Additionally, immigrants facing language and cultural barriers were effectively locked out of the mainstream economy. NDC offered the tools necessary for the neighborhoods to overcome these challenges.

PROGRAMS AND SERVICES

NDC tapped into the entrepreneurial energy already present in the low-income neighborhoods. It designed the *Neighborhood Entrepreneur Training Program* (NETP), a sixteen-week program offered in the neighborhoods served by NDC. The program, which met in each neighborhood, trained the entrepreneur in the skills necessary to operate a small business. Under the guidance of a professional business trainer, the entrepreneur-in-training studied management, bookkeeping, marketing, and other important areas of business. Participants, with incomes less than 80 percent of the area median, were residents of an NDC neighborhood and were committed to operating their businesses within that neighborhood. Structuring the NETP around participants' neighborhoods was not simply an incidental element of the NDC program. Mihailo Temali, executive director of NDC, insists, "I have never in my whole life of growing up and living and working in inner city neighborhoods, found that people who are from there or live there hate their neighborhoods. They love their neighborhoods. They live there by choice." Graduates of the NDC program had a special interest in the revitalization of their own community. They felt a particular sense of ownership and responsibility toward the betterment of their neighborhoods

NDC also offered the *Ethnic Entrepreneur Training Program* (EETP) throughout the St. Paul and Minneapolis area. NDC felt that the challenges facing the large American Indian, Hmong, Latino, and Somalian communities in the Twin Cities were best addressed from within those communities. Many of the potential entrepreneurs operated businesses in their homeland and simply needed assistance maneuvering through the bureaucracy and legal system of the United States. Predictably, language was also a unique challenge for many of these ethnic groups. Even entrepreneurs who were able to develop a high level of English fluency following their move to the Twin Cities found the use of their native languages in the classroom to be of benefit.

Mr. Ramon Leon, a Mexican American graduate of the EETP and the founder of Mexam Upholstery, was most appreciative of the Spanish courses despite his well-honed English. Mr. Leon explained that difficulties in comprehension are not necessarily due to the use of new words, but with the way in which new concepts are presented in non-native languages. "Concepts from Spanish to English change, so sometimes it is more difficult for me to understand in English than in Spanish." The EETP was designed with these particular needs of the people it served in mind, and it quickly found success.

Additionally, the EETP alleviated problems NDC faced when blending different ethnic groups in training sessions. Ethnic prejudices obviously exist in all cultures, and this often led to disruption and frustration in the training program. NDC discovered that a program directed toward a particular ethnic group was more rewarding for participants while reducing unnecessary ethnic and racial conflicts.

A third program offered by NDC was *RECIPES for Business Success*. This program attempted to serve the needs of those interested in developing a food-related business. Adherence to food and safety regulations often requires a considerable amount of education and experience. One NDC staff member talked about the difficulty in acquiring all of the necessary licenses for the entrepreneurs in her program and the way in which it exemplifies the importance of a program such as RECIPES. She said, "Trying to figure out which businesses need city and state licenses, which need only city licenses, and which need only state licenses—it is challenging!" She continued by telling the story of one NDC staff member who found it necessary to camp out at the state agricultural department in order to get the answers needed to move forward with an entrepreneur's plans.

One NDC staff member was reacting to this experience when she shared this reflection: "And to think that we speak English and some of us have been working with small businesses for years and years. I feel like I am a relatively intelligent person and I should be able to figure out how these processes work, and we're still having difficulty! I think that really spoke to me about how difficult this really is for anyone to get into business, let alone someone who is facing having to learn another language in order to cross some of those barriers." The RECIPES program acted as a liaison between those who are knowledgeable about food-related issues and NDC entrepreneurs traversing the complicated governmental regulations. It brought together entrepreneurs' visions with the people able to make such visions accessible. Additionally, the RECIPES program assisted entrepreneurs by reviewing the business skills necessary for a successful food enterprise and the complicated process of adapting a recipe to feed hundreds rather than simply the immediate family.

Since its inception, NDC program graduates have opened 338 businesses. The sixteen-week programs, however, were shown to not provide enough training for many of the entrepreneurs to operate a successful small business. Many of the individuals participating in the programs had learned to survive for years on the margins of society. It often remained difficult to train these participants and convince them of the professional methods being suggested by NDC staff. Yet NDC remained committed to these entrepreneurs and continued to offer personalized assistance as each business evolved. One NDC graduate understood this to be a "commitment to help until we can walk by ourselves." This sort of long-term support and continuing education was clearly necessary if NDC graduates, often referred to as alumni, were to be successful.

Continuing technical assistance was also necessary as the small businesses encountered new challenges. Many of the obstacles faced by new businesses could have required the assistance of costly professionals. NDC developed relationships with accounting firms, law firms, and advertising agencies throughout the Twin Cities that assisted the struggling entrepreneurs, all at little or no cost to graduates of the program. In addition, NDC continued to review the business plans of the often-expanding ventures, coupling the education and experience of both the professional business trainers and the entrepreneurs.

Finally, NDC offered many of their program graduates loans to realize their goals. NDC was able to finance entrepreneurs who did not have the education and collateral that would be necessary at most lending institutions. Utilizing federal, state, and private funds, the small businesses affiliated with NDC received nearly $2.5 million in loans. Financial supporters included the U.S. Small Business Administration, the State of Minnesota Department of Trade and Economic Development, the Catholic Campaign for Human Development, the McKnight Foundation, and the St. Paul Companies, to name just a few of the more than twenty funders.

Following the offering of a loan, NDC stood by their borrowers through the difficult process of birthing a business, when loan default often occurs. Loans were restructured and business practices honed until success was achieved and the repayment process could continue. Though loan repayment was obviously important for NDC to continue its support of new entrepreneurs, it was central to the mission of NDC to keep businesses in the neighborhoods creating employment opportunities, even through difficult periods of default. Therefore, the success of a new business was given priority over the timely repayment of a loan. This policy would not have been possible with a bank as the creditor and was an important element in the success of NDC alumni businesses.

ACHIEVEMENTS

According to Mihailo Temali, NDC was for the entrepreneurs "a door to their dreams." The services provided by NDC focused on the creation of employment opportunities, encouraged the revitalization of neighborhoods, formed new leaders for these neighborhoods, and offered a place for the community to gather and be strengthened by one another. NDC helped rebuild neighborhoods from within, and its success was tangible. More than twelve hundred neighborhood residents were trained, with 338 businesses established, a 28 percent rate of success. Of these businesses, 77 percent were founded by persons of color and 49 percent by women. These businesses returned $10 million annually to the local economy. On average, each business created 3.5 jobs, returned almost $2,500 a month to its neighborhood economy, and had an annual payroll of $56,064. Additionally, 23 percent of the businesses have located in formerly vacant buildings, effectively reversing neighborhood blight and creating an increase in commercial traffic that has a direct relationship to the reduction of crime. All of this success came from and remained in the community, repeatedly strengthening each street and neighborhood touched by an NDC graduate.

The formation of successful small businesses impacted neighborhoods in other, less tangible ways. Residents of many low-income neighborhoods are often forced to turn outside their community for role models. NDC encouraged program participants to engage their communities and become local leaders for their neighborhoods. Mr. Leon, the founder of Mexam Upholstery, exemplified the commitment that NDC alumni made to their communities. Mr. Leon sat on the board of directors for the Mercado Central, a Latino retail cooperative, and the Whittier Emergent Business Center, a small-business incubator. He was also an active member of the Isaiah organization, a social-justice organization; Interfaith Action, a community-organizing group; and St. Cyril Catholic Church, a Spanish-speaking parish in his neighborhood. Committed and ambitious men and women, like Mr. Leon, were able to gain visibility through their entrepreneurial endeavors and found ways to positively influence their neighbors. In a 1998 survey, 75 percent of NDC alumni described themselves as role models for their community.

Many of the businesses founded by NDC program participants offered their community not only employment opportunities, neighborhood revitalization, and leadership opportunities, but also a place for residents to meet and develop a sense of community. Important political issues relevant to the community were discussed at local retail shops. Health and crime issues were addressed at neighborhood restaurants. The elderly enjoyed the company of their peers at local coffee shops. NDC-supported businesses directly influenced the development of living, vibrant communities within the Twin Cities.

CHALLENGES

The achievements of NDC, though numerous, came with great difficulty. Many challenges faced the organization as it attempted to open the doors to each entrepreneur's dream. A foundational issue encountered by NDC was that of making contact with the potential entrepreneurs, who were often poor, uneducated, or both. It is relatively easy to locate but often more difficult to establish relationships with the disenfranchised ethnic groups that are typically the focus of NDC's efforts. NDC employed a unique model to open up communications. It partnered with fourteen neighborhood organizations and three ethnic community groups. Each partner was an established presence in the neighborhood who was aware of the unique needs of each community. These organizations approached NDC and invited them to enter their neighborhood or ethnic community. Such partnerships allowed NDC to reach the people of St. Paul and Minneapolis while simultaneously allowing it to remain focused on entrepreneurial development rather than community organizing.

NDC and some of its alumni also faced the many legal challenges that immigrants in America often experience. NDC did not question the residential status of program participants. Its concern was the social and economic revitalization of inner-city neighborhoods. The contributions of both legal and illegal immigrants were valued as important elements in building a community. However, some successful alumni struggled with the threat of deportation due to their illegal status. NDC remained committed to these entrepreneurs during their legal struggles. Organizing the press, politicians, and local leaders, NDC was successful in creating support for alumni immigrants. Individuals with successful businesses (in one circumstance, multiple businesses) were able to continue to contribute to their neighborhoods and city by becoming legal residents through the efforts of NDC.

THE INFLUENCE OF CATHOLIC SOCIAL THOUGHT

Important elements of Catholic social thought were clearly present in the mission of NDC. The call for economic justice heralded by both scripture and church documents was actualized in the development of small businesses in low-income neighborhoods. NDC encouraged the fair distribution of wealth and resource ownership; the success of the entrepreneur was given priority over the protection of the capital investment; and the grassroots nature of the program respected the principle of subsidiarity. It is important to note, however, that NDC had no particular religious affiliation, and the staff members of the organization were grounded in a number of traditions and operated from a variety of motivations. Therefore, to more fully understand the work of NDC it will be helpful to look at the people who animated the organization.

Mihailo Temali, executive director of NDC, founded the program in 1993. Temali grew up in an immigrant family in the urban center of St. Paul and belongs to the Serbian Orthodox Church. He feels that his immigrant experience and his religion are interwoven. The self-reliance and determination shown by the millions of immigrants in the United States during the early part of the twentieth century, according to Temali, was fostered and encouraged by the immigrant church community. Around the country, many Orthodox churches aided newly arrived immigrants with networks and support. Through their connections and support, immigrants found vital resources that led to good jobs and employment. The church worked to empower those who arrived in this country without money or education.

In many ways, Temali understands NDC to be the organization that is able to offer assistance to the newly arrived immigrants today, similar to how the church acted when his parents immigrated years ago. In the same way that the church community offered meaningful assistance to Temali's parents, who relied on their own initiative to succeed, NDC offers this same assistance to struggling individuals who desire the American dream of success, independence, and participation in the larger society. It appears that, for Temali, the sense of community and valuable networks from his church served as an early example of how communities are invaluable to new immigrants and others without resources and connections they need to advance. The work of the church and the efforts of NDC are as interwoven as his immigrant experience and his religion.

Temali's experience of the church, however, goes beyond its role as a means of support during times of difficulty and transition. He articulates the call of Christianity by stating, "What you do for the poorest, you do for me. What you do for the least educated, you do for me. When you have clothed the naked, you have clothed me." He is personally inspired by this. Though not all of the staff, board members, and entrepreneurs are grounded in this tradition, Temali does feel it can be found in the work of NDC.

One staff member clearly articulates a similar motivation for her work with low-income entrepreneurs. Though raised in the Catholic tradition (in fact, her mother is active in social justice work with the Dominican Sisters), she does not remain affiliated with the church. Religious faith does not play a role in her work. She is, however, passionate about justice. She feels a just economy is necessary for a just society, and the resources she is able to place in the hands of the entrepreneurs will move society toward her vision of justice. She feels this work for justice is revolutionary and requires the efforts of strong leaders who are able to create change. This staff member understands the work of NDC to also be revolutionary because it addresses and transforms the unjust distribution of resources in society.

When considering the Catholic social tradition, this staff member acknowledges that organizations such as the Catholic Campaign for Human Development do offer practical assistance in the work for social justice, but she feels the Catholic Church is just beginning to live out its teachings on justice in the world. She hopes the church is fully embracing the ideal that "to be spiritual you must be just."

A second staff member draws the inspiration for her work from the entrepreneurs with whom she works. According to her, the risks that the small business owners take are not simply for financial gain but come from a desire to inspire their communities. She finds this selfless approach to business and the neighborhood to be her primary motivation for being a part of the process. This staff member spent thirteen years in Catholic schools and acknowledges that her desire to work for justice finds its foundation in her

Catholic tradition. Although she says that she does experience tension between her relationship with the Church and her work for justice with the urban poor, she points out that nearly half of NDC staff were raised in the
Catholic Church, and she recognizes the influence that Catholic social
thought must have also played in their life endeavors.

Finally, it also seems important to briefly consider the motivation and vision of a person who is served by NDC. Mr. Leon is attempting to speak for
all of the marginalized men and women served by NDC when he says, "We
have the same dreams; we have the same goals. We also deserve to be
treated with dignity and respect." He feels that it was this respect that was
given to him by NDC. He says, "We come [to NDC] without a penny in our
pocket and we receive the opportunity to help ourselves, not [through] social services, but they help us to use our own skills and abilities to be productive."

Mr. Leon credits NDC with enabling him to support his family and reach
his dream of economic security. Yet Mr. Leon credits NDC with even more.
He says, "I don't know if I'll ever be rich, or even a millionaire, but my faith
is stronger than ever." Speaking of the men and women who went through
NDC's program with him, Mr. Leon insists that it was "our faith which was
the main thing that moved us." Almost simultaneously, he insists that "our
Church never let us down, even when no else believed in us." Mr. Leon
seems to see NDC and the Church as intimately related. He proudly asserts
that he turns to Jesus Christ as his inspiration. "Jesus Christ," he says, "struggled against everything." He also proudly acknowledges that, along with Jesus, NDC aided him in his struggles "against everything."

The work of NDC parallels much of the Catholic social thought encountered in this book. Though the organization is not explicitly affiliated with
any religion, NDC appears to actualize the theory and ideals of the tradition.
Many of its staff members and entrepreneurs are directly motivated by their
encounter with Christianity and Catholic social teachings. However, it is clear
that others within the organization, while maintaining a strong commitment
to justice, think the Church can make (greater) progress in fully living out its
teachings in this area. These unique and diverse dynamics make for an interesting case study from which to approach Catholic social thought.

NOTES

1. This study was performed in the Summit-University neighborhood of St. Paul,
MN. It is interesting to note that 20 percent of those operating in the underground
economy were interested in moving their businesses outside of their homes.
2. The data were made available by NDC and published in 1992 by The Metropolitan Council in a study entitled "Trouble at the Core."

9

Oakland Community Organizations' "Faith in Action": Locating the Grassroots Social Justice Mission

Joseph M. Palacios

In the poor San Antonio District of Oakland, California, the parish of St. An-thony's has been an anchor for generations of Catholics. It was in this neighborhood that the Oakland Community Organizations (OCO) was formed in 1973 as a network of local organizing committees (LOC) to help improve the community. St. Anthony's parish, along with other Catholic parishes of OCO, helped change the work from "community organizing" to "faith-based community organizing." What do those terms mean to you? Do you see the work as part of a democracy?

This case study tells part of the story of a faith-based community organization in one parish. The reader will first learn about the approach of the parent organization to OCO, the nationally famous Pacific Institute for Community Organization (PICO) (see the Resource Section), and the civic participation processes they promote (for example, one-on-ones and model-teaching the practical skills needed to run a one-hour meeting). The material presented by Professor Whitmore on "participation" is applicable here. Executive Director John Baumann, S.J., expresses part of PICO's philosophy: "We are moved to justice to make the world right for our family." As you re-call the earlier essays and case studies, what are some other motivations for "doing justice"? What do you know about "biblical justice"?

Based on research through the "one-on-one" approach, the OCO, and St. Anthony's LOC as part of it, took on an education agenda for four years. Parents felt powerless in the face of deep problems in the Oakland Public School District. The campaign included Advent and Lenten consultations, where participants learned a "continuum of behaviors related to civic participation." There were public actions that incorporated passages from scripture, artistic symbols, "rallying cries," and the actual meetings. Do you see these as effective strategies? How do these activities in the larger arena relate to what Weigert discusses about faith and the involvement in the political and public arenas?

The faith-based community organizing approach, so central to St. Anthony's LOC, "allows for an ongoing reintegration of social issues, parish pastoral cycles and processes, and leadership development." Professor Massaro noted the various names of the see-judge-act model. Do you see that played out in this case study? What more would you like to know about it in practice? Finally, the deliberate and explicit integration of "faith in action" is the dominant motif of this case study. As one woman expressed it, "My religious life must be related to improving my family and my community." How does this explicit focus compare and contrast with that found in the other case studies?

INTRODUCTION

St. Anthony's is the second oldest parish in California's East Bay. Founded in 1871, the parish serves a neighborhood that reaches from Lake Merritt to the Fruitvale neighborhood of Oakland, California. The San Antonio District of the city of Oakland is comprised of about 35,000 people of whom approximately 70 percent are Hispanic, 10 percent black, 10 percent Asian, and 10 percent white. However, in the immediate neighborhood of St. Anthony Parish the population is largely immigrants from Mexico, Vietnam, and Cambodia. The housing stock of the neighborhood mirrors demographic changes of the district: from stately turn-of-the-century mansions that once housed the wealthy and powerful of California but have now been cut up into apartments for the immigrant working poor; to the 1930s' and 1940s' California bungalows for Oakland's white middle class, now housing the Latino, Filipino, black, and white working-class, single-family homeowners; and to modern 1950s' and 1960s' apartment complexes housing many of the Mexican and Asian immigrant working class. The parish name of St. Anthony actually determined the name of the neighborhood, San Antonio. The San Antonio District is the oldest Mexican neighborhood in Oakland, and for that reason from the 1970s until 1995 there were four Latino priests who have served as pastor of St. Anthony's.

The San Antonio and the Fruitvale Districts were the first neighborhoods to form the Oakland Community Organizations (OCO) in 1973 as a network of local organizing committees (LOC), thus making OCO one of the oldest and most continuous community organizing efforts in the United States, particularly in the West. In the first few years, the organizing was neighborhood-centered and utilized local churches to recruit members and to use their facilities for meeting spaces. The early organizers were two California Jesuit priests who had been trained in Chicago by the key organizers of Saul Alinsky, the originator of community organizing in the United States. The California Jesuits wanted to create a similar organization to that of Alinsky's Woodlawn organization in Chicago. The old-timers of St. Anthony's LOC recall that in the early days of the community organizing (the late 1970s) they were concerned with the proliferation of liquor stores and prostitution in their community, especially along the two main boulevards of the district. By the 1980s, the liquor store and prostitution issues were replaced by new issues of crack-cocaine houses in the middle of the neighborhoods and gang violence that came along with drug dealing.

OCO has been highly successful in training local lay people in the "Alinsky method" of pragmatically oriented civic activism based on the "one-on-one." Saul Alinsky (1909–1972) believed in the observation of Alexis de Tocqueville in *Democracy in America* that Americans can be motivated to serve their fellow citizens by tapping into their "self-interest rightly-understood" or their "enlightened self-interest." The fundamental premise of the Alinsky method is that when members of a community discover their common self-interest, then they can work in a concerted effort to achieve that interest. OCO's mission is to organize the interests of disempowered people into an associational life and into civic institutions that represent its constituency.

"FAITH-BASED COMMUNITY ORGANIZING" AS THE FOUNDATION FOR LOCAL SOCIAL-JUSTICE TEACHING AND IMPLEMENTATION

How did "faith-based" community organizing come about, and how has it been sustained? At St. Anthony's Parish and other Catholic parishes of OCO, the appropriation of sacred symbols and the scriptures for social purposes has been an essential component of "faith-based" community organizing. Indeed, the almost unconscious American instinct to do this was a key reason that OCO's parent organization, the Pacific Institute for Community Organization (PICO), moved from a neighborhood-based community organizing model to a faith-based model in the early 1990s. PICO provides OCO and its other affiliate organizing committees with their professional community organizers. Most importantly, PICO offers semi-annual national training institutes for local clergy and lay leaders utilizing the principles of Saul Alinsky. John Baumann, S.J., PICO's long-term executive director, has described the fundamental drive of the organization in the following way:

> In its own way, PICO too, is a family—a place where people can find their own true voice. It is a place where all people are treated as individuals deserving of respect and love. And, like a family, PICO looks out for its own. We are all filled

with anger when we see conditions that foster fear, hatred, and despair. We are
moved to justice to make the world right for our family. And we realize that the
power to change the world rests in our capacity to unite as family, as community, and as children of God.

For PICO, faith-based community organizing draws upon a pragmatic approach of getting new members from religious congregations and the theoretical desire to integrate religious culture, social-justice teaching, and the
scriptures into the life of community organizing as a way of providing ongoing meaning for the disciple citizens.

The skills developed by PICO and other Alinsky-type civic organizations
have a primary cultural perspective on American civic culture that has a normative orientation toward incorporating its members into U.S. civil society.
This normative orientation sets the tone for what becomes the foundational
cultural milieu for Catholic social-justice teaching and implementation at the
local level of a parish or neighborhood.

The normative orientation of PICO can be seen in its educative mission to
"empower" its members to implement grassroots change in American public
spaces, such as school boards, city halls, police departments, and governmental bureaucracies. In this sense, PICO training in civic participation is a
school for the behaviors necessary for active members of civil society. This
is what Alinsky himself called "popular education"—that is, education and
mutual understanding among various groups in order to gain a "new appre-
ciation and definition of social issues."

The primary civic behaviors and skills of PICO as popular education include:

- *One-on-Ones*: A method introduced by Saul Alinsky of interviewing a
  person's neighbors to find out their self-interests, which initiates the organizational network of trust ("relationship building") wherein each
  member is important through the identification of the issues related to
  his or her self-interest in the grassroots development of trusting relationships and common values and interests.
- *Public Prayer*
- *Credentials*: A process at every PICO gathering in which a leader re-
  views the organizational identity, its membership status, and its own
  self-identity vis-à-vis *other* power relationships in the community.
- *Research*: The process of systematically evaluating one-on-one's to determine issues for the organization to develop and execute with the
  cooperation of other organizations, elected officials, academics, other
  professionals, and governmental bureaucrats.
- *Action*: The specific activity of creating a "target" for research, i.e., holding the targeted public institution accountable through a gathering or a
  mass meeting that can be organized at various levels: the local unit,
  areawide, citywide, state-wide, regionally, or interorganizationally.

- *Accountability*: The development of a challenging process for organizational discipline as both an internal activity of the organization and an outside activity of holding a target accountable.
- *Negotiations*: Usually a behind-the-scenes process of lay leaders and organizers meeting with targets to forge agreements prior to an action so that agreements can be ratified at the action.
- *Evaluations*: At the end of every meeting of an LOC, Research Meeting, or Action, an evaluation is made by the leaders and organizers present in order to hold accountable the various participants of the event and to improve communication and critical reflection among the leadership.

On the day-to-day level of LOC meetings, the PICO model employs a standard methodology of conducting a meeting or action that becomes a fixed cultural ritual or repertoire. The rules of order for a meeting are not taken for granted because they are viewed as constitutive of the democratic process. By experiencing the democratic process at meetings, the participants learn democratic values and skills as a new kind of discourse that will integrate with the social teaching of the Catholic Church—particularly with the key doctrinal elements of participation and association that are fundamental to achieving more abstract doctrinal elements such as the dignity of the human person and solidarity. The methodology of a one-hour meeting includes the following: call to order; prayer; organizational credentials (the city-wide organization is identified along with how many congregations and families are involved, and the mission of the organization is stated); opening remarks; discussion of agenda items; discussion of action items; polling of commitments to do one-on-one's; closing remarks; and closing prayer. Newcomers are folded into the organization by involvement in the practices of civic participation as habits of the organization that facilitate a well-organized and effective process. Newcomers are not given overviews of organizational philosophy as an ideological formation. Rather, particularly through the one-on-one, a newcomer is given the experience of being able to articulate one's self-interest with a willing listener who also shares his or her interests. PICO follows the belief that democracy should be built upon "the principle of self-interest rightly understood."

At every St. Anthony's LOC and city-wide OCO meeting, a "credential" is read to start the meeting that reflects the power of the organization: "OCO is an organization of 35,000 families in the City of Oakland in 32 churches. . . ." Over the years, OCO has become the largest civic organization in Oakland and can claim for itself a successful track record of "victories." As one of the lay founders of OCO states,

Those were simple beginnings, the issues were less complex and local—stop signs, stray dogs, run-down properties—but the seed was planted, the soil was right, and it was bound to grow. As we began working together as groups to resolve issues, first in our own neighborhood, then with others who had identified similar problems, we were, and still are, constantly challenged to move beyond, to stretch our horizons, and to develop leadership qualities we didn't even know we had!

OCO's victories resulted from a strategy of mediating the self-interests of the local LOC's and the institutional structures of urban life, such as the police and fire departments, city council, school board, zoning boards, the Catholic Diocese of Oakland and other religious bodies, the business sector, and philanthropic foundations such as the Catholic Campaign for Human Development. This strategy can be seen as a leveraging mechanism that places the organization between the people as citizens with interests and the institutional players of a community. Thus, the local LOC and OCO define the problems that emerge from one-on-one's as "issues" that become the basis for connecting the constituency to the institutional structures with the goal of effecting long-term institutional change in the existing institutional structures. The goal in a victory is that all the players "win": the constituency gets a problem solved, and the institutional players can claim that they are not only doing their job but also working on behalf of the grassroots. OCO is not interested in running programs or building new institutions. Rather, it wants the existing structures to work for the people they are intended to serve. The one-on-one's keep the organization always current on the issues, so that once an issue is won the organization can easily move to another issue.

In the late 1990s, OCO initiated a major education initiative that had come about through one-on-one research in the Oakland community regarding the plight of the Oakland Public School District. In the early 1990s, the school district had achieved national notoriety because the school board had attempted to make Ebonics a second language and also because it had gone into receivership by the state of California. Adding to the district's problems were some of the lowest scores in California on the state's standardized tests in reading and math in 1994 and 1995. The one-on-one's revealed that parents felt powerless in the face of the school district's entrenched bureaucracy and the seeming obstinacy of the teachers' union. OCO leadership knew that the education agenda of its constituency would not be an easy issue to tackle, but it had to be taken on or else the children would never get a quality education in the public schools. "For the Children" became a constant rallying cry at OCO meetings.

INTEGRATING CIVIC SKILLS WITH FAITH-BASED CONTENT AND CULTURAL DYNAMICS

Through the bottom-up, experiential process of civic participation, the cultural system of practices, beliefs, and ethos is put into effect as training, as a school for civic participation. The above practices serve as a model for civic participation for PICO that functions across various lines of cultural, religious, community, political, and ideological variance among its members and local units and provides for an experiential solidarity among the various members—solidarity as organizing principle, as well as solidarity in relationships or public friendships. Furthermore, this cultural system functions as an "American" model of civic participation that is normatively embedded in the public life of democracy and that has its own language and practice of participation that need to be learned in order to "make democracy work."

OCO has relied on St. Anthony's to produce key Latino leaders for the citywide organization. In the spring of 1996, the local organizer recruited two new members, a Mexican male, Manuel, and a Mexican American female, Silvia. (Pseudonyms are used throughout.) These two new members helped bring a new vitality to the group. By the fall of 1996, the LOC and the organizer began to strategically plan for the recruitment of new members, since it was clear that many of the old activists had changed parishes. That fall, one of the old activists, Diane, a white female who speaks fluent Spanish and who is very Mexican in culture and style, returned to active participation. The LOC made a decision to utilize the liturgical year of 1996–97 to begin a process of parish renewal in the Latino community by holding parish-wide meetings on Sunday mornings following the Spanish Mass. It should be noted that the pastor did not attend LOC meetings until 1999. However, he faithfully paid the parish dues to OCO, and the organizer kept him informed of his activities in the parish. He never impeded OCO activity, but when he got involved in the organization in 1999 he brought new energy into the meetings by introducing multi-lingual music to get the people motivated. More importantly, by being present as the pastor he brought a new legitimacy to the organization, especially for the Vietnamese parishioners.

Scott (the lead organizer) had observed that on Sundays following the 9:30 a.m. Spanish Mass many parents escorted their children to the Catholic school for religious instruction held from 11:00 a.m. to 12:00 p.m. every Sunday during the school year. Many parents waited in the gymnasium during this time. Scott suggested to the LOC that they might target these parents as potential new members. With this idea, the LOC decided to offer an Advent retreat utilizing the themes of the December 12 Feast of Our Lady of Guadalupe. The retreat was entitled "On the Road to Tepeyac" (the hillside in Mexico City where Mary as an indigenous woman appeared to Juan Diego in 1531), signifying the idea that Latinos are on a continuous journey of faith. The idea was to connect themes of neighborhood social-justice issues with the religious practices associated in the Mexican community with Advent, Guadalupe, and Christmas.

"The Road to Tepeyac" theme for the meetings was an attempt to integrate the liturgical cycle, the social justice image of Our Lady of Guadalupe that has developed in the United States, and the legitimation of social concerns vis-à-vis common religious symbols and impulses of the Mexican immigrants. This

type of integration is quite common in American pastoral practice and planning based on a pragmatically oriented pastoral life driven by the practical
question, "How do we get more people to our meetings?" The use of saints
and feast days by Catholic pastoral workers for various social objectives, particularly in immigrant communities, is common in U.S. Catholic history. The
appropriation of Our Lady of Guadalupe for social purposes in the United
States is a significant development in the evolution of the meaning of the ap-
parition. U.S. Hispanic theologians such as Virgil Elizondo, Andrés Guerrero,
and Jeannette Rodriguez have brought new meaning to Guadalupe based on
her message of compassion for the natives of Mexico and her social location
as an indigenous woman in the Spanish conquest. This kind of social-justice
theological reflection is not at all common in Mexico, even though Mexican
national identity has been historically driven by the Guadalupe story—
particularly in the image of Father Hidalgo, the founding father of modern
Mexico who led Mexico into independence under the banner of Guadalupe
and the red, green, and white flag of the new nation-state on September 16,
1810. Thus, the appropriation of Guadalupe for OCO objectives would be
part of the ordinary construction of a social justice cultural milieu for the Mexican in the United States.

EFFECTS OF CONSULTATION MEETINGS
AND RECRUITMENT OF NEW MEMBERS

As a result of the Advent and Lenten consultations, Latino participation in the
LOC maintained a steady group of about ten regular members (up from a
low of four). Also, the effects of the discussion of more lay-oriented initiatives seemed to take hold: development of the Spanish choir for the Spanish
Mass; greater involvement of the Mexican immigrant parents in the planning
for the Our Lady of Guadalupe fiesta in December 1997; the beginning of the
training of children as altar servers; and another consultation of the laity during Lent of 1998. All of these activities were lay-initiated and executed with
the support of the organizer, the priest, and the religious educators. Each
success in lay leadership brought another project.

From October 1997 through March 1998, three consultations were organized by the LOC to focus on the issue of parental involvement in the local
public schools. Specifically, Scott and the LOC leaders needed to listen to
parish opinion on the formation of a "village center," an all-purpose community center utilizing the spaces of the local public junior high school. Organized similarly to the previous Sunday-morning consultations and aimed
at the parents, the dynamics of these two meetings were strikingly different
from the initial meetings. Again, from forty to fifty parents were in attendance, most of whom had attended the 1996 Advent and the 1997 Lenten

consultations. Old-timers were not involved in these meetings. Though many parents seated themselves and talked to their children at the periphery while waiting to be invited into the central meeting space, some parents did chat in small groups and went to the arranged seats once their children went to the classrooms. Particularly at the last March meeting, almost all of the participants seemed to easily participate in the basic behaviors and dynamics of a PICO-OCO meeting: socializing with other adults before the meeting; moving into the meeting space on time and with attention; and becoming actively involved in the various behaviors and practices of holding a meeting, such as setting up and moving chairs, raising one's hand to speak, sitting in sharing groups, and expressing their opinion.

Over the course of eighteen months, there were eight consultation processes with Mexican immigrants held in the Catholic school gymnasium. The participants learned a continuum of behaviors related to civic participation: entering the meeting room; finding a place to locate oneself; entering the meeting space; participating in a variety of consultative and democratic processes (expressing one's opinion, casting a vote, volunteering for an activity); socializing with one's peers, being helpful, and so on. These behaviors may appear to be very commonplace in American civic life, but for Mexican immigrant urban compassions in Oakland these behaviors were not "natural" or easily adopted.

Participants were brought into the public meeting space through personal invitation by an outside leader. They were told where to sit, how to participate, and how to express themselves. They learned the civic process by *doing* the civic process. In this sense, the OCO leaders provided a basic civic education for these Mexican immigrants in the introduction of primary civic behaviors that make a meeting in the Alinsky model work. As well, they integrated cultural themes and social-justice teachings of association, participation, and solidarity as matters of practice.

The introduction of skilled civic participants, such as other Latinos involved in other parts of the parish, helped introduce to the immigrants other, more "social" aspects of civic participation: chatting with one's peers, enjoying refreshments together, and being helpful in setting up and taking down chairs and tables, preparing refreshments, and cleaning up. These old-timers modeled social skills for the newcomers who, at least in this situation, were uncertain, oblivious, or nervous about such social behaviors.

Over time, the parents had adapted themselves to entering, participating in, and enjoying a certain style of public meeting. Not only had they learned the primary skills for civic participation, they had learned to become citizens together, seeing each other as peers and becoming involved with each other's opinions, values, and commitments. They began to see and experience that they themselves can effect change in their localities. Specifically, they saw that to expect a Spanish-speaking priest to be hired in the parish and solve all of the problems of the Latino community was not only unrealistic but was also not the best reason for having clergy in the parish. They began to realize that the meetings they were attending were giving them skills and voice that they could apply to the situation in the parish and in the community, as evidenced in the incremental changes that the Latino laity are making in the parish and community.

While the word "solidarity" was never used by the organizers or the participants of these processes, the entire organizational process illustrated the way solidarity evolves. In the small groups, the participants were engaged in a primary solidarity of getting to know and trust each other through the identification of their self-interests. During the first meetings, people were self-selective in choosing small groups and moved to ones of familiar faces. As time went on, the participants, except for the youth, became more conscious of ideas and values, which became more important than the comfort of familiar faces. This was manifested in the behavior of joining integrated small groups of old-timers and newcomers based on common interests—another aspect of solidarity. Over the months, some of the participants became more active in OCO activities related to the neighborhood but that were also citywide. Both the LOC and new leaders became more active and integrated into the larger civic organization that deals with city government, the school district, the business community, and philanthropic foundations. This evolution from the small and simple to the large and complex demonstrates the movement from mechanical to organic solidarity. Also in this evolution, a theological sense of solidarity as friendship and comradeship developed in the building of new public relationships. One cannot underestimate the change that some of the immigrants experienced in their lives. As one immigrant Mexican woman expressed,

> Before I started going to these meetings, I saw myself just with my husband and children. I really didn't have any friends outside the house. Now I want to be involved in improving life for my children and the community. I never thought of the Church as a place for bettering our lives, because that is not what the Church does in Mexico. My religious life must be related to improving my family and my community.

"FAITH IN ACTION": EVOLUTION OF PICO FAITH-BASED COMMUNITY ORGANIZING

PICO's faith-based process allows for an ongoing reintegration of social issues, parish pastoral cycles and processes, and leadership development. Basically, PICO's faith-based model helps balance the pragmatism of the Alinsky community organizing model with renewing processes drawn from the liturgy, religious education, and cultural practices. All throughout the education campaign (1996–2000), the OCO professional community organizer worked with the local leaders (priests, nuns, pastors, and the laity) to find ways to integrate "faith in action"—the integration of social justice principles and processes with the social issues of the community. One organizer, Scott, was very concerned that the faith dimension needed to be institutionalized in the ongoing processes of PICO national training, OCO issue formation, and local LOC processes. In early 1999, he introduced the first articulated faith component into national leadership training held for Spanish-speaking leaders in Oakland, California. He had attended a summer institute in 1998 at the Franciscan School of Theology in Berkeley on multicultural ministry. There he had been introduced to the biblical reflection process of "see, judge, act" of the European Catholic Action Movement that became very popular in the Latin American *comunidades de base*. The process is very easy to teach: oral recitation of a scripture passage, time to reflect on it, sharing of what it means in everyday life. The process can be augmented by individuals or small groups making posters to symbolize their reflections. At the national training, he utilized the poster method. Scott asked the participants to take a social issue that they were working on in their local LOC's and utilize the scripture reading of the loaves and fish (Matthew 14:13–21) to illustrate the issue. Once the process was explained, the participants working in small groups quickly went to work using poster paper and colored markers to complete the task. At the completion of the posters, each small-group leader explained to the entire assembly what the poster signified. Every group made an application of a scriptural principle to the social issue chosen.

Scott continued to make this kind of "faith-based" contribution at the LOC meetings and in planning large OCO actions. He had really taken to heart as a practicing Jew the concepts of biblical justice that he had learned at a PICO trainers' meeting also held in the summer of 1998, the first concerted attempt of PICO to institutionalize faith-based social justice concepts, albeit Catholic ones, in the ecumenical organization. For Scott, the idea of "right relationships" was intimately associated with how one-on-one's should be conducted and how local solidarity should be constructed. Indeed, "wins" for PICO-OCO should be on the principles of biblical justice. As an organizer, Scott realized that the techniques of "see, judge, act" and games and processes were important tools to use at meetings in order to convey these principles and experience them in the educational process itself.

Over the course of three years, a subtle but significant change occurred in the OCO city-wide organization as the faith-based dimensions were more integrated into the organizational culture, particularly more articulated faith-testimony and faith-principle dimensions. For example, at an Oakland City Council meeting that OCO activists attended in 1999 in order to lend city support to the building of a supermarket in West Oakland, one of the professional organizers—a black liberal-Protestant pastor—actually spoke about food as a fundamental human right in such a way that left one council member later in the meeting articulating the access to good food as a human right. Two years prior, the issue would have been framed by OCO leaders more in terms of equal access to food and would have appealed to the emotions of the council members with testimonies of senior citizens taken advantage of by the high cost and inferior quality of food sold at the small, corner liquor-grocery stores in the neighborhood.

Over the course of three years, the OCO professional group developed a melding of Catholic social teaching, black liberal-Protestant biblical justice emphases, and a general Christian spiritual emphasis on common prayer and discernment. The organizers themselves saw their work as a social justice vocation, and they, as well as their membership, wanted "more" from community organizing—the "more" being spiritual meaning in their own lives. As one Catholic-school educated Latina feminist organizer in her mid-twenties, who was not active in a parish, conveyed: "Through organizing we're doing God's work." She felt quite comfortable finding scriptural passages to use at her LOC meetings. One of her favorite sections of the Bible is the Exodus story of Moses and Pharaoh. She had used this text to help her LOC see the need for research on an issue—that "to let my people go" requires necessary footwork to prepare for the journey.

Since 1997, the PICO national organization has spent time working with pastors to develop a more articulated faith-based organizational culture. According to the national PICO leaders, Protestant pastors do not have difficulty understanding and using the principles of biblical justice and the principles of Catholic social-justice teaching (solidarity as an organizing principle, dignity of the human person, human rights, association, participation, the right to organize, the dignity of human work, etc.) as the theological foundation of PICO's evolving faith-based culture. And Catholic priests and women religious learn how to express the biblical foundations of their faith in a more emotive way through the influence of the black Protestant pastors. At St. Anthony's, Father Rick's homiletic and prayer style often evokes the call-response technique of African American preachers that brings people into the emotions, as well as the content, of the scripture texts. This technique brings the scripture back to its origins in the oral tradition: the scriptures convey stories of people's real lives.

At an OCO public action, the dynamism of scripture and testimonies of real people often become integrated into a common message. During the campaign for homework centers, a passage from Joshua 6 on the siege of Jericho was utilized to convey that the power of the people would prevail over the forces of resistance to changes in the Oakland Public School System: the people would march around the walls of the school district headquarters (Jericho) until the walls fell. At these actions, a mural of the walls of Jericho was placed behind the speakers' tables so that the membership could visualize their "faith in action." And during the course of the meeting the leader, a black male leader in his sixties who at the time was the chair of the OCO steering committee, would let out a rallying cry in both English and Spanish "For the children! *¡Para los niños!*" Everyone would respond back in kind "For the children! *¡Para los niños!*" Over the course of a one-hour rally, this cry sounded like a clarion call for political battle. The politicians and school-board members in attendance could certainly feel the emotive power of the membership.

The constant reference to Joshua and Jericho conveyed a different kind of seriousness to OCO's objectives: the membership not only wants social change, but they are exercising their faith at the same time. No politician or bureaucrat has been willing to get into a public debate regarding the faith dimension of OCO. They know—as well as the press and the general public—that OCO is actually an organization in civil society that draws its membership from religious congregations, even though OCO does not represent the congregations. Indeed, if anything, city council members, school board members, and even the mayors of Oakland affirm in varying ways their respect for the membership both as citizens and as active church members.

In the beginning phase of building a so-called faith-based organization, the PICO and OCO staff did not have a strategic plan on how to incorporate faith dimensions into already successful neighborhood- and congregation-based models. However, they knew that many of their affiliate pastors and some of the most active laity wanted more from the organization as a religiously inspired type of social justice program. This basic impulse is driving the ongoing evolution of PICO-OCO faith-based community organizing.

During the last few months of 2000, OCO was beginning to face a challenge to the meaning of faith-based organizing because it had become a partner with other community organizations in pursuing its charter- and small-schools initiatives. OCO actually had initiated the first charter school in the Oakland Public School District in 1994, which helped set a statewide policy for charter schools in California. By 2000, there were many more organizational actors wanting to participate in charter schools. OCO "partnered" with the local leaders of the Village Centers—which it had initially got off the ground but that had now become their own organizations—and with nonprofit development agencies. The new partners did not have faith-based organizational cultures, nor did they have broad-based memberships, as did OCO's Local Organizing Committees, in the congregations. However, the partners brought with them expertise on educational-reform issues and new people, particularly from the non-Christian Asian communities and from the growing non-religious minority, professional, and artistic communities moving into the San Antonio District. At stake in the integration of these groups was the faith-based focus of OCO. The new partners did not like the prayers and scriptural readings at OCO meetings and did not want them at joint meetings. However, as three OCO organizers reflected upon in an evaluation, these basic faith-based behaviors could not be negotiated if OCO was to be involved—primarily because the membership would not want to be involved in strictly secular social action. The prayers and scripture, as well as the presence of the pastors, brought a legitimacy to civic activity, especially for the Latino immigrants and the black Protestants and Catholics. They were not eager to be involved in planning another such action without guaranteeing the faith-based dimensions of the OCO organizational culture.

More than anything, OCO as a social-justice cultural milieu has provided a location for ordinary people to be trained in social justice in order to make social, cultural, and political institutional changes in Oakland and California. OCO has built local solidarity and has achieved institutional change for the common good. As part of the national PICO network, it is "reweaving the fabric of America's communities." OCO delivers not only practical change through civic education and empowerment, but also helps integrate Catholic social-justice teaching into the fabric of American life.

10

COPS: Putting the Gospel into Action in San Antonio

Patrick J. Hayes

San Antonio, Texas, is home to the famous COPS (Communities Organized for Public Service), the oldest member of the Industrial Areas Foundation, a network of community-based groups across the United States (see the Resource Section). Merging with Metro Alliance in 1989, the COPS/Metro Alliance has been working to organize parishes and congregations since the early 1970s to help them get action on issues that affect their daily lives. Holding public officials accountable for their decisions is a key. How do you imagine that being possible? What do the essays in Part I contribute to this discussion?

One of the early issues the community wanted addressed was flooding that occurred in the city's poorer neighborhoods. While many residents of the south and west sides of the city knew a family who had a drowning victim, "no single complaint could move the city to do anything about it." Why do you think this would be so? You will learn the approach COPS actually took to address this issue; think about the means they used and how you evaluate them.

While San Antonio does have high-wage jobs, poorer communities are often not able to take advantage of them. The concern about jobs emerged in house meetings, and in response COPS/Metro Alliance created an intensive, supportive job-training program in 1992. The training, as you will learn, is not just about good wages. It's about a sense of self-worth, about the community supporting its members, and about a new model for partnering business, education, and community action. This hearkens back to the material of professors Massaro and Whitmore. What do they suggest the Catholic social tradition has to offer on this topic?

Finally, you will encounter the concept of a "living wage" in this case study (a concept that is at the heart of the Baltimore case study that follows). Before you read this case, think about what a living wage means to the Catholic social tradition as discussed by Professor Whitmore, and what you think about it. What do you think wage "guidelines" would contribute to this conversation? Is there a living wage in your community? Should there be?

THE CONTEXT OF COPS/METRO ALLIANCE

Communities Organized for Public Service (COPS) and its partner organization, Metro Alliance, are catalysts for social change in San Antonio, Texas. They emerged from the organization of several Catholic and Protestant churches, schools, and community groups to promote the development of human capital in their city. Each church or organization is a dues-paying member either of COPS or Metro Alliance, to which they have historically affiliated. COPS organized the west and south sides of the city in the early 1970s, and Metro Alliance organized in the north and east sides in the early 1980s.

COPS/Metro Alliance is a grassroots association that forms part of the Industrial Areas Foundation (IAF), a larger network of community-based groups across the country. IAF provides leadership training in organizing local communities and can function both as a watchdog group or an advocacy group. COPS is considered the "flagship organization of the IAF" and is its oldest member, affiliating in 1974. Metro Alliance, a partnership of two previous organizations, the Metropolitan Congregational Alliance and the East Side Alliance, merged with COPS in 1989. COPS/Metro Alliance has an office in the city's west side and a paid staff of two lead organizers, Elizabeth Valdez and Allan Cooper. All other participants are volunteers.

COPS/Metro Alliance is based in San Antonio, the nation's ninth largest city, with a population of about 1.2 million in the 2000 census. An additional 450,000 people encircle San Antonio in outlying areas. It is the fastest-growing community in Texas, spurred on by recent job growth, notably the addition of 1,100 management-level jobs brought in by SBC Communications. SBC, a company that established its corporate headquarters in San Antonio in 1998, is now the fourth largest employer, infusing the Alamo City with some 8,000 jobs. Such a large increase in the work force means that housing starts are also up. Currently, it's a buyer's market. In 1999, the average selling price for a house in San Antonio was about $91,000, or nearly 30 percent below the national median. It is possible to attain a high wage in San Antonio. Financial institutions and insurance and real estate companies have shown the largest percentage growth among leading employment sectors, adding 3,200 new high-wage jobs to the economy between 1999 and 2000. The median age in metropolitan San Antonio is 32.5. The total civilian labor force is almost 780,000. The average annual unemployment rate was at 5 percent in 1996, whereas in April 2000 it had dipped to 3.1 percent.

It would seem that companies want to do business in San Antonio, and perhaps this is confirmed by *Forbes* magazine designating San Antonio as the eighth-best place to do business in its annual survey of two hundred locales (a move up from number thirty-six in 1999). One annual-cost-of-living index indicates that San Antonio falls below the national mean for a family of four making $60,000, compared to other major American cities that consistently exceed the annual cost of living. For instance, a similar family in San Francisco would need to make an additional $30,000 per year in order to afford the same goods and services in the Bay area as their counterparts are able to purchase in San Antonio. Perhaps because the cost of living is so low, the city also makes an attractive host for a large tourist and convention industry. Not surprisingly, San Antonio is expected to grow at a rate of 1.9 percent through the year 2010.

Admittedly there are many good things happening in San Antonio to make living there attractive. But like many other major cities, there are many people living below the poverty line. While San Antonio's unemployment rate is very low, there is a poverty rate of 22 percent, the second highest among the nation's fifteen largest cities. Nearly half of these impoverished citizens are between the ages of eighteen and fifty-nine. Couple this with an illiteracy rate of 15 percent of the total population, about 150,000 people. Eleven percent of the population has less than nine years of formal education. Many of these individuals are Mexican-Americans who often have been treated as "second-class citizens," even though they maintain a numerical majority.

Beatrice Cortés, a past president of COPS, acknowledges that maltreatment of Mexican Americans has "always been there; it's still there." The reality of exploitation is unmasked when San Antonians seek to explain why their city's jobless rate is so low: one in three of the city's residents end up in low-skilled, low-wage, service industry jobs, and the majority of these laborers are of Mexican descent. Clearly, not everyone is reaping the benefit of the Alamo City's prosperity.

However, certain measures are being taken to close the gap. COPS/Metro Alliance is a collective of thirty-five member institutions (mostly churches and schools) and concerned citizens interested in improving the quality of life for all San Antonians. Projects to which they commit themselves seek to change social structures where there have been perceived injustices or demonstrable disparities. In twenty-five years of organizing, COPS/Metro Alliance has influenced the beginning or continuation of thousands of initiatives and has maintained a respected presence in the San Antonio political arena. Over the last quarter century, COPS/Metro Alliance has helped channel nearly a billion dollars in infrastructure development to the inner city. This case study will point to a few of these projects.

THE HISTORY OF COPS/METRO ALLIANCE

"Thank God for the Church! Thank God for Ernie Cortés!" exclaimed Virginia Zamora, a long time COPS advocate and parish leader in South San Antonio. Indeed, there would be no history of COPS without Ernesto Cortés, the current director of the Southwest Region of the IAF, and his ability to persuade the churches to act on their words. After graduate work at the University of Texas, Cortés returned to his native San Antonio and decided to work against complacency. He was taken with Saul Alinsky's methods for organizing, which Alinsky employed in Chicago neighborhoods in the 1940s. Alinsky founded the IAF in Chicago, and when he died in 1972 the work was carried on by Edward Chambers, the current national director. There are now over sixty IAF organizations throughout the United States and Great Britain.

With the blessing of the Catholic hierarchy, Cortés began organizing parishes in 1973 through house meetings and talking with priests and pastors. These meetings would sound out the concerns of parish leaders for individual neighborhoods based primarily in San Antonio's west and south sides. Cortés' efforts began to be known throughout the Southwest, and in 1976 he moved to East Los Angeles to organize there. A recent roundtable discussion recalled Cortés' influence. "Ernie gave us power to be leaders by showing us how to use our anger," said Mary Piccione, a COPS cochair. "Ernie taught us the validity of anger, that when it is focused it can be productive," noted Andres Sarabia, COPS' first president. Their anger focused on public officials and manifested itself by holding them accountable for their actions in civil government.

Belgian-born Father Walter D'heedene, CICM, also spoke of Cortés' work during the initial organizing period from his vantage as pastor of Sacred Heart Parish on the city's west side.

> When I became pastor of Sacred Heart, the very next day I met Ernesto Cortés. He showed me what it means to be in touch with people. He showed me that the tools of organizing can be applied to parish life. It's helped me to talk to people, have house meetings, the one-on-ones. This is something that you don't learn in the seminary, even though you can read books about it. Experiencing it and reflecting on it is just so precious.

For his parish, Father Walter has encouraged what has come to be known as congregational development.

> Congregational development in our deanery usually manages to bring together 40–60 people from our parish. This type of organizing has really made me a better priest and a better leader. It helps us to grow in faith, and for me it allows me to live out my priesthood and all the possible dimensions that the priesthood has. We did one program for parish renewal. One weekend we had about 70

people—it made me think of Christ who sent out the 72 disciples—to do house blessings. Some said, "We're blessing houses? Isn't that for priests?" But I said, "No, no, the laity will do this." We would knock on doors and ask if people wanted us to bless their houses. They had 300–400 houses they blessed! It was great: neighbor meeting neighbor! We can fall back on the stories of this one event. We can get things done because of our common experience. Small things, to be sure, but these add up. . . . Our people employ Catholic social teaching by showing solidarity with one another. You know, our poor, when someone dies and they can't pay for a funeral, they go around and people just generously contribute. . . . I think the social teaching of the Church makes a lot of sense.

By 1974, Cortés had developed a small group of parishes with mutual interests, all of which had a personal stake in the outcomes of their city's political agenda. He also had the willing cooperation of many diocesan priests, such as Father Albert Benavides, who eventually directed COPS' "Water Action Committee" (Benavides later drowned in a swimming accident, and his legacy is memorialized in a park and literacy center named for him). Intent on preserving the thrust of Saul Alinsky's motto, "Never do for others what they can do for themselves," Cortés sought to bring people into tension with the issues that affected them in order to move them to respond out of their own self-interest. Issues continue to drive COPS efforts, says Andres Sarabia:

The issues may change but the fundamentals of leadership don't change. Everybody has pain. We create forums where people can express their pain. In order to create change you've got to suspend judgment. You've got to say everything is valid. Leaders can control their anger. They can control their pain and how they express it. Jesus sure expressed a whole lot of pain and anger through his ministry and lifetime and he caused a lot of reaction. His displays of anger are still valid 2,000 years later. Issues are at the heart of Catholic social teaching. They make the unjust uncomfortable. When issues arise, they confront injustice and make those who are causing injustice uncomfortable with what they are doing.

One such issue was flooding in the city's poorer neighborhoods. Flooding affected about 100,000 people. Every resident of the south and west sides knew a family who had at least one drowning victim, but no single complaint could move the city to do anything about it. In June 1974, Cortés and a half-dozen others met with city officials to move on the Six-Mile Creek drainage project on the city's south side. When nothing happened, COPS sprang into action. Assembling hundreds of supporters drawn from a number of parishes from the west and south sides, Cortés helped residents demand attention from some of the city's power elites. The first step was to do their homework in preparation for meetings with city officials. COPS members learned that drainage projects were already drawn up and that funding already had been secured for some of the projects as far back as 1945. The city had simply diverted these funds into other projects on the more affluent side of town. As the floods continued that August, COPS leaders shamed city officials into drawing up an immediate response. Four hours later, the result was a $47 million bond package for fifteen drainage projects, a bond that passed in the November elections thanks to COPS' voter-registration efforts. Since then, hundreds of other repairs have been made to the city's streets and are ongoing in some areas of the city even today.

That same month, Cortés and friends assembled in their first convention to formally constitute COPS. They drew about 2,000 leaders from parishes and other groups and elected Sarabia as the first president. He maintains that the rains have always been a sign of victory for COPS. When the convention was finished, participants celebrated by going to a large hall that was still under construction. "We had a hard rain that night. The roof leaked. People were dancing in water puddles."

The force of numbers has been a significant part of COPS' success. COPS members continued to show up at city meetings, by the dozen and by the score and by the hundreds. Locals still speak of the action taken in 1975 when hundreds of COPS members lined up at the teller cages of the Frost Bank, one of the city's most venerable institutions, to change pennies into dollars. Then they moved to the end of the line to change their dollars back into pennies. This brought the bank to a grinding halt and made bank President Tom Frost take notice. Now an ally to COPS/Metro Alliance, Frost came to see that teaming up with social advocates was not antithetical to economic development, but a necessary part of it. Because it is business that drives San Antonio politics, collaboration with the economic sector is key to raising the social welfare of the city. Representing the interests of over 90,000 families in the Alamo City makes COPS/Metro Alliance a major player on almost every issue affecting the region, from stop signs to economic development. Beatrice Gallego, a former COPS president, confirms that "COPS has made an impact *on the process* of city decision making." Three recent initiatives illustrate this.

PROJECT QUEST

While many of the efforts COPS/Metro Alliance has undertaken deal with the city's infrastructure, such as bridges and drainage systems, many more engage people themselves—or "human capital,"—in the words of COPS members. One of the longest-running programs that COPS/Metro Alliance developed and has fought to sustain is Project Quest. An outgrowth of the concerns expressed in house meetings, Project Quest is a long-term (two-year), intensive, supportive job-training program begun in 1992. Participants are drawn from the community and must meet certain basic criteria to enroll, such as coming in under the national poverty level, having a poor work history, and/or being a single parent. There are about a thousand graduates of Project Quest who earn an equivalent number of course credits to an associate's degree that may be transferred into a four-year college if they choose to pursue that option. Otherwise, they may be placed in career fields like health care or information systems.

Project Quest is an example of what Paulo Freire called "transformative education." Not only does a participant obtain the requisite knowledge and skills needed for the job market, Project Quest offers counseling and other assistance to clients to bolster confidence that they can achieve their educational and professional goals. Going from a feeling of desperation to the realization that achievement is possible is one of the outcomes that clients experience as they go through the program. It is not simply a matter of cultivating a "can-do" attitude, but of restoring self-respect. A sense of self-worth, while hardly quantifiable, is certainly promoted through the earning potential of Quest graduates. The current average hourly wage at placement is $9.97. One of the goals of Project Quest has been to work toward placing graduates in jobs that pay a livable wage, ones that enable them to support their families and that provide a career path with marketable skills in case their initial placement becomes unsatisfactory or is eliminated.

Antoinette Favorite, a Quest graduate now working as a computer network administrator, remembers what life was like before her enrollment in the program. "I had been injured on the job and lost my job because of that. At the same time I was separating from my ex-husband and had no income. I've always wanted to go back to college but could never afford it. I needed help with day care, too. Project Quest helps with day care and that allowed me to go to school full-time."

"People have fallen through the net so many times," notes Virginia Ramirez, a Project Quest board member and COPS activist. "In our house meetings we learned that in order for Project Quest to succeed, we needed to have counselors who could assist participants in getting the supports they needed. . . . The community is always there supporting them one hundred percent." In 1995, the average cost per participant was over $10,000, but the investment is returned within three years in the form of taxes and the removal of these individuals from public welfare roles. But Project Quest is doing more than reducing welfare roles. "We're doing the Lord's work here," Ramirez continued, "to work with those who cannot help themselves." That involves a financial commitment that will assist in the payment of tuition, counseling staff, child care, and, on an emergency basis, rent and utilities.

Favorite first learned of Project Quest from an announcement from the pulpit one Sunday. A member of Macedonia Baptist Church in the city's west side, Favorite says that getting involved in Project Quest was a privilege.

Although the demands on her time and family life were significant, the impact that Project Quest had on her and her family has been beneficial:

> Today I can financially support my family without any federal assistance. I pay
> for child care. I pay for health insurance. I pay for rent and everything that
> comes along to maintain a family and I'm doing it by myself. This takes some of
> the pressure off. The financial stress is alleviated. You can enjoy life just a little
> bit better. I don't have to work two jobs. I'm home more frequently and I can
> help my kids with their homework because I have more free time. Going
> through Project Quest actually mattered a great deal to my family. I'm the kids'
> role model. I no longer have to argue with them to do their homework because
> they saw their mother working hard on her homework. They realize that education
> is so important for improving the quality of their lives.

Project Quest represents a new model for partnering business, education, and community action. Now both employers and local colleges are bound in mutual relationships because of Project Quest. Employment and training experts from the University of Texas system and the United States Department of Labor have worked with college departments and employers to change curricula to adapt to current and long-term needs. Jobs that require highly skilled workers are filled from among a pool of "Questors" who enroll in college courses that train them specifically for the kinds of jobs employers are seeking to fill. Businesses give grants to continue the work, but state and city monies are also used. Project Quest was launched through a $2.5 million grant from the State of Texas under Governor Ann Richards who personally supported the initiative. Some funding is dedicated to the analyses of emerging industries to keep pace with the demand of these employers for high-skilled workers. This allows for a steady stream of placements with high earning potential, breaking the cycle of poverty and allowing individuals to move toward self-sufficiency. Additionally, businesses can remain productive while the city's tax base can be expanded. Finally, funding can help increase the numbers of Project Quest participants, the likelihood of which is now assured given the city's investment in one of COPS/Metro Alliances' other projects, the Human Development Fund. Further information on Project Quest may be obtained through its web site, www.questsa.com.

THE HUMAN DEVELOPMENT FUND

Among its other achievements, COPS/Metro Alliance has sought and obtained millions of dollars from the city's general fund in order to invest in an overall vision for the city. It now seeks to expand the services it has set up already through the assistance of city government and neighborhood schools. The vision of a better San Antonio is reliant on the Human Development Fund (HDF), a road map for this vision. A holistic, synthetic approach to human living, the

HDF emerged from a concept known in Spanish as *lo cotidiano*, which means a sense of attending to commonplaces, to that which occurs and recurs daily. Beyond jobs or infrastructure, the HDF looks to support San Antonio's quality of life in all its dimensions and for all people across the life span. The city agrees. City council members voted unanimously to invest a record $6.87 million in HDF projects in 1999, a $2 million increase from the previous year.

Current HDF initiatives focus on San Antonio's economy. The vision is to create an economy where every family has the opportunity to earn a living wage. To that end, education becomes central. HDF supports Alliance Schools, a COPS/Metro Alliance model program bringing together all stakeholders in public education: students, parents, teachers, administrators, and the neighborhoods in which these schools are located. Here the focus is on student success and the reduction of San Antonio's high dropout rate. The After School Challenge permits a safe and enriching learning environment during after-school hours. The San Antonio Education Partnership is a scholarship program that offers high schoolers an incentive to stay in school and achieve good grades. With a "B" average and a 95 percent attendance rate, any student can obtain up to a four-year scholarship to a local college. Adult education is also key. Project Quest serves as the connection to a living wage. Pre- and post-natal counseling helps new parents to develop effective early childhood education through a program called Smart Start.

These cornerstone initiatives cost money. COPS/Metro Alliance continues to work with city government and the business community toward passage of a sales tax that would establish the creation of the Human Development Fund. Although this has yet to be realized, COPS/Metro Alliance has a good record that promotes the overall vision and need for investment. There are indications that student retention rates and test scores are up. School safety and neighborhood safety are being seen as hand-in-glove issues, with the result that there is greater stability in each. There are over 4,000 scholarship recipients from ten of the city's high schools who would not otherwise have been able to attend local colleges. Research indicates that the more education a person receives, the greater their earning power can be. Tracking over six hundred graduates of local colleges who have benefited from the scholarships indicates that their combined earning is over $12.5 million, contributing $3.5 million in taxes annually. With such benefits on record, the city is being prompted to expand these initiatives to dozens more Alliance Schools and all thirty-six high schools in San Antonio.

THE LIVING WAGE

It is hard to imagine that any corporation would want to pay high wages to employees. Simple economics tells us that cuts into profits. But what economics doesn't speak to are the realities that are caused from keeping wages too low. Not only does this affect the employees and their families, whole communities are disenfranchised by their inability to contribute both as taxpayers and as consumers. "People are working two or three jobs to make ends meet and you have to say, 'wait a minute, what is going on? What's happening to the family, what's happening to the children when people have to work on Saturday and Sunday?' The economy that is going so well overlooks our poor people who are not benefiting from it," noted Father Walter D'heedene.

This scenario is why COPS/Metro Alliance has consistently stood for a "living wage"—earnings that allow a family of four to live reasonably well without resorting to working additional jobs or sacrificing basic necessities (this could range anywhere from health insurance to special dietary needs for the elderly members of a family and so on). They argue that this is the best way for San Antonio to fix its image as one of the nation's poorest cities and, concomitantly, a city where "cheap labor" is plentiful. Moreover, they contended, any corporation would want to relocate to a city that has a high standard of living, one index of which is the ability of its employees to have a decent earning potential, and so the living wage ultimately would bring in more business to the community.

This has not been an easy sell in city hall. The prevailing economic strategy has been to grant generous tax abatements to new businesses in exchange for the promise of supplying a certain number of job openings that would be filled by city residents. The theory is that "any job is a good job." However, corporations will not only enjoy tax breaks, they also will pay new employees low wages.

Recently, a major hotel decided to build in San Antonio and was given the customary tax breaks. COPS/Metro Alliance organizers decided to challenge the city's policy. Their stance was that if businesses were going to receive abatements, they had to pay their employees a living wage. So far, organizers have secured from city officials wage "guidelines" that all businesses should adhere to if they are going to employ area residents. The guidelines state that if tax incentives are going to be granted to a business then at least 70 percent of the workforce employed by that company must be paid a living wage. While these guidelines have been on the books for years, they do not have the force of law and are frequently overlooked. City government cannot mandate a living wage, but organizers wanted officials to be accountable to the guidelines, which said that if businesses did not meet a minimum standard, they would be ineligible for abatements.

What would be a living wage for San Antonians? Some say that the federal Bureau of Labor Statistics offers a good hourly standard, between $9.43 and $10.43 for nondurable and durable goods. This is almost twice the federal minimum wage. COPS/Metro Alliance realizes that raising the bar will not come about without the assistance of businesses. Tim McCallum, an accountant and COPS organizer, noted that this issue presents a direct challenge to social structures that have been the status quo for most of the last century, particularly changing from a corporate profit motive to mutual collaboration. "Who needs an accountant when nobody makes any money? My interest is in a thriving economy. When that thrives, I thrive."

CONCLUDING REFLECTIONS

The leadership of COPS/Metro Alliance has gained some wisdom from their activities, including their failures. Neighborly engagement with issues is an often-uncertain process or even painstaking in terms of getting together at all. But COPS leadership training has at its core a spirituality that enables shy or withdrawn people to get past their initial anxieties. Spirituality is not simply a gimmick to get people moving. It affords participants the opportunity to see reality more clearly, more freely, more courageously. COPS/Metro Alliance is not merely engaged in political issues, but the correction of injustice. The imperative of working for justice has the added benefit of being meaningful. This creates a kind of reciprocal development. Beatrice Cortez, another former COPS president, sums it up in the following way: "My faith never had the meaning it has today. You don't live until you've lived for others. This was part of what my parents taught me. COPS is the one that connected me to church in terms of scripture and my responsibilities and understanding my baptism."

NOTE

This case study is dedicated to the memory of Cassandra Lopez and Denise Marmolejo, both 14, found dead near Sacred Heart Parish on June 30, 2000.

11

Coalition of Immokalee Workers

Kathleen Dolan Seipel

The state of Florida often conjures up images of sun, water, and fun. There are other realities, however, including the working conditions and opportunities of agricultural workers. In Immokalee, a city in the southwestern part of the state, during the height of the October-to-May growing season, there are over 10,000 such workers living there. With hard physical labor, these farm workers earn an average annual wage of $9,000. How do they fare?

This case study helps you understand the challenges facing the farm workers and the approaches they and their supporters have taken to rectify what many see as an unjust system. With a concern for basic human needs and drawing on methods of popular education, church leaders started to focus on the farm worker population in the 1970s. Seeking initially to provide direct service needs, these leaders recognized that the system needed to be addressed as well. The distinction that Professor Massaro elaborated on between charity and justice sheds light on this. Joining with other groups, the Coalition of Immokalee Workers was eventually created to advance the well-being of the farm workers and their families. Trilingual meetings drew the workers; they started to discuss and analyze their situations. How does this work relate to the "see-judge-act" method Professor Massaro explicated?

One of the first actions that the Coalition of Immokalee Workers took was a work stoppage in the fall of 1995, an attempt to act collectively—"We are all leaders" is a core principle—and to protest the decrease in its hourly picking wage from $4.25 to $3.85. The workers were not successful at this point; no overall change in workers' wages resulted. Why do you think this was so? Could they have done something differently? What did that experience teach them?

A deep concern of the workers dealt with public acts of violence. You will learn how the group decided to respond to a beating of one of the workers by a "crew leader." That event galvanized the group and led to a protest march, greater organization, and eventually to a shift in the relationship of power with employers. How does Professor Whitmore's discussion of "marginalization" and "moral agency" fit in here? How comfortable are you with various definitions of "power"?

Finally, dignity, solidarity, and social change are core themes in this case study: "Awareness + Commitment = Change." What does this case study, along with the framing essays in Part I and the other case studies you have read, add to your thinking about these concepts and the relevance of the Catholic social tradition?

INTRODUCTION

The town of Immokalee sits in the northwestern corner of the Florida Everglades, about twenty-five miles inland from its larger and better-known neighboring cities along the southwestern coast. To get to Immokalee from Fort Myers, one has to travel east on Route 82, a long and lonely road that is lined on either side by orange groves and tomato fields for as far as the eye can see. After a few miles on this road, it doesn't take long to notice that agriculture is the dominant industry in this part of the state. Close to one-third of the tomatoes grown in Florida come from this area. Route 82 ends at Route 29, another long, straight road that cuts north to south through the large expanse of cultivated land. Turning south on Route 29 will bring one down Main Street in the town of Immokalee. On either side of Main Street, there are stores, fast food restaurants, and doctors' offices—the first signs of population since leaving Fort Myers. Although a relatively short distance separates Fort Myers and Immokalee, they appear to be a world apart.

Between October and May, the height of Florida's growing season, over 10,000 agricultural workers live in Immokalee. Each morning, they wake before 5:00 A.M. to meet in large parking lots where buses and vans will come to take them out to the fields. After a long days' work in the sun, the workers return in the evening to receive their daily wage. The workers earn between $50 and $80 a day. If the weather is bad, there is no work at all. The average annual wage of farm workers is estimated to be about $9,000, well below the poverty line. The cost of living in Immokalee is high. Without access to transportation, workers shop for their staples at places within walking distance, usually at stores that keep their costs high because they have a captive market. At the end of the day, workers return to overcrowded trailers and apartments with monthly rents of $1,000 or more. In order to keep enough of their wages to feed their families, workers must make difficult trade-offs as they earn and spend their money.

Using the wages of the farm workers to measure how justly the agricultural industry is functioning, many have concluded that the industry fails the test that the church has laid out. The Coalition of Immokalee Workers was created as a vehicle for workers themselves to bring about an agricultural system that functions more justly for all who contribute to its profits.

THE BIRTH OF THE COALITION OF IMMOKALEE WORKERS

The roots of the Coalition of Immokalee Workers can be traced to many different sources, including popular education movements in Haiti, ecclesial base communities in Latin America, and the social teachings of the Catholic Church.

Many people connected with the social justice work of the Catholic Church remember Fr. Richard Sanders as one of the earliest influences on the ministry with farm workers. Fr. Sanders moved to Immokalee's Our Lady of Guadalupe Parish in the 1970s and opened the parish to Immokalee's farm workers in ways that had not been done before, speaking Spanish and learning Haitian Creole so he could communicate with the workers. Fr. Sanders also opened a social-service center and a food kitchen within the church. The social-service center became Guadalupe Social Services, which currently operates under the auspices of Catholic Charities for the Diocese of Venice. While Guadalupe Social Services sought to address the overwhelming direct service needs of the farm-worker population, Sr. Eileen Eppig, SSND, the agency's first director, recognized the need to hire staff members to focus on changing the systems that kept the workers poor and oppressed. In 1984, Sr. Barbara Pfarr, SSND, John Witchger, and Maria Teresa Gaston joined the staff at Guadalupe Social Services. While Pfarr and Witchger were responsible for much of the organizing work, Gaston recalls that the entire staff of Guadalupe Social Services also supported social-change efforts. "We all wanted change. The organizing was born out of a clear understanding of the mission of the church," she said.

Since the late 1970s, as the work of the farm laborers contributed to the growing profits of the agricultural industry in southwestern Florida, the wages of the workers had remained unchanged. As the cost of living continued to rise, it became increasingly difficult for farm workers to make ends meet. They worked no less, but their work did not reap the compensation needed to meet the workers' basic needs. For years, various community agencies like Guadalupe Social Services and Florida Rural Legal Services had been working to fill in the gaps between the workers' wages and their cost of living. Agencies assisted workers in the retrieval of unpaid wages, provided access to health care for workers who lacked insurance or the means to pay for care, and tried to help workers with their basic needs of food, shelter, and clothing. Seeing that workers' wages were at the root of the poverty in Immokalee and that direct services often provided a subsidy to companies who paid their workers too little, a group of interested agency representatives and workers began talking about ways to build an organized community of workers who could act as a unified force on their own behalf.

Those involved in the examination of organizing models at this stage included farm workers who had experience with the Haitian Peasant Movement, Guatemalan Food Cooperatives, and Mexican Base Communities; representatives from Guadalupe Social Services and other Catholic Social Justice groups; and Greg Asbed and Laura Germino, who arrived in Immokalee in the early 1990s to work with the Florida Rural Legal Services. Both had experience working with migrant workers in Virginia. Asbed, who speaks Spanish and Creole, had spent several years working with a peasant organization in Haiti, which used methods of popular education. Another pioneer of the Coalition was Pedro Lopez, who had experience in his homeland of Guatemala with cooperatives. Many of the other workers in Immokalee had been exposed to popular education in Latin America and the Caribbean and in base communities in their home countries. People within the group that supported the development of organizing in Immokalee examined many different models. Some received training in faith-based community organizing or union organizing.

IMMOKALEE: FROM PLACE TO COMMUNITY

An initial challenge to organizing Immokalee's farm workers was that, despite the fact that they lived in the same small town, many of the workers lived in isolation from one another. The isolation was related to several different factors, including the diverse ethnic roots of the workers—the majority of whom come from Mexico, Guatemala, and Haiti, and speak several different languages—and the temporary nature of agricultural work, which keeps vegetable and fruit pickers moving to different areas of the country throughout the year to find work and which limits workers' connection to the communities in which they live. Some of those who lived in Immokalee before the community began to organize have compared it to a frontier town from the days of the Wild West—every worker for him or herself. As workers struggled to survive from day to day, many of them felt that they could not trust others in the community. Laura Germino, a community educator with Florida Rural Legal Services, characterized the lack of trust among the workers as the result of "people living very separate lives even though they all rode on the bus [to the fields] together," rather than any active racial tensions among the groups.

In the early 1990s, workers began to come to trilingual meetings that were held in the offices of the Guadalupe Social Services. For many of the workers, these meetings provided an unprecedented opportunity to communicate with each other across ethnic lines about the issues that affected them. Through discussions and analysis, the workers began to recognize their common experiences—they all struggled to meet their basic needs while their wages remained low and they worked in poor conditions. The Coalition of Immokalee Workers' ability to unite a diverse group of workers as an organized voice to advocate for their own interests is what has enabled it to be a powerful force for social change. As Laura Germino stated, "When your wages get cut, it doesn't matter what race you are, so those theoretical discussions turned into practical matters."

THE COALITION TAKES ACTION

The strength of the emerging Coalition of Immokalee Workers was first shown publicly in November of 1995 when a major grower decreased its hourly picking wage from $4.25 to $3.85. This action motivated the workers to initiate a work stoppage. On the morning of the strike, workers gathered to demonstrate against the wage cut. Although the initial plan was to refuse to work for only the company that had reduced its wages, the workers spontaneously decided to protest against all of the growers that hired labor from Immokalee. During the protest, each company bus that came into Immokalee during the strike left for the fields with only a few workers. For five days, workers decided that it was more important to speak out against the injustices affecting all of the farm workers than to collect their own wages for the day. Because the workers acted collectively, they had no appointed spokesperson or identifiable rabble-rouser. Several different workers addressed the crowd through a megaphone, and others spoke to the press. Through their collective action in speaking out for themselves and their co-workers, the workers stayed true to the core principles of the organization—"We are all leaders" and "From the people, for the people." Although there was not an overall change in workers' wages as a result of the work stoppage, Laura Germino recalls the strike as the first significant opportunity for the workers' community to "flex their muscles" and show that "a new day was coming."

Many Coalition members said that their day-to-day working conditions changed dramatically after the workers began to meet and participate in collective action. One major shift was in the interactions between workers and crew leaders in Immokalee fields. Each day, farm laborers do their work in teams that are managed by individual crew leaders. Before the Coalition became organized, it was a common practice for crew leaders to arbitrarily withhold wages from the workers. Members of the Coalition began to counteract this practice by collectively and nonviolently confronting such crew leaders to demand the back wages.

Another element of farm-labor culture was the use of public acts of violence to keep workers submissive. According to Laura Germino, Florida Rural Legal Services would see five to six cases annually of workers who had been beaten by their crew leaders. Individual prosecutions would cost the crew leaders a fine, but would not deter the practice. That changed in 1997, when a worker entered the office of the Coalition with his shirt and face bloodied from a beating he had received at the hands of a crew leader. On that day, the members of the Coalition decided to take collective action against the violence that had taken place. After meeting to decide what action they would take, 500 workers marched to the home of the crew leader to protest the violence. Since that demonstration took place, Florida Rural Legal Services has not heard of any other reports of violence against the day-haul workers in the region's fields. Through organizing, the Coalition began to establish a relationship of power with their employers.

THE HUNGER STRIKE

For years, the town of Immokalee remained completely isolated from its neighboring cities along the southwestern coast of Florida. The majority of the residents living in the middle-class and upper-middle-class communities of Fort Myers and Naples never knew anything about the lives of the workers who lived there. This changed in December of 1997 when six members of the Coalition began a hunger strike that drew the attention of the entire state of Florida to the plight of the farm workers.

The six men who went on strike started their fast on December 18, after the Coalition had initiated two previous work stoppages during the same growing season. The strikes were called to pressure the area's major tomato growers to agree to negotiate with the workers on the subject of their wages. The work stoppages prompted one of the growers to negotiate with the Coalition and to increase their picking wage by ten cents per bucket in a first-ever community-based negotiation process. After the other major tomato companies did not respond to the Coalition, the workers decided to begin a hunger strike. The decision to have the hunger strike was made according to one of the Coalition's mottoes—"From the people, for the people." The initial idea was proposed by one of the members and then discussed at several community meetings before it took place. Those who volunteered to strike made the commitment to represent their fellow workers "for as long as it takes."

It did not take long for the hunger strike to draw widespread public attention to the lives of the farm workers in Immokalee. The strike itself was a powerful symbol. The men who were on the strike stated that their fast represented the starvation that results from substandard wages. By putting their

own bodies on the line, the strikers tried to persuade the companies to recognize their humanity and agree to negotiate. When the growers refused to
meet with the Coalition, it seemed that they were also rejecting the humanity of the workers that harvested their products. The workers' weakening
bodies illustrated a stark contrast to the strength of their employers. As the
days passed, the images of the six starving workers that spread throughout
the state of Florida on television news and in print stirred the interest and
emotions of many people outside of Immokalee. Kathleen Kirley, a Catholic
educator from the Fort Myers area who first heard about the Coalition
of Immokalee Workers during the strike, said she was "astounded" by the
fact that people were on a hunger strike and was moved to find out more
about it.

During the strike, several churches in Southwest Florida formed a group to
provide a vehicle for area faith communities to learn more about the concerns
of the farm workers. In Naples and Fort Myers, churches invited the workers
to share their stories with their congregations. In early January 1998, two
weeks into the hunger strike, St. Ann's Catholic Church in Immokalee held an
ecumenical service for 600 people who came out to support the farm workers. Coalition leader Lucas Benitez, who spoke at the service, remembers the
hunger strike as an event that exposed many Florida residents to the injustices
faced by the workers for the first time. "Not even after hunger strikers were
hospitalized did the growers acknowledge their presence and agree to come
to a meeting," Benitez said. "This injustice was witnessed throughout Florida
and people began to come and see for themselves what was happening."
Laura Germino also said that the attention given to the hunger strike from the
press and the churches connected people outside of Immokalee to the struggle of farm workers in a new way. "It was as if the consciousness of the non-
agricultural communities (e.g., Fort Myers, Naples) was raised," she said.

Kathleen Kirley visited some of the churches when the strikers were there
and formed new relationships with people connected to the struggle of the
farm workers. As those relationships deepened, Kirley believes that bridges
were built between Immokalee and other parts of Southwest Florida. Kirley
now works regularly with the staff of the Coalition to educate others about
how Catholic social teaching supports the workers' campaign for justice. Kirley says she is motivated to do the work because of her relationships with
people in the Coalition. "The words of Catholic social teaching are given life
in community," she says. Kirley sees the encyclicals and pastoral letters as
"empowering." "Catholic social teaching honors lay people and the sacred-
ness of all people in the world." After being in relationship with members of
the Coalition, she explains, "you have to look at the situation of the workers
and ask 'why shouldn't the workers have the same things I do?'"

As the hunger strike continued, several influential leaders made public
statements that encouraged dialogue between the growers and the workers

that would bring the hunger strike to an end. A week after the strike began, Bishop John Nevins of the Diocese of Venice sent letters to the Coalition and the growers association asking for both sides to meet. Offering a site for the negotiations, Bishop Nevins expressed hope that open dialogue would allow for free discussion of both workers' and growers' concerns, and that this would lead to a fair and just result for all. A week after Bishop Nevins sent his letters, Lawton Chiles, then governor of Florida, sent a letter to growers asking for them to dialogue with the workers.

The strikers ended their fast after thirty days when former President Jimmy Carter sent a letter to urge growers to negotiate with the workers. The association that represents the agricultural companies operating around Immokalee rejected the request, saying that "the wage paid to any farm worker is the proprietary business concern of that individual's respective employer and fundamentally constitutes a private relationship between employee and employer" and that the association "does not participate in any way with the establishment of farm wages rates." While the growers did not change their position, the Coalition won a tremendous amount of public support through their strike. On a material level, the hunger strike generated such public attention to the issue of farm worker poverty, that Jeb Bush was moved when running for Governor to visit with Coalition members and take action once elected to push growers to grant a second five-cent raise. The farm workers in Immokalee were no longer isolated. New relationships were built between workers and people from all walks of life in communities throughout the state and the country who were committed to stand with the farm workers in their struggle for dialogue and a living wage.

THE GROWTH OF THE CAMPAIGN

The hunger strike motivated religious leaders from Southwest Florida to form a group called "Religious Leaders Concerned" to continue to educate their congregations about the lives of the farm workers and to encourage dialogue between the growers and the workers. Beginning in the summer of 1998, the group worked with the Coalition to organize pilgrimages that gave church members from Fort Myers, Naples, and Bonita Springs the opportunity to come to Immokalee and listen to the workers as they shared their experiences. As the church members met the workers face to face, the invisible barriers that had once separated Immokalee from other Southwest Florida communities began to break down. A more neighborly spirit began to develop between residents of Immokalee and Fort Myers and was reported by local press in their coverage of the pilgrimages.

Once the spotlight had turned to Immokalee during the hunger strike, statewide public support continued to back the workers. The more the public knew about the conditions of the workers, the stronger was their call for change. After the wage increase, the Coalition continued to fight for the right to dialogue with area growers. While a number of public officials have met with members of the Coalition, the association representing Florida's fruit and vegetable growers has continued to refuse to negotiate with them. Despite the increase in the per-bucket picking wage, the position of the Coalition was that the system would remain unjust until there is a change in the relationship between workers and growers and they can sit at the same table to negotiate.

The Coalition has continued to build on its relationships with people throughout the state of Florida through its "Campaign for Dignity, Dialogue, and a Living Wage." The Coalition has led marches through several Florida cities, raising the consciousness of many Florida citizens about farm-labor issues and gathering support for the Campaign. In February 2000, the Coalition organized a two-week, 230-mile march from Fort Myers to the headquarters of the Florida Fruit and Vegetable Association in Orlando. Along the way, the workers held "town meetings" where residents of the communities in which they stayed had the opportunity to meet the workers and get to know why they were marching. Lucas Benitez described this march as "an important solidarity-building and education opportunity in the history of the Coalition." Laura Germino stated that she was "struck by how Floridians from all walks of life were overwhelmingly supportive of people who looked nothing like them . . . you can draw inspiration from the fact that the great majority of the population can see the extraordinary injustice of what is going on."

In January 2001, the Coalition of Immokalee Workers participated in a march with several other groups representing Florida's farm workers to the governor's mansion, calling for the governor to encourage Florida's agricultural business to negotiate with the farm workers. This march marked the first time the groups had collaborated in an event of this scale. It also showed the power of relationships, which connected local farm labor communities to others throughout the state. The Coalition has developed relationships on a national scale through student organizations and other campaigns working toward economic justice. As more people throughout the country show their support for a living wage and dialogue between farm workers and their employers, the Coalition continues to expand its base of leaders.

MODEL OF SOCIAL CHANGE

The Coalition uses the following formula to describe the process of social change: "Awareness + Commitment = Change." The first part of the formula, awareness, refers to the belief that the base of social change occurs at the level of the individual, when the individual is aware of his or her dignity and worth as a human being and as a worker. The Coalition's weekly meetings actively encourage all members to contribute as educators and decision makers. The Coalition's slogan, "We are all leaders," proclaims the importance of each individual member for the strength of the organization. As Coalition organizer Greg Asbed explains, "change has to take place in each person" in order for change to occur on the level of the community or the industry. More than the mobilization of bodies, the Coalition's goal is to mobilize "selves."

Using methods of popular education, the workers actively participate in an analysis of the conditions of their work and the state of their community. The methods include popular theater, videos, and drawings. In one of the skits the Coalition uses at its community meetings and street fairs, some of the workers act out a scene that shows interactions between growers, crew leaders, and workers. One actor plays the role of the company boss, known as *"Don Tomate"* ("Mr. Tomato") and wears a papier-mâché mask of a tomato-shaped face over his head. Another actor plays the role of the crew leader. Others play the workers who are picking tomatoes. The skit keeps the audience engaged, not only because it is funny and entertaining, but also because it illustrates experiences all of the workers can relate to. As Alejandro Benitez, a member of the Coalition's Board of Directors, explains, the skits are "representations of actual experience as well as animation that opens the eyes of the workers" who begin to think critically about the conditions in which they work. At the end of the skit, the members of the audience are asked to critically analyze what they saw in the skit, "What do you think?," "What does it mean?," "How do the growers see us?," "How do we see ourselves?" In their analysis, the workers educate each other on the issues and motivate active participation in the continued work of the Coalition.

In other gatherings, the members of the Coalition watch a video and then discuss how the themes in the video are related to their own experience. For example, the Coalition looks to the work of historical civil-rights leaders to understand their own struggle and learn about ways to bring about social change. The workers have watched videos that tell the stories of leaders like Mahatma Gandhi, Martin Luther King, Jr., and Cesar Chavez. Most of the members of the Coalition are well versed on the lives of these figures and the movements they inspired. Manuel Rodriguez, the president of the Coalition's Board of Directors, explains that the stories provide inspiration and generate practical ideas as the workers learn how nonviolent protest can effect social change. "We have to continue on their path, we are following in their steps," he says. The workers know that they have an important place in the long procession of movements that have fought for justice and human dignity in society and that others will learn from their actions just as the Coalition has learned from those who came before them. "There will be people who come after us that we also can support," Rodriguez says.

The Coalition also uses *dibujos*, or drawings, as a tool for discussion. The *dibujos* are one of the most-used tools for popular education because they can be widely distributed and they are accessible to everyone, regardless of their level of formal education. The *dibujos* usually appear on the flyers that are posted all over Immokalee to announce meetings and public actions. Like popular theater, they depict realistic elements of the lives of the farm workers and the agricultural economy and challenge the viewer to react to what they see. Through the tools of popular education, the Coalition constantly encourages the workers to critically analyze their surroundings. Manuel Rodriguez explains that the ideas the workers share with each other in their analysis are so important because they sharpen the common awareness that "we are human beings, and we deserve respect, dignity, and a good wage so we can take care of our families." The "classroom" of popular education can therefore travel with the workers well beyond the city limits of Immokalee, Florida as they continue to analyze their work and their community life.

Participatory education and the increased level of awareness that comes out of it often inspire a commitment to action. Commitment is the second element in the formula for change. Through their commitment, the members of the Coalition build their collective strength and power, which leads to changing relationships within the community and in their work. Although members of the Coalition participate in leadership training, they become skilled leaders by participating in public actions and collectively evaluating their effectiveness. Several years of consciousness raising and commitment have in fact brought about many important victories for farm laborers in Southwest Florida. Tomato pickers saw their first wage increase in twenty years. Coalition organizer Lucas Benitez has received national recognition from the Catholic Campaign for Human Development and the "Do Something" Foundation for his leadership. Members of the Coalition have met with public officials on the local, state, and national levels and have won the active support of religious leaders throughout the country. Increasing numbers of citizens in the nation now stand in solidarity with the struggle of their neighbors in Immokalee who harvest the food that feeds their families.

CONCLUSION

The Coalition continues to animate and train leaders and hold weekly meetings that have strengthened and expanded its base of members. They also continue their campaign for dialogue and fair wages, expanding networks of solidarity and putting pressure on international companies that purchase Florida tomatoes to modestly increase what they pay for tomatoes so that farm-worker wages can, in turn, be increased. The Coalition has also supported and developed many innovative grassroots efforts that have contributed to an improved quality of life for Immokalee's farm workers. They run a food cooperative out of their main office, which sells staple foods to members at much lower prices than the town's retail markets. Coalition members have also developed a labor cooperative to harvest watermelons during the summer months. Without a crew leader, the members of the harvesting crew can earn more wages collectively. Through their collaborations with the Florida Rural Legal Services and the United States Department of Justice, the Coalition of Immokalee Workers has also contributed to the federal convictions of several ringleaders of slave-labor operations that they uncovered.

There are still great challenges ahead for the Coalition of Immokalee Workers and other groups of farm laborers working to improve their wages and work conditions. Farm workers continue to be the poorest-paid and least-protected workers in the United States. As Virginia Nesmith of the National Farm Worker Ministry has stated, "It rots at the very core of our country when the people who produce the bounty of our country often can't afford to feed their own families." Efforts to organize are further challenged by the transitory nature of farm labor, which keeps vegetable and fruit pickers from becoming rooted in any single community. This is why the Coalition's strong emphasis on personal consciousness raising through popular education has been successful. Greg Asbed stated that the most important principle in the work of the Coalition is the dignity of the human person. "All of the work of the Coalition is aimed at two long-term goals—to help low-wage workers realize their worth in the broader society and to assist workers in building their strength, in southwestern Florida and anywhere else they may travel." No matter where the workers go, their ability to analyze their surroundings in terms of how well their dignity is being upheld will stay with them. As Laura Germino described, workers who have traveled to other areas of the country have become leaders in those areas because of what they experienced in Immokalee. "They became so aware of their ability to control their own destiny, they became very vocal spokespeople for workers' rights. . . . You cannot take away from people a mental change or the desire to right a wrong."

From the early meetings of workers at Guadalupe Social Services to the statewide marches for worker justice, the greatest strength of the Coalition of Immokalee Workers has been their ability to build a community of leaders who actively participate in an analysis of the social and economic systems that affect them. As stated in the encyclical *Pacem in Terris* (no. 26) "the dignity of the human person involves the right to take an active part in public affairs and to contribute one's part to the common good."

12

Baltimore: BUILD and the Solidarity Sponsoring Committee

Kathleen Dolan Seipel

When economic, cultural, political and social changes occur in metropolitan areas, some people are left behind, with limited opportunities for improving their situation. Some of the changes have to do with transportation and housing decisions, which relate to what Mr. Rusk described in his essay. When the changes happened in Baltimore, a group of concerned clergy and community leaders looked at, as Professor Massaro urges, the "signs of the times" and rallied to try to bring about positive change for the low-wage workers. These mostly service employees had weak job security and working conditions that left them isolated. The coalition tried to help the workers by getting a "living wage" policy enacted by the government. This case study describes that story and the subsequent challenges the group faced.

Do you know what the federal minimum wage is and how much a worker makes in a year at that level? Do you know the federal level of poverty, say, for a family of three? Compare those two and then think about what Professor Whitmore discussed in terms of a "just wage." In addition to the living wage work, this case study alerts us to the issues of "payday loans" and what happens to "temporary workers." What do you know about those two areas? What can and what should be done in the face of all these concerns in light of Catholic social teachings?

A particular vehicle for bringing about change is community organizing, which takes different forms as you are learning. In this case study, as in that on COPS in San Antonio, the IAF plays a significant role. The Baltimore church-based organizing will bring to mind the PICO model in the Oakland case study as well. What commonalities do you find in the community-organizing approaches you are encountering?

Finally, this case study offers an example of collaborative decision making. We have examined in some of the other cases the question of who should be involved in determining what the important issues are in a given area, as, for example, in the Chicago case. Here we see an example of where the workers in a "temporary employment agency" helped determine the rules for management of the business. In both cases, the Catholic social teaching on the conditions of fulfillment for the common good and the idea of "participation," discussed by Professor Whitmore, come to mind.

INTRODUCTION

In November 1993, the *Baltimore Sun* newspaper quoted a Maryland politician as saying that nothing "short of a revolution" would boost the wages of Baltimore's service-economy workers "into the living wage category."[1] Just thirteen months later, when the city council passed an ordinance that guaranteed a living wage for employees of Baltimore City contractors, an alliance of Baltimore churches, community organizers, labor organizers, and workers showed that a revolution was indeed underway—not just in Baltimore, but all over the nation.

Since the Baltimore City Council passed the living wage ordinance in 1994, dozens of states, counties, and municipalities have passed similar legislation in their local areas across the country. "Living wage" is the term they use to describe a wage with which a worker can support him or herself and his or her family without having to rely on government subsidies to meet basic needs. These laws, and the movements that have brought about their passage, are based on the premise that employment at the federal minimum wage, which has failed to keep up with inflation since the 1970s, is not sufficient to keep low-wage workers above the poverty line.

The living wage revolution began in Baltimore, Maryland—a city that, like many major cities on the eastern seaboard, has undergone major changes in the last fifty years as its economic base has shifted from manufacturing to the service industry. In 1950, Baltimore was one of the United States' leading industrial centers. It was the country's sixth largest city, and over one third of its workers were employed in manufacturing. The manufacturing sector provided opportunities for relatively unskilled workers to have steady employment at wages that provided for a middle-class standard of living.

However, in the 1950s and 1960s, Baltimore began a transformation that would continue for the remainder of the century. As the economy began to shift to the postindustrial era, major employers left the city as the suburbs began to grow. By 1995, Baltimore had lost almost 75 percent of the manufacturing jobs it had in 1950. Between 1950 and 1995, thousands of Baltimoreans left the city to live in new suburban developments. This led to a major shift in the racial composition of the city. In the 1950s, African Americans from the rural south came to Baltimore seeking economic opportunity. At the same time, whites left the city in droves for the surrounding suburbs. As new highways and suburban development increased at a rapid pace, city neighborhoods and retail centers were left with unemployment, a deteriorating housing stock, and increases in crime and public health problems.

In the 1970s, Baltimore city leaders initiated major plans to redevelop the city, focusing especially on the city's Inner Harbor, with hopes of transforming the area into a tourist and retail center. The city used tax cuts and special subsidies to attract businesses and developers to downtown. In 1980, "Harborplace," a collection of shops and restaurants, opened in the Inner Harbor, and development soared as tourists and real estate developers flocked to the area. In the 1990s, development continued in the area as two major sports stadiums were built and the convention center was expanded. For tourists and workers in the downtown office buildings, the city had undergone a successful face-lift in the last two decades of the century.

However, many residents of Baltimore saw it as a city with two faces. While the Inner Harbor benefited from major development, people in neighborhoods outside of this area continued to struggle with a myriad of social problems connected to poverty. As a city known for its close-knit neighborhoods, many of Baltimore's communities were torn apart by drugs, crime, poor education, inadequate health care, and dilapidated and vacant housing.

This is the picture of the city that Baltimore's Solidarity Sponsoring Committee (SSC) sought to change. Believing that many of the city's problems were connected to a lack of decent jobs for its residents, SSC leaders aimed to rebuild Baltimore's neighborhoods by uniting its workers and their families to fight for a living wage and better employment opportunities. This is their story.

THE STRUGGLE FOR A "LIVING WAGE"

The Solidarity Sponsoring Committee was born out of an alliance between Baltimoreans United in Leadership Development (BUILD), a church-based community organization, and the American Federation of State, County, and Municipal Employees (AFSCME), a union of public service employees. Before the Solidarity Sponsoring Committee was initiated, BUILD was developed in Baltimore City as a broad-based coalition of churches, community leaders, and service sector workers. This coalition first drew Baltimore's attention to the plight of people employed as service workers in the revitalized downtown area by calling for a living wage for these workers.

Since 1977, BUILD has been a leading force for social change, calling the attention of city and state politicians to the needs of Baltimore's neighborhoods and establishing programs for various community needs, including education, affordable housing, and child care. Affiliated with the Industrial Areas Foundation (IAF), a national network of community organizations, BUILD acts on the basic organizing principles that the IAF teaches, especially its central philosophy: do not do for people what they can do for themselves.

In 1992, clergy within BUILD began to discuss what they had been noticing as a trend throughout Baltimore city. They observed that many of the city residents who were using church-sponsored soup kitchens, food pantries, and emergency shelters were employed in Baltimore's downtown area. In increasing numbers, workers needed assistance from churches to provide for their families' basic needs. BUILD clergy and organizers began to meet with the custodians, security guards, hotel workers, and other employees of the downtown service economy to learn more about the situation. Fr. Joe Muth, BUILD leader and pastor of St. Matthew's Catholic Church, explained that it was challenging to meet with the workers because they were isolated from each other. "You could not go to one factory to find all of the workers in one place like in the old days," he said. Workers came downtown in different shifts to different floors of several high-rise buildings. In order to dialogue with the workers, BUILD clergy and organizers served tea and hot cocoa to workers at bus stops and outside downtown buildings when the overnight shifts changed. They met with workers at shelters and soup kitchens and talked with hundreds of low-wage workers throughout the city.

Reverend Doug Miles, a BUILD leader and pastor of Koinonia Baptist Church, recalled that the city clergy, who had initially formed a crucial base of support for the city's redevelopment plan when it was proposed in the early 1970s, had come to the conclusion that the plan had not reaped the benefits that the city had promised—to replace lost manufacturing jobs with good jobs in the growing service economy. "What we discovered was that many of the persons working downtown were working part-time, temporary jobs, and that the majority were working at the minimum wage," he explained. According to Fr. Muth, the clergy discovered that the downtown jobs not only produced a wage gap, but also broke down community institutions. "People could not get to church, were not with their families, and had to shift their children [to various day care providers]" because of their work schedule.

Angry that the public money used to support subsidies for downtown redevelopment had not provided jobs that paid enough for workers to be able to support their basic needs, BUILD developed what it called a "new social compact."

The new Social Compact proposed "that jobs in the heavily subsidized downtown service sector pay a living family wage, that they have a career track, and that a pool of funds for benefits and training for downtown workers be created. . . . We simply demand that all corporations requesting and enjoying public assistance through subsidy must in turn provide jobs that pull people out of poverty."

As BUILD leaders continued to meet with and recruit workers, they held a series of large public events at which they asked public officials for a commitment to cut off subsidies to corporations unless they would agree to adhere to the "new social compact." While Mayor Kurt Schmoke and other public officials said that they supported the general goals of the BUILD campaign, they claimed that they did not have the power to force downtown corporations to pay a living wage.

Then, in December 1993, City Council President Mary Pat Clarke introduced a bill that would set prevailing wages for service work done under city contract. The mayor, facing a challenge in the next election from the city council president, agreed to assemble a task force to study the impact such an ordinance would have on the city economy. After continued pressure from workers and community leaders, the city government unanimously approved the "living wage" bill in December 1994. Employees of city contractors would begin to see their paychecks increase when the law took effect the following July.

THE BIRTH OF THE SOLIDARITY SPONSORING COMMITTEE

During the fight for a living wage, BUILD leaders recognized the need to build an organization for low-wage workers. On May 22, 1994, leaders from BUILD stood with leaders from the American Federation of State, County, and Municipal Employees (AFSCME) at a well-publicized event in an East Baltimore church to announce that they were joining forces to create such an organization—the Solidarity Sponsoring Committee. It was Pentecost Sunday, a day containing symbolism that the BUILD clergy regarded as no mere coincidence. As Rev. Miles recalled, "preachers sounded like labor organizers and organizers sounded like preachers. . . . It was really a day of Pentecost celebration."

Rev. Miles believes that the development of the Solidarity Sponsoring Committee gave more back to both of its parent organizations than either of them contributed. While BUILD contributed the broad-based, organized support of church and community leaders, "Solidarity (SSC) helped to reinvigorate the BUILD organization and helped us reground ourselves in the issues where the church ought to be." While the support of AFSCME provided important resources for SSC, financing the organizing campaign and assisting in the development of the organizers, AFSCME gained a more solid base of members that could stand against a growing movement toward the privatization of work done by public sector employees. Miles also believes that Solidarity gave AFSCME some needed direction, saying that "it helped AFSCME reground itself in union organizing principles."

After the "living wage" ordinance took effect in 1995, the SSC continued to be active on issues that affect low-wage workers. They drew public attention to contractors who did not comply with the ordinance, which in turn led city leaders to take action, threatening to revoke the contracts of any businesses that did not pay its employees what they were owed.

WELFARE REFORM

In 1996, President Clinton signed the "Personal Responsibility and Work Opportunity Reconciliation Act of 1996." This marked a historic shift in the environment of low-wage employment. According to the new law, welfare recipients were required to work or engage in an "approved work activity" for at least twenty hours per week within two years of their start in the program. This legislative change introduced a new challenge for the Solidarity Sponsoring Committee. With the new law, businesses could hire Welfare-to-Work participants to replace existing workers who were being paid the living wage. For employers, this would produce a great savings in their personnel costs. Welfare-to-Work participants could be hired on a probationary basis during which employers would have to pay them only a small stipend (averaging about $1.50/hour) in addition to the welfare benefits the state paid. SSC members feared that this would provide employers with a steady supply of sub-minimum-wage workers without an obligation to provide permanent employment.

Although there was a federal prohibition on the displacement of workers, Solidarity leaders recognized that employers were able to get around the prohibition because its wording was too vague. They spoke out against the practice of worker displacement, writing newspaper commentaries and holding public meetings—and when the Solidarity Sponsoring Committee spoke out, Maryland public officials responded. In June 1997, Governor Parris Glendening issued an executive order, the first of its kind in the nation, officially prohibiting displacement, stipulating that Welfare-to-Work subsidies should be used to create new jobs, and establishing an enforcement mechanism under which workers who believed they had been displaced could file grievances.

TAKING ON THE CHECK-CASHING INDUSTRY

In 1999, the Solidarity Sponsoring Committee turned its focus toward Maryland's check-cashing industry. As many banks have closed their branches in inner-city neighborhoods, check-cashing businesses have taken on the role of the primary financial institutions in these areas. Solidarity leaders specifically targeted check-cashing centers that offered "payday loans." These short-term, high-interest loans allowed customers to borrow against their next paycheck by writing postdated checks for the amount they were borrowing in addition to the fees for the loan. For example, if a customer needed an immediate $300, he or she would write a postdated check for $379. If customers did not have the money when it was due, they could often roll it over into a new loan by paying the fees on the loans. By continuing to take out payday loans, customers could accumulate debts of thousands of dollars. As Solidarity leaders investigated this practice, they calculated that the fees that check-cashing centers would charge on payday loans amounted to an annual percentage rate of 400 percent or higher. Maryland law limits the APR on small loans to a cap of 33 percent. Because the businesses had not been regulated in Maryland, state financial officers did not have the power to sanction check-cashing businesses that violated consumer-lending laws. Solidarity saw this as a way the working poor were being exploited.

Members of the Solidarity Sponsoring Committee went to the Maryland state capitol in Annapolis to call the attention of state legislators to the practice of payday lending. As a result, state delegates introduced several bills in the 2000 legislative season to curb the practice and to regulate the check-cashing industry. At the same time, lobbyists for the check-cashing industry were active in Annapolis. Their influence led to the introduction of a bill that would exempt payday lenders from the 33 percent APR lending cap. The Maryland Senate Finance Committee soundly rejected this bill the day after they heard from a panel of advocates for the working poor, led by the Solidarity Sponsoring Committee.

Solidarity organizer Scott Cooper described this campaign as a great opportunity for the organization to build power and cohesion by working together on an issue that was so important to all of its members. Solidarity leader Marvin Lee saw the campaign as a concrete way to do something to help his own community. "I was able to get in there and fight, to make a difference," he said. "Now I look at my neighborhood . . . and I speak to senior members, to young members, to all members, and I could feel how they were overjoyed to know that no longer were they [the payday lenders] going to be sucking us dry."

Organizers and leaders from the Solidarity Sponsoring Committee are currently in the process of meeting with major banks to set up basic accounts so that members can have access to convenient and affordable financial services.

SSC EMPLOYMENT AGENCY, INC.

Temporary employment is the largest growing workforce in urban areas across the country. As the economy changed from a manufacturing base to a service base, many workers who once had full-time jobs as custodians and other service workers found themselves in the temporary-labor pool. Using temporary and part-time services to do the work of a formally full-time employee continues to be a popular cost-saving practice for government and private employers. Most temporary workers do not have health insurance or other benefits and are left with little to no chance of advancement in their jobs.

The Solidarity Sponsoring Committee sought to affect the temporary employment sector by establishing their own worker owned and operated temporary agency. With the help of the Catholic Campaign for Human Development and the Annie E. Casey Foundation, the SSC Employment Agency, Inc. was launched in 1997. Avis Ransom, who has been the director of the agency since its founding, said she was initially motivated to work with SSC because she saw it as a good business decision. She was contracted to do the initial feasibility study—to look at whether a collectively owned temporary employment agency could be profitable in Baltimore City. Ransom then constructed the business plan and was asked to become the agency's Executive Director.

After Ransom took on her role as the director of the SSC Employment Agency, she began to view her position there as the answer to her prayers. She remembered the feelings she would have when she participated in her church missions to poor Baltimore City neighborhoods. Although she felt like these visits were meaningful, she said she had mixed feelings when she left the neighborhood.

> I would leave people pretty much in the same physical, financial, economic, and educational situations that I had found them in. They would be spiritually lifted, but they would be just as hungry and just as poor.... I felt like I could do more and I felt like the institutions that were backing me could do more substantive work to address the problems of people I was meeting and developing relationships with.

Ransom saw the opportunity to lead the SSC Employment Agency as an important way to use her educational background while she worked with Baltimore church and community leaders to make a long-term difference in people's lives. "It allows me to contribute in a way that is not [charity]," she says proudly. "I earn a living while I do this, so it is a mutually beneficial exchange between me and people that live in Baltimore City who would have a more difficult time gaining an economic foothold without me being their partner."

One important way the business has developed is through the use of grassroots organizing methods as a foundation of its management practices. Ransom calls one of these methods "the rounds." The first interaction workers have with the SSC Employment Agency is as part of a group of nine or ten other people who come together for orientation and training. The group opens with prayer, and Ransom introduces herself to the group. Ransom explains that she tries to share something personal about her life during her introduction. "I allow myself to be a bit vulnerable and open in front of strangers, and people often follow with the same kind of openness." This establishes a culture in which individual workers begin to form relationships with each other. "I'm amazed often to hear people share that they are addicts and ex-offenders . . . and it's often responded to with claps and cheers and encouragement from other members of the group who understand how difficult it is to be open about that in an organization in which you hope to get employment."

Another SSC management practice that is based on grassroots organizing methods is a decision-making model that involves the workers in the management of the business. Ransom recalled that customers identified three main problems in their experience with the temporary workforce—workers arriving late; workers arriving unready to work because of appearance, lack of skills, or because they were under the influence of substances; and fewer workers arriving than had been ordered by the customer. Ransom presented these issues to the workers and asked them to come up with solutions. What came out of this request were solutions that she believes have made the SSC Employment Agency the best at what they do in the city. The first of these was to tell workers that they were expected to arrive one hour before the start of work. Ransom says that clients often realize that the workload is heavier than they originally thought it would be and end up starting workers right away. She says that this would also make time available for workers to develop relationships with each other through prayer circles and conversations. The second solution was for SSC to screen workers before the customers screened them. The third was for SSC to order more workers than the client asked for. While clients often use the extra workers, those who do not get to work will get two hours' pay for coming to the work site. Ransom explained that if she had come up with these rules and presented them to SSC employees, they would most likely have rejected them, but the fact that the suggestions came from them added to a sense of collective ownership in the success of the business.

Another key to the success of the SSC Employment Agency is its establishment as a worker-owned cooperative. Ransom says that the sense of ownership that the workers have inspires them to work hard and gives them the authority to address co-workers whose actions might damage the image of the company and its relationship with clients. For SSC employee Marvin Lee, the worker-owned structure of the agency allows him to be able to contribute skills that he was not encouraged to use in other places he has worked. He says that it gives him a sense that he is a part of something great. "I want to see this company become the best at what we do . . . and I want to be able to say I was a part of it, I helped it grow and helped it rise."

RECONNECTING COMMUNITY

The establishment of the Solidarity Sponsoring Committee was a response to what religious and community leaders recognized as a community coming apart at the seams, as workers and their families were isolated from each other and had little time in their schedule of multiple jobs to be connected to community institutions. Solidarity's model of social change was to reweave the community fabric through a process of individual meetings and relationship building.

Renee Brown, Solidarity leader and custodial worker at the World Trade Center in Baltimore's Inner Harbor, first heard about Solidarity when two of her co-workers began talking to an organizer who came to their building when their shifts changed. Brown's interest was piqued, and she also began to converse with the organizer about issues that she now knows in intimate detail. "[The organizer] came down with hot cocoa and talked to us about a living wage, first right of refusal, and a benefit package," Brown recalled. As Brown started attending Solidarity meetings and participating in actions, she began to see a change in her workplace—not only due to the policy changes that brought about a living wage, but as a result of the relationships that formed among the workers. "We began to talk more, get more personal, and get to know each other's families."

As a result of the relationships among members of the community, Solidarity leaders have become active in many community issues that are not directly related to their own jobs and wages. Marvin Lee, a Solidarity leader without children, has become active in the "Child First" campaign, a BUILD initiative to improve the city's provision of educational and health services to children. He has also been involved in "School Counts" which has led the state of Maryland to allow educational hours to count as work experience for the Welfare-to-Work program. Lee explained that these initiatives are important to people who are important to him—his sister, his fiancée, people in his neighborhood—and therefore these relationships connect him to the issues. Solidarity has sought to reilluminate those connections among people so that members can participate together on a range of issues that affect themselves and others in the community. As organizer Jonathan Lange explained, the organization "approaches people as whole people with a series of issues. The same people who are worried about low wages are also worried about the quality of the school their kids are going to, and also worried that they can't find a decent affordable house, or that there are drugs sold on the corner."

When members develop relationships with one another, they begin to see that they have common interests for their families and their communities. Recognizing their common ground, they have the strength to work together for social change. As Avis Ransom explained, "social change requires connecting the segments of society that, for whatever reason, those in power drive wedges between. We find our common interests when social change happens." Fr. Joseph Muth agreed; "What happens is people begin to know each other across economic class lines and racial lines and church denomination lines, people begin to sense their power in a way they never have before and begin to recognize that they can do something." Members of BUILD and the SSC have shown that social change happens when people, drawn together in community, recognize their common interests and goals and decide to work for those goals.

CHALLENGES

While the Solidarity Sponsoring Committee has been an effective force in improving the lives of Baltimore's working families, it has also faced formidable challenges along the way. Most Solidarity organizers and leaders said that the biggest initial challenge was to gain the trust of the workers, to show that this was not just another group making promises it could not deliver. They did this by staying true to the "iron rule" of organizing: "do not do for others what they can do for themselves." By developing relationships with workers, hearing their stories and encouraging them to listen to each others' stories, the organization gave the workers the tools they needed to effect social change. True to its name, the Solidarity Sponsoring Committee built its power through the efforts of diverse groups of people—workers, church members, labor organizers, and community organizers supporting each other toward the same purpose. As Solidarity worker Renee Brown stated, organizers "did not come to us and promise us the living wage," but they did say they would stand with the workers to fight for it.

The leadership was in the hands of the workers—they formed the backbone of the association, supported each other, and recruited new members from their work sites. However, recruitment and sustainability within an employment sector with high turnover and instability has continued to present another challenge. Over the last six years, close to 4,000 people have joined the organization. The solid base of membership is about 150–500. Most Solidarity leaders said that their most important resource to deal with the challenge of turnover is having enough trained organizers to do the work of building leadership within the organization. They explained that organizing low-wage workers is extremely labor intensive because it involves meeting with individual workers, who are often disconnected from their co-workers, rather than working through an established institution. Solidarity organizer Scott Cooper explained that the workers are currently seeking ways to build a stable base of power by establishing a workers' center with staff to organize benefits and provide job training. While workers have expressed interest in building such a center, they are challenged by their commitment to their organizing foundation. They do not want to be another social service agency that provides only for immediate needs without building long-term power. Rev. Miles stated that the biggest challenge Solidarity faces as it continues to grow and build power is that it might be led away from its foundations in relational organizing. He said that it is vital to the organization "to stay grounded in its own principles of organizing and in who it is."

CONCLUSION

BUILD's fight for a living wage and the creation of the Solidarity Sponsoring Committee show how the principles promoting the rights of workers, solidarity, and community participation can work together to rebuild communities. Fr. Joe Muth explains how he believes their work connects to Catholic social teaching:

> BUILD naturally has a way of doing things to build up communities and rebuild people's lives that is very much steeped in Catholic social teaching. The kinds of things that have been preached about for 100 years, that is what we've done with SSC. The Church's labor documents have been all in it and through it even though we didn't do it because everybody in the SSC can quote Catholic social teaching, but because what they've done really celebrates what Catholic social teaching is all about.

The SSC Employment Agency illustrates how opportunities can be created for previously marginalized workers to have a real stake in the growing economy. These models look beyond emergency provisions for Baltimoreans who are most in need and work to transform the city by building on the capacities of its low-wage workers to work together to change the systems that keep them poor. In the Catholic social teaching writings of the last 110 years, the Church has recognized these elements and lifted them up to show how the church can work most effectively for social change in the community.

NOTE

1. James Bock, "BUILD seeks 'living wage' for downtown workers," *Baltimore Sun*, 21 November, 1993, 2B.

13

Students Against Sweatshops

Christopher C. Kelly

This last case study takes a different approach from that of the previous ones. Instead of examining a single group in one city to determine how it works to bring about positive social change in light of the Catholic social tradition, this case study examines the national collegiate anti-sweatshop movement and explores, in particular, the involvement and motivation of leaders on seven different college campuses. How might (or might not) this be seen as an instance of what Professor Massaro identifies as the "see-judge-act" process? As Professor Weigert said in the introductory essay, we live in a "glocal" world. How do you see connections between the local and global worlds in this case study, and what does the Catholic social tradition proclaim?

A major factor in the story of the sweatshop movement is attention paid by various media, from the national press and television to the college or local newspapers and magazines. How much access do ordinary people have to the media? What can be done to provide greater access?

Two of the protagonists in this story were part of groups that went to Central America; those trips dramatically influenced them. As Professor Weigert suggested in her opening essay, "experiential learning" offers a unique vehicle for "transformative education." How do you judge such experiences? Have you had any yourself, whether in the United States or elsewhere?

On several of the campuses students opted for nonviolent actions, ranging from "sleep-outs" to "sit-ins" to "hunger strikes." For some people, such actions are counterproductive; for others, they offer the most viable and worthy alternative. How familiar are you with the history of nonviolent action? Have you ever participated in such actions? What does the Catholic social tradition say about nonviolent struggles?

Finally, various leaders articulate ideas about their models of social change. As you read this last case study, reflect back on the essays and the other case studies: are you ready to explicate your model of social change? What role, if minor or major, does the Catholic social tradition play in that? How will you contribute to the development of this rich, still not well known tradition?

INTRODUCTION

The garment factory workers were frightened. They were poor and illiterate, most all of them women and children, and they toiled in terrible conditions. Their jobs were to cut and sew fabric that would eventually be sold as clothing in America. They earned pennies for their labor and dared not speak out against abusive owners for fear of losing their jobs. And it cost them their lives.

Late one afternoon, a fire trapped them on the top floors of their factory. Many leaped to their deaths from windows to avoid the encroaching flames. Others were found huddled near locked exit doors. In the end, 146 workers lost their lives in the inferno.

Thanks to intensive media coverage and grassroots organizing efforts by an angered public, Americans quickly learned of the dangerous working conditions in this and other factories known as "sweatshops." A new anti-sweatshop movement swept the nation. Protestors called for improved working conditions and protections for vulnerable workers, and real change began to take place.

This incident could have happened anywhere around the globe today where sweatshop abuse is epidemic—including Thailand, Mexico, El Salvador, Indonesia, and China. But those 146 victims perished in the United States—in 1911. They were immigrants who worked at the Triangle Shirtwaist factory in New York City's garment district.[1] And the tragic fire that took their lives spurred changes in U.S. public policy that provided workers with unprecedented protections still in place today.

As a new century dawns, college students across the United States are helping to bring about similar changes regarding global sweatshop abuse. Most are active in campus groups dedicated to grassroots organizing around justice issues; still others serve as campus task force members or elected student-body leaders who study sweatshop issues and have the power to recommend policy changes. All have one goal in common: to ensure improved working conditions for laborers who produce apparel with their school's logo. Their success stories help call attention to the global sweatshop issue and could very well impact public policy for decades to come.

Catholic social teaching has long supported the rights of workers. In 1891, when the Industrial Revolution was in full swing, Pope Leo XIII issued *Re-*

rum novarum (The Condition of Labor), the first comprehensive document of social justice. *Rerum novarum* focuses specifically on the rights of workers, who faced exploitation in the factory and great poverty at home. Throughout the twentieth century, the church reinforced the concepts of *Rerum Novarum*, particularly as disparities grew between rich and poor nations. In 1961's *Mater et magistra* ("Christianity and Social Progress), Pope John XXIII called upon industrialized nations to give aid to poor countries, citing the need for cooperation and interdependence. In *Populorum progressio* (The Development of Peoples), Pope Paul VI in 1967 called for increased development in poorer nations as a method to help the poor avoid violence and revolution. In 1987, Pope John Paul II pointed out the realities of global debt, unemployment and underemployment, and the economic gap between the Northern and Southern Hemispheres in *Sollicitudo rei socialis* (On Social Concern).[2]

Despite the Church's support, and over one hundred years of well-developed Catholic social teaching on the dignity of work and the rights of workers, and a century of progress in workers' rights, sweatshops continue to flourish, especially in developing countries. A sweatshop is essentially any workplace where workers are subject to extreme exploitation. This includes hazardous working conditions, arbitrary discipline and a lack of a living wage, benefits, or basic human rights.[3] Today they exist around the globe for a variety of reasons, including the availability of cheap foreign labor, consumer demand, international trade policies that encourage developing nations to create export industries, and local factories that cut costs by pushing laborers to produce goods as quickly as possible. The end result is forced overtime, low wages, punishment and fines for slow work and mistakes, forced child labor, and other abuses.[4]

From 1987 to 1999, U.S. apparel imports increased from 47 percent to 61 percent of the $101 billion wholesale apparel market, a cutthroat industry where consumer demand for cheap clothing means retail giants continually seek cheaper sources of labor.[5] In fact, the four largest U.S. retailers—Wal-Mart, Kmart, Sears, and Dayton Hudson (owner of Target and Mervyns) account for almost 66 percent of U.S. retail sales. Contractors for these companies routinely open and close factories around the world, most often in developing countries where labor costs are extremely cheap. As a result, workers have no bargaining power. They work long hours in horrid conditions for wages that are sometimes substandard even in their local economy, and face the prospect of having the contractor close the factory and move to another country where labor costs are even cheaper.[6]

In the early 1990s, human rights groups in the United States began to focus on the international sweatshop issue led by the National Labor Committee for Worker and Human Rights (NLC). This group, headed by Charles Kernaghan, initiated an independent monitoring movement and outlined the first components of a corporate "code of conduct" for factories that produced apparel to be sold in the United States. The code included the right to organize, full disclosure by companies of the names and addresses of factories that make their products, inspections by independent monitors and decent wages.[7]

But it wasn't until 1996 that Kernaghan and the NLC were able to make the sweatshop issue a national topic, after he exposed the Honduran sweatshops that used child labor to make the Kathie Lee Gifford line of clothing sold by Wal-Mart. Later that year, the Clinton administration seized upon the issue and organized the White House Apparel Industry Partnership (AIP), with representatives from the garment industry, labor unions, and consumer, and human rights groups called to study the issue. Their final report, released in November 1998, included a proposed workplace code of conduct and established the Fair Labor Association (FLA)—funded primarily by the apparel industry—to implement monitoring guidelines.[8]

FLA member companies agreed to the outlined code of conduct as a way to police international factories that produced their apparel. The code required those factories to pay a prevailing local minimum wage, limited hours of work to no more than sixty per week, and banned child labor, slave labor, and union busting.[9] The FLA also designated major accounting firms to enforce the code through monitoring guidelines that included announced and unannounced visits, allowed companies to select which facilities would be inspected, and agreed to keep factory and monitoring reports secret in order to protect competitive advantages.[10]

Over one hundred college and university administrations quickly sought to affiliate with the FLA, and with good reason. The collegiate licensing industry is a $2.5 billion business, with companies like Nike and Champion paying royalties to hundreds of schools through a trademark company called the Collegiate Licensing Corporation (CLC) for the right to use the campus logo on apparel, hats, and jackets. By early 1999, the CLC stood ready to implement the FLA code and monitoring guidelines.

But college students had already seized upon the issue. In the fall of 1997, a group of students at Duke University called Students Against Sweatshops held a sit-in and succeeded in convincing the university to require that manufacturers of items with the Duke label not use sweatshop labor. They worked with administrators to create a Duke University "code of conduct" that went further than the FLA code, calling for full disclosure and independent monitoring of factory locations. Their victory quickly spread to other campuses, and by the summer of 1998 a national umbrella organization was formed called United Students Against Sweatshops (USAS), eventually growing to over 150 chapters.[11]

USAS took the sweatshop issue to a new level over the next year, demanding through sit-ins and other actions on a number of major campuses that school officials adopt a stricter code of conduct than the one proposed by the FLA. They called for manufacturers to fully disclose factory locations that would be monitored by human rights organizations, developed specific language to ensure women's rights, and insisted on a living wage for workers who produce clothing bearing the university logo.[12]

They also reflected the electronic age of activism, developing similar strategies through the use of listservs, Web sites, laptops, and cell phones. The movement has a strong bond with organized labor, and many of the USAS student leaders previously received grassroots organizing training through internships with the AFL-CIO.[13] Many of these leaders gathered during 1998 and 1999 to draft an alternative organization to the FLA called the Workers' Rights Consortium (WRC), which would incorporate all of the USAS demands to fight sweatshops. In October 1999, USAS members formally called upon their universities to join the WRC and withdraw from the FLA.[14]

The following case studies, based primarily on phone interviews conducted over the period of December 2000 through May 2001, examine the accomplishments of seven student leaders as they grappled with specific issues related to their school's involvement with the WRC and the FLA. Six were members of local USAS chapters; one was appointed to a task force to study the issue at her university. All have a commitment to social justice that sustained them as they worked to help oppressed factory workers around the world.

CARA HAYES: GEORGETOWN UNIVERSITY

Georgetown University, in Washington, D.C., is the nation's oldest Catholic university. This Jesuit school has 6,418 undergraduates and 3,298 graduate students (excluding the law and medical schools), and boasts a diverse student population from across the United States and around the world. Fifty-two percent of the combined student population is female, and 15 percent are minorities; another 17 percent are international students. Most students are from the east coast, with a concentration located in the middle Atlantic states.[15]

Cara Hayes, a sophomore from Long Island, N.Y., serves as the campaign director for the Georgetown Solidarity Committee (GSC), where she serves as the committee's contact to local and national labor. Two years before she arrived on campus, GSC helped establish the campus movement against sweatshops, along with Duke University and the University of Wisconsin. Early on, when the university joined the Fair Labor Association (FLA), GSC members worked hard to capture the administration's attention about the injustice of sweatshop labor being used to produce the school's apparel. In 1998 and 1999, as the GSC grew in numbers and strength, administrators also considered adopting the Collegiate Licensing Corporation code of conduct.

This time the students demanded full public disclosure of abusive factory locations as part of the code of conduct, something the administration did not initially favor.[16] Twenty-seven GSC members held an eighty-four-hour sit-in at the university president's office, and in the end both sides compromised. The school endorsed the CLC code, but agreed to terminate its contracts with manufacturers who failed to disclose factory locations within a year. Administration officials also demanded that the CLC show substantial progress "on the issues of full public disclosure, living wage, universal compliance and independent monitoring."[17]

When Hayes arrived at Georgetown in the fall of 1999, GSC was working hard to convince the administration to leave the FLA and join the Workers' Rights Consortium (WRC). She became aware of the anti-sweatshop movement when she heard three factory workers from El Salvador speak at the school about their attempts to unionize, and the threats made against them. "I was really moved by what they had to say and their strength in a really difficult situation," she said, and immediately sought to become involved.

The university formed a Licensing Implementation Committee to study the issue, and when administrators gathered to make the FLA/WRC decision, Hayes and other GSC members organized a silent protest to call attention to the plight of exploited workers. Their activism helped achieve a significant victory when the school announced its decision to leave the FLA and join the WRC. Since then, Hayes has found the challenges of maintaining the WRC commitment to be stimulating. "I was excited about understanding the world in a different way and was never exposed to something like this. The more I found out, the more I had a personal need to be involved," she said.

A number of important issues had to be overcome in order for the movement to succeed. Included were strong university ties to the corporate world and a lack of connectedness between students on campus and sweatshop workers in a foreign country. "It's hard for a twenty-year-old kid from Manhattan who is studying business at Georgetown to feel something for the Nicaraguan *maquila* worker," said Hayes.

Thanks to a journey to Nicaragua on a *Witness for Peace* youth delegation in March 2000, Hayes learned first-hand about life with a family whose existence is dependent upon sweatshop employment. *Witness for Peace* is an organization that is dedicated to changing U.S. policies that contribute to poverty and injustice in Latin America and the Caribbean.[18] "People can't tell me I'm exaggerating, because I've seen it. People who want to get involved with this kind of thing need to get out there and experience what these people experience, or else you'll never be able to really give truth to what they are living or give voice to their needs."

GSC faced a number of internal issues in achieving its goals, including how to deal with emergency actions that required immediate planning. "Sometimes the urgency of the situation can make it really hard to organize around," she said, "because actions that are effective and wide-reaching and really powerful sometimes take a lot of planning." Fortunately, they have been able to rely on support from other student organizations to help in their cause, including networking with student government leaders to provide support and further legitimize the movement.

Media involvement also played an important role in GSC actions, particularly the student newspapers (*The Georgetown Hoya* and *The Voice*). Hayes noted that campus perceptions are critical, especially in frequent stories about the anti-sweatshop movement. "If you are out there all the time and see articles all the time about Solidarity, sometimes you need to reserve public relations stuff for when you really need it."

At Georgetown, where Catholic social teaching is included as part of some courses, Hayes has taken a course in the theology of social justice, and is minoring in justice and peace studies. She believes that being spiritual is as important as being religious, and described as "completely arbitrary" the life she was given and the privilege she was born with, just like the lives of the sweatshop workers around the world. "Everyone shares in that humanity, and we are all linked spiritually," she said.

She is inspired by the people at *Witness for Peace* and by their philosophy about forming partnerships and helping developing countries form sustainable economies. Social change comes about when activists are able to convince those who have power to work together on issues that they both care about. External pressure—including protests, teach-ins, or demonstrations—must be combined with effective help from the judicial and legislative branches for true change to occur. "The key to really bringing about change is to show the people that this is in the interest of everyone, why it should affect them too, why they should care about it," she said.

The biggest challenge facing GSC as they head into the future is to keep everyone active and involved in the movement. Since her trip to Nicaragua for *Witness for Peace*, Hayes often thinks about the family she stayed with while there. "I hope my work here will be able to make their lives better in some way."[19]

TOM STRUNK: LOYOLA UNIVERSITY CHICAGO

Loyola University Chicago is a 130-year-old Jesuit institution with over 13,000 students and one of the largest Jesuit communities in the world. The Lake Shore Campus, where most of the students live and attend class, is located in the diverse working class Rogers Park neighborhood on Chicago's north

side. Tom Strunk, a Ph.D. candidate in classical studies who has been involved with USAS since 1998, is a campus leader in the movement and a
member of the USAS national coordinating committee.

Strunk first learned about USAS through an anti-sweatshop activist at
Georgetown University, and quickly took a leadership position at Loyola. He
had three initial challenges: to educate the student population about the issue; to convince the Loyola administration to join the Workers Rights Consortium and to reject the Fair Labor Association; and to develop a code of
conduct for the factories that the university licensed its clothing to. He succeeded in all three areas.

He initially believed that getting Loyola to join the Workers Rights Consortium wouldn't be too difficult, but quickly learned that students on campus
didn't have a lot of power. Eventually he became a member of the university's
Fair Labor Task Force and helped shape its current policy on the subject. "To
me this has been a very powerful experience," he said, "because when I first
began it, I thought, 'I'm one person, what can I do? Do I have the personal
ability to convince my fellow students that this is something to think about
and act on, and can we then go to the administration and get them to do what
we want?' I had doubts about all of that, but by going through this I've realized one person can do a lot, and that's a very powerful lesson to learn, and
I think a lot of us at Loyola have learned it."

Educating the Loyola campus was essential. "Before we were around, this
was never talked about," he said. "We had to educate them as to the possibilities of what we could do." The other challenge was to take the issue to
the administration and get them to act. "It's going to those people that have
power and somehow getting them to make the decision that you think is the
right one, and somehow exerting some sort of pressure on them to do that.
Sometimes it's doing a sit-in or giving them some piece of Catholic social
teaching that says 'this is bad, it's bad for workers and we shouldn't be doing this as a Catholic university,'" he said.

Strunk credited the relationship between Loyola's task force members and
then-University President John Piderit, S. J., with helping move the issue forward. "We sent him e-mails, met with him personally at one point, and let
him know we were willing to take direct action. He listened to us." Fr. Piderit
approved the establishment of the Fair Labor Task Force and appointed the
university's licensing director as its chairperson. Strunk said the process,
which at many universities can be antagonistic, was fair at Loyola. "It's gone
cordially at Loyola because we don't bring in millions of dollars in terms of
our apparel sales, and we let the administration know we were very committed to this."

When starting out, Loyola's students had no resources but instead relied
on other USAS chapters in terms of communication and meeting other students to learn of their experiences as a learning tool. "We learned of unions

to ally ourselves with, such as UNITE, and organizations like Jobs with Justice, who talked to us. The university's ministry office provided us with space, and the Jesuit community was helpful as well in terms of support."

The news media covered the story of the sweatshop movement at Loyola, especially as the students engaged in solidarity actions in support of sweatshop movements at other schools. "The *Chicago Tribune* did a first-page story on the student anti-sweatshop movement as a whole, after students at the University of Wisconsin-Madison were arrested for a sit-in. We went into a building at Loyola and hung banners from the windows in support of the Wisconsin students, and when we did that, it appeared in the story on local activism. The *Sun-Times* broadly covered us as well, and we got into several other smaller publications. We got on TV once, when we did a "sleep-out" in support of Purdue University students who were fasting and sleeping out in order to get their university to join the WRC. We sent out a press release, and a news channel came out and filmed us." He described the sleep-out as a good action that helped bring attention to the Loyola students' goals, especially since the university committee was set to vote the next day on whether to join the FLA. At that meeting, Loyola decided not to join.

Catholic social teaching and the Jesuit tradition at Loyola helped the students achieve their goals. "As a Catholic university there's talk about opting to help the poor, and that's where we felt we belonged, rather than with Nike and Reebok. We didn't want to be walking with the multi-national corporations." Strunk is also inspired by Dorothy Day and the Catholic Worker Movement, and by the Church's historical support for workers' rights reinforced in *Rerum novarum*. A practicing Buddhist, he has been moved by the Church's commitment to justice and Loyola's willingness to be engaged in its community.

He is also inspired by those who are directly involved in the struggle—exploited workers who have little or no money and few resources, but who are "standing up and are willing to get fired and go to jail" to improve their lives, he said. He cited three chief positive outcomes to the activism on campus: creating a greater awareness of workers' issues among Loyola faculty and students, joining the WRC, and demonstrating that students could do things to improve their university within a cultural context. "We are very respected on our campus for both our organizing ability, but then also for our role in educating the community about this," he said. The chief negative outcome, he believes, is global: sweatshops still exist.

In spring 2001, Loyola adopted a formal code of conduct for the factories that produce their clothing, with full public disclosure to ensure compliance. "USAS has listened to the needs of the workers, and has tried to respond through solidarity. The WRC is hoping to put the power with the people on the ground and to have us in the U.S. help them."[20]

MARIA CANALAS: UNIVERSITY OF NOTRE DAME

The University of Notre Dame, in South Bend, Indiana, is a national Catholic university that has been described as "a place where the Catholic Church could do its thinking." With a history of excellence in research and in undergraduate and graduate programs, the school today has a combined enrollment of over 11,000 students from all fifty states and over eighty foreign countries.

Maria Canalas, who hails from Plymouth, Massachusetts, and Pleasanton, California, is a third-year graduate student in physical chemistry and former president of the Notre Dame Graduate Student Union. In 1999, the university president appointed her to the newly formed Task Force on Anti-Sweatshop Initiatives to study the growing issue of sweatshop labor. Canalas was one of only two students appointed to this fifteen-person committee, along with administrators, faculty, and representatives of university-licensed apparel manufacturers. She found the task to be overwhelming at first. "It was a baptism by fire," she said, of having to learn the complicated issues that were multi-national, multi-corporational, and multi-cultural.

In 1996, Notre Dame was the first school in the nation to establish a code of conduct for factories that produced university apparel. The task force carried this commitment one step further shortly after being formed by voting to join the Fair Labor Association (FLA). "We decided early on that we would join any organization that would further the cause of anti-sweatshop initiatives," Canalas said of joining the FLA. "Being one of the nation's most recognized Catholic schools, we wanted to have some influence, so we jumped right in."

Not everyone on campus reacted positively to the FLA. One group in particular, the Progressive Student Alliance (PSA), started organizing the campus on behalf of leaving the FLA and joining the Workers Rights Consortium (WRC) instead. The task force wasn't initially convinced that joining the WRC was the right way to go. "At the time they were loosely formed and not well organized, and we took a more cautious approach. It was clear to us what the purpose of the FLA was; it wasn't with the WRC."

In the months that followed, the task force developed a closer relationship with the WRC's national representatives, while the PSA worked hard at organizing the campus. This included holding rallies and demonstrations, meeting with the university president, leafleting students and lobbying task force members to vote in favor of joining the WRC. Canalas initially wasn't swayed, but later cast a critical vote in support of also joining the WRC. "I looked at what the WRC wanted to accomplish, and what we as a task force initially said—to join any organization that would try to improve the conditions of the workers—that's when my vote swung."

Canalas' decision showed how close the issue was on campus: In March 2001, Notre Dame President Fr. Edward Malloy approved the recommendation of the task force in favor of also joining the WRC. "It was made clear that joining the WRC would not impact our membership in the FLA," she pointed out. "It was important to bring everyone to the table. The FLA is missing the labor organizations and a lot of the NGO's (non-government organizations), while the WRC doesn't want to have anything to do with the business and corporate side. I think you need to be able to sit down and talk and rationalize and make your best case for what to do. To me it was very important to stay a member of the FLA as well as to join the WRC."

The sweatshop issue is very important to Canalas. "I became educated very rapidly," she noted. "We wanted to ensure that Notre Dame clothing was manufactured and distributed under humane working conditions. Every human life has dignity, and we wanted to ensure that workers were treated justly and fairly, and that our school's apparel was produced under morally high standards."

The task force tackled a number of issues, including full public disclosure of factory locations, an appropriate factory monitoring system, and the right of factory workers to obtain a local living wage. Members voted to insert a clause in the school's code of conduct that necessitated the right for workers to organize, based on a trip Canalas and other members took to El Salvador in 1999. They toured three factories, and members were not fooled about the conditions. "We knew this was their best," she said. Inserting the right to organize into Notre Dame's Code of Conduct led to one dramatic change: "No Notre Dame merchandise can be manufactured in countries lacking the legal right to organize, most notably China. We also realized the importance of setting up a monitoring system. We couldn't rely on other people's words." The Notre Dame group knew that they had to get into factories quickly in order to identify relevant issues and implement change as soon as possible, if necessary.

The work of the task force has often received front-page coverage in the university newspaper. "We've also released open letters to the Notre Dame president, and the local news picked them up," Canalas pointed out. "Our work has also been featured in *The Chronicle of Higher Education* and *Notre Dame Magazine*. I don't go out seeking media attention, but if a news release goes out and I'm asked to comment, I will." As the sweatshop issue reaches more and more Americans, Canalas recognizes that change in the way business is done is inevitable. "The more they know, the more outraged they are, the more they want something changed," she noted. And yet no set standard exists from country to country. "Our aim is to improve the conditions for the workers. We don't want to close the factory down so that the worker doesn't have a job. It's a balancing act that requires diplomacy."

Faith plays a large part in her motivation, with role models including Mother Teresa and Archbishop Romero, along with fellow Notre Dame students who are committed to improving the lives of workers around the world. A key source comes directly from Archbishop Romero of El Salvador, who said: "No to violence, yes to peace." Canalas said that "Christ invites us not to fear persecution. In El Salvador we know what the plight of the poor means. That speaks to me."

As the task force continues its work, she foresees a continued emphasis on monitoring factories that produce Notre Dame apparel and the continued development of programs that will effectively support workers at the local level. "It's important to communicate, educate, and enlighten," she said. "Being on the task force, I've seen firsthand that student activism is alive and well and committed to change."[21]

MARIKAH MANCINI: PURDUE UNIVERSITY

Purdue University, located in West Lafayette, Indiana has an enrollment of close to 39,000 students. With historic strengths in agriculture and engineering, the school today offers hundreds of academic disciplines and excels as a research-based institution. Affordable in-state tuition, a central location only a few hours from Chicago and Indianapolis, and membership in the Midwestern "Big Ten" athletic conference help attract many to the campus. About 60 percent of its students are from Indiana; another 27 percent are from out of state, and about 13 percent are from other nations.[22]

Marikah Mancini is a doctoral student in economics from Minnesota who helped create the anti-sweatshop movement at Purdue. Inspired by a social concerns Bible study class she took in 1999 at a nearby Catholic parish, Mancini gravitated toward the "sweat-free campus" campaign sponsored by USAS. She volunteered to work with the national group that helped form the Workers' Rights Consortium (WRC), and in the fall of 1999 organized Purdue Students Against Sweatshops (PSAS). "We were pretty clueless, but ended up searching around and doing what we could with the campaign," she said of her early organizing efforts.

Initially, Mancini and other PSAS members focused their actions on getting Purdue to pass a factory code of conduct, and to agree to join the WRC. They also funded the group themselves to help keep the movement alive. In the spring of 2000, PSAS began to spread the message on campus about the WRC, and on March 27 commenced a camp-out and hunger strike to get the administration to become a member. Eleven days later they reached an agreement that eventually led to formal Purdue recognition of both the FLA and the WRC.

The hunger strike was a turning point in the PSAS activism. "It helped interest and educate the campus, but polarized it as well," Mancini said. "The campus was more aware that sweatshops were an issue." The hunger strike also encouraged and inspired student activists on other campuses, with administrators reaching agreements on joining the WRC after observing how well organized the students were.

But something else happened at Purdue: An opposition group formed in response. Here Mancini found that media coverage, mainly from the Purdue University *Exponent* campus newspaper, focused on the controversy instead of the issues surrounding why the strike was taking place. "The way the coverage came out was very harmful. We didn't see that happening when we planned the action," She said. "The focus was on the controversy between the opponents and supporters of PSAS."

Mancini learned of the importance of developing a good relationship with the news media, particularly for the way an action will be perceived on campus. "It's very easy to look at it and say, 'it worked at the University of Michigan, it will work here,' but every campus is different. We knew if we did anything that was technically illegal, we would be perceived as hooligans and our message would be completely disregarded."

The Catholic Church plays an important role in the inspiration for her work. Initially uncomfortable with her activism, she gradually understood the responsibility and obligation she had "to continue to do God's work." Mancini cites a particular passage from the Old Testament that dealt with the concept of social sin. "We all have a part in this," she recalled as the theme of the passage, "and we are all guilty and have a responsibility to do something about these things."

Why has the sweat-free campaign worked so well? Mancini credits a model for social change that emphasizes personal responsibility and the effectiveness of small groups working together. "Social change happens through small groups of people who need to change things they have control over," she said. "As students you can impact how things are done at your university."

Today PSAS is working hard to stay focused on the issues at hand. Mancini hopes her successors will keep pressuring the administration to actually get factory locations sent to the WRC, and to have Purdue pay their dues to remain in the consortium. Other local actions in the name of solidarity continue to show promise. During the past year, USAS (including Purdue) in the Midwest protested at Kohl's department stores in support of workers in Nicaragua who were illegally fired. Mancini also hopes to keep the PSAS group focused on Purdue-specific issues. "In the long term, I just hope to see a more educated and open student body to these issues, and an organization that 'keeps living' and stays active."[23]

MELISSA BYRNE: ST. JOSEPH'S UNIVERSITY, PHILADELPHIA

St. Joseph's University is a nationally recognized private Jesuit university located in Philadelphia, Pennsylvania. With 3,750 undergraduates, the school emphasizes a liberal arts foundation in a tradition of Jesuit service to others. The school offers attractive majors in the arts and sciences and a popular school of business. Most students are from the Philadelphia area.[24]

Melissa Byrne, from Vineland, New Jersey, was an undergraduate at St. Joe's who helped organize the United Students Against Sweatshops campaign on campus. She enrolled at the university in 1997, when no real movement against sweatshops existed. Then, during a semester spent at Boston College in the spring of 1999, Byrne learned about the USAS movement and felt inspired to bring about change at Saint Joe's.

In the fall of 1999, Byrne and another St. Joe's anti-sweatshop student activist leader joined with students from Philadelphia-area colleges, including Temple, Penn, Bryn Mawr, and Haverford to form a coalition called No Sweat. This organizing group called attention to the sweatshop issue and helped convince the Philadelphia City Council to pass a resolution calling on their schools to join the Workers' Rights Consortium and to reject the Fair Labor Association.[25]

Byrne was inspired by the success of the city council's resolution. "We got more involved, and we came back to our campus and started tabling and leafleting and educating the students," she said. Byrne said that despite what she described as "awesome" Catholic social teaching at the Jesuit campus, she described the culture as conservative and more geared toward volunteerism than activism. "But today it's more proactive than it's been," she noted.

In the Spring of 2000, the St. Joseph's Students Against Sweatshops committee grew to about ten core activists and gathered the support of some faculty members. Their major action that semester was an overnight "sleep-out" on the lawn in front of the main administration building, designed to call attention to the plight of workers toiling in sweatshops, and to convince the administration to join the Workers' Rights Consortium. "We decorated a statue of St. Joseph, the patron saint of workers, to say 'hey, here's the patron saint of workers but we're not upholding the rights of workers,'" Byrne noted. Following the sleep-out, the administration turned to an ad hoc committee on labor (formed in 1999) to further study the issue. The committee, composed of students and faculty members, recommended joining the WRC, but Byrne said the school's president opted to join both the WRC and the FLA.

Months later, the students also participated in actions at the campus bookstore to continue calling attention to the issue. To keep the movement going, the St. Joseph's students relied on funding from some other organizations on campus, and brought Saint Joe's alumnus and anti-sweatshop activist Jim Keady back to campus to speak. Keady was a graduate student and assistant soccer coach at St. John's University in New York, who decided to resign from his position rather than wear the Nike sponsorship logo. His appearances helped increase interest in the movement.[26]

Byrne feels that one of the biggest successes of the campus movement was helping to educate incoming freshmen and sophomores about the importance of the issue. They accomplished this through the use of listservs to communicate to the students, as well as through the use of Grass Roots Organizing Workshops (GROWS) to keep new students trained. "They realized it was more than just volunteer work," she said. "It's great to go to a soup kitchen and feed somebody, it's great to tutor somebody after school, but if you're not able to attack the problems that cause people to have to go to soup kitchens or be tutored, you're not going to understand the problem. You're not going to find a solution."

Byrne feels that the administration's apathy toward the anti-sweatshop movement on campus proved to be a large obstacle and failed to focus on the plight of the worker. Despite Catholic social teaching in the classroom and support for social justice issues in general, Byrne believes the administration remains conservative in its pursuit of a better life for workers. She is a passionate believer in justice causes who was inspired as a young teenager by nonviolence issues and the tragedy of the Holocaust. She recently returned from a civil-rights pilgrimage in the South, and is encouraged, however, about issues of diversity being raised on campus and their impact on the sweatshop movement. "Students are saying, 'why is our campus not diverse, why are we 91 percent white?' People are starting to ask those questions now."

Although faith doesn't play a large role in her motivation, she believes strongly in the power of nonviolence to effect change and that people shouldn't be exploited. She's inspired by Fr. Roy Bourgeois, a Maryknoll priest who is founder and director of the School of the Americas Watch, and by the Berrigan brothers. She also believes that the truly radical approach to bring about social change is through the effective use of nonviolence to attain goals. "It's really about achieving dialogue," she said.

The biggest obstacle facing USAS in general and at Saint Joe's in particular is turnover among activist students due to graduation. "We're not the ones being oppressed by the sweatshops," she said. "We need to keep up the passion and the dedication on the subject. There are so many other issues going on, it's hard to choose. There's a lot to do out there. Also, being on different college campuses, we need to maintain the focus and keep it going."

In the short term, she hopes that more students at St. Joe's will be educated about the importance of being on the WRC. "It's not just a college issue," she added. "The general public needs to be educated as well." In the long term, she hopes that workers' lives will benefit from concrete policy changes.[27]

MOLLY MCGRATH: UNIVERSITY OF WISCONSIN–MADISON

The University of Wisconsin–Madison, located in the state capital, supports over 40,000 combined undergraduate and graduate students, and over

10,000 faculty and administrative personnel. Most of its undergraduates are from Wisconsin, and slightly over 9 percent of those enrolled are minorities. Today the university claims a national leadership role in the anti-sweatshop movement, citing a commitment to full public disclosure of manufacturing locations, the study of living wages, and protecting the rights of all workers, especially women.[28]

Molly McGrath, a recent Wisconsin graduate who today serves as the director of the University of Wisconsin Labor Center, helped initiate the anti-sweatshop movement on her campus. She was a third-year Women's Studies major in 1998 when she first heard Charles Kernaghan of the National Labor Committee speak at the school and became interested in the movement. Some months later she and less than a dozen other students began a campaign to establish an anti-sweatshop code of conduct for Wisconsin. "We met weekly and went about the campaign sort of haphazardly at the start," she recalled. "I didn't have a lot of experience with the issue before that, so my very basic hope was that the work we were doing would actually support people in other countries to improve their economic conditions. It seemed so far-fetched to me at the time, and less far-fetched to me now. I feared that it was futile because the source of the garments was so far away."

There were a number of issues that the Wisconsin students faced as they began their campaign. The question of race was one that had a large impact. "The sweatshop movement is made up largely of middle-class white students, and when approaching the question of race, it's been hard for people to deal with. Why do mostly white students pick up this issue?"

Another issue was the need to obtain student support early in the process to make the campaign a success, especially from those who appeared interested but remained non-committal. "The question was, 'is what we are doing actually supporting people in improving their economic situations in developing countries?' That's hard for people to grapple with, especially students who aren't involved in the issue. They'd rather see something that they can have a direct improvement in, such as homelessness."

To overcome these hurdles, the students relied upon the wisdom of 1960s-era student activists who had been involved in social protests, and from the labor movement to develop their organizing skills. They engaged in discussions with social activists from the 1960s, and with antiapartheid activists from the 1980s for ideas and support in building the foundation for their campaign. Older activists even joined e-mail discussion groups on the subject, while the labor movement provided practical organization-building assistance. Due to this encouragement and mentoring, the Wisconsin students maintained a positive approach in their quest for justice.

In 1999, they achieved their first victory to establish a code of conduct through a direct action—in this case, by occupying an area outside of the university chancellor's office for four days. Later that year they engaged in another sit-in that resulted in fifty-four students being arrested, an emotionally difficult experience for those involved, but one that helped sway the administration to join the Workers' Rights Consortium.

Media involvement helped the Wisconsin movement and the national movement as well, thanks to coverage in local and national papers. Student newspapers at Wisconsin reported on the actions and helped to legitimize the campus movement, while newspapers in Madison also covered the actions. "I'm glad people are reporting on the issue because it makes it important. Sometimes I agree with what they write and sometimes I don't," McGrath said.

The Wisconsin students developed a sense of pride in their accomplishments and in helping to improve the lives of workers in other parts of the world. Participants developed into organizers, and the movement's success attracted new students to the cause. McGrath, too, learned organizing skills and achieved a sense of personal development while learning how to view the group's goals realistically and pragmatically.

Perhaps that's because she draws inspiration from her background in women's studies, with role models who have clearly effected change during their lifetimes. They include historic figures in the U.S. women's labor movement, like Elizabeth Gurley Flynn, who helped organize immigrant women garment workers in New York in the early 1900s, and 1960s student activist Elizabeth Martinez, who today helps advance the cause of justice for people of color.

She believes strongly in the Catholic social teaching concept of "the dignity of work" in what she does. "It plays a huge role in how people are trying to explain to others about why working in a sweatshop is bad, because people aren't working with dignity; they are treated with disrespect and harassed," McGrath noted. The biggest challenges facing the movement today at UW–Madison—and across the country—include a lack of power and resources and the potential for a backlash from powerful organizations and governments globally that call for a multi-faceted movement to succeed.

Today, USAS at Wisconsin continues its fight in support of the global anti-sweatshop movement and is working to gain university approval to support the rights of workers to organize at apparel factories monitored by the WRC.[29]

SARAH JACOBSON: UNIVERSITY OF OREGON

The University of Oregon (UO), located on 280 acres in Eugene, has a combined undergraduate and graduate enrollment of over 17,000 students. Sixty-seven percent are state residents, and 13 percent are students of color, but this public university also boasts representation from around the world thanks to especially strong programs in the arts and sciences. Relative to its size, the UO has been ranked number one in the United States among major public universities in international-student enrollment.³⁰ Eugene, and its neighboring city, Springfield, are located in the Willamette Valley, an area known for its strengths in agriculture, small businesses, and wood products. The area is also known for its high quality of life, outstanding natural environment, and a host of progressive activist organizations.³¹

Sarah Jacobson, a 2000 UO graduate who now is an organizer for the Eugene-Springfield Solidarity Network, a Jobs with Justice organization, was a junior in 1999 when she first became involved with the anti-sweatshop campaign. At that time she led the school's Human Rights Alliance (HRA), whose focus was on broad-based social justice issues. Oregon had not yet opted to join the FLA, and the WRC had not yet been developed by students as the non-corporate alternative, but the UO activists, inspired by the successful sit-in at the University of Wisconsin, decided to invite administrators to a meeting on the subject. "That's really when we learned how the university works," she said, describing what she termed a "hostile" response to their initiative.

In the weeks and months that followed, as the university established an advisory licensing task force to study the issue, Jacobson realized that only through activism would real change occur. Her group networked with other USAS activists from around the country and learned more about how to achieve broad student support for the anti-sweatshop campaign. They organized on campus, demanded full disclosure from factories that produced Oregon apparel, and insisted that the university join the WRC.

Jacobson described three especially important issues faced by Oregon's Human Rights Alliance. The first was the struggle to gather broad student support, especially from students of color, and to include diverse views from within the group. The second was learning about the university's decision-making process. Finally, the alliance sought to build relationships directly with those who make university apparel. "We wanted to respond to the needs of the workers to organize and have a voice in their workplaces," she said.

Early in 2000, the students set an April 1 deadline for joining the WRC and engaged in a campus-wide educational program on the subject. "We talked to thousands of students and faculty members and held a referendum in March, and won that election by a 75 percent majority," Jacobson said. With no decision pending from university officials, however, the activists held a rally and occupied the administration building to call attention to the issue. Over the next few days, numerous students were arrested for the occupation.

Here the Human Rights Alliance relied on media attention to help their cause, particularly from the local newspaper, the Eugene *Register Guard*. "The whole occupation was a big spectacle," Jacobson noted. "We'd invite the press to come at five o'clock because we'd purposely placed students inside the building to get arrested. It was about generating press attention to build public support." She said that the alliance also received unexpected backing from the campus newspaper, which previously had not been friendly to their cause, when the administration balked at making a decision on the issue.

Their action produced an initial victory: a few days later the university agreed to join the WRC. Controversy quickly erupted, however, when Oregon alumnus Phil Knight, founder of Nike, withdrew a $30 million gift to the athletic department as a result of the school's decision. "It really polarized the campus," Jacobson said. In September 2000, the university president announced that the school had also joined the FLA. Six months later the Oregon Board of Higher Education ruled that no public university in the state could set environmental or labor standards to evaluate who they can do business with, effectively eliminating the University of Oregon from joining either the FLA or the WRC.

Despite the setback, Jacobson believes that universities and students have the potential to use their position to support social movements around the world. "I've learned a lot about organizing and understanding our relationships with power and how it can be obtained legitimately or illegitimately," she said. Despite pervasive racism and sexism in today's society, Jacobson believes a focused group with different views can create a more just world. "It's amazing to work with other people," she noted. "When you struggle through, being democratic, acknowledging privilege, or really challenging ourselves and each other, when that works, it's powerful and amazing." She developed allies during the campaign, including leaders of labor groups, human rights groups, and women's rights groups, and noted that members' experiences, faith, position, or cultural background also led them "to act for, or on behalf of, or in the interest of, other people as allies."

Jacobson is inspired by a family history of social activism that has been strongly influenced by relatives who survived the Holocaust. "What does faith mean in the post-Holocaust era? For me it means social change and driving toward a more just society and sustainable world." She is familiar with Catholic social teaching, having worked with the farm-worker movement in Oregon, and has been exposed to people of all faiths who are motivated for social justice and change. Among the leaders that serve as role models for her is Ramon Ramirez, president of Oregon's farm worker union, PCUN (*Pineros y Campesinos Unidos del Noroeste*, translated as Northwest Tree Planters and Farm Workers United). Women activists in her local community, particularly those who focus on immigrant issues and who are working to create social change also serve as role models.

In the near future Jacobson hopes that the campus will be able to organize and reverse the recent decision by the board. She also envisions a long-term relationship between the university and the Eugene community, and with communities in the global south, to help increase understanding about issues related to the environment, women's rights, and labor rights. "Building real relationships and learning about other communities with totally different experiences in the global economy will contribute to a broader, deeper understanding in this community of how to act on our privilege to create social change."[32]

CONCLUSION

As of 2003, the WRC has 117 member schools; the FLA has 178. A number of schools maintain membership in both organizations. Students are now playing a major role in helping to shape global policy related to sweatshops. Eric Brakken, who was a student leader at the University of Wisconsin and now serves as director of the national USAS office, sees issues of race and class as the top challenge for the future. "There needs to be a long-lasting commitment by students and young people to issues of social and economic justice," he said. "Building a base of folks over the long term who are intricately connected to those issues, both in terms of their background, their families, and their communities, and who are going to retain their commitment over time, will allow the movement to sustain itself and build alliances over time."[33]

Catholic social teaching emphasizes the significance of this solidarity in our relationship with others. Solidarity ". . . insists that we are one family; it calls us to overcome barriers of race, religion, ethnicity, gender, economic status and nationality. We are . . . one in Christ Jesus (cf. Gal. 3:28)—beyond our differences and boundaries."[34] Students opposed to international sweatshops clearly express their solidarity with those who labor to make their school's apparel. They also acknowledge the privilege that exists in their own lives and their responsibility toward improving the lives of the workers. As Brakken pointed out, "the people who are making these garments bearing our logo are our age and, in many cases, younger than us and, in many cases, women. There's a special sense of solidarity because of that. When we enter the university, we graduate with a chance of having a better life. For these young women in those factories four years later, they're not necessarily going to be any better off or have that same kind of chance for a better life."[35]

NOTES

1. UNITE! and the Kheel Center, "The Triangle Factory Fire," School of Industrial and Labor Relations, Cornell University, http://www.ilr.cornell.edu/trianglefire/narrative1.html (accessed 17 July 2001).

2. "The Busy Christian's Guide to Catholic Social Teaching," *Salt of the Earth*, (November–December 1991). Cited with permission of Claretin Publications, 205 W. Monroe St., Chicago, IL 60606 (800-328-6515).

3. "On the March to End Sweatshops," *Co-Op America Quarterly* (Fall 1999):14.

4. *Co-Op America Quarterly,* 68.

5. A. Bernstein, "Sweatshop Reform: How to Solve the Standoff," *Business Week,* 3 May 1999, 186.

6. Richard Applebaum and Peter Dreier, "The Campus Anti-Sweatshop Movement," *The American Prospect* 10, no. 46 (September 1999): 1–9. http://web6.infotrac.galegroup.comhttp://www.prospect.org/print/V10/46/dreier-p.html (accessed 10 July 2001).

7. George M. Anderson, S. J., "Fighting Against Sweatshop Abuses: An Interview With Charles Kernaghan," *America* 182, no. 19 (27 May 2000): 7–12.

8. Applebaum and Dreier, "Anti-Sweatshop Movement," 1–9.

9. Jennie Capellaro, "Students for Sweat-Free Sweatshirts," *The Progressive* 63, no. 4 (April 1999): 16.

10. Applebaum and Dreier, "Anti-Sweatshop Movement," 1–9.

11. Applebaum and Dreier, "Anti-Sweatshop Movement," 1–9.

12. Capellaro, "Sweat-Free Sweatshirts," 16.

13. Applebaum and Dreier, "Anti-Sweatshop Movement," 1–9.

14. Steven Greenhouse, "Students Urge Colleges to Join a New Anti-Sweatshop Group," *New York Times,* 20 October 1999, 23.

15. Georgetown University, "Georgetown University at a Glance," http://communications.georgetown.edu/facts/ataglance.html (accessed 24 November 2003).

16. Andrew Milmore, Georgetown '01, "The History of the Georgetown Solidarity Committee," http://www.georgetown.edu/organizations/solidarity (accessed 17 July 2001).

17. Clay Risen, "Administration, Student Activists Release Details of Compromise," *The Georgetown Hoya,* 10 February 1999, http://www.thehoya.com/news/020999/news7.htm (accessed 17 July 2001).

18. "Witness For Peace," http://www.witnessforpeace.org/hist.html (17 July 2001).

19. Cara Hayes, phone interview by author, 7 February 2001.

20. Tom Strunk, phone interview by author, 14 November 2000.

21. Maria Canalas, phone interview by author, December 2000, 18 June 2001.

22. Purdue University, "Purdue University Facts Online," http://www.purdue.edu/oop/facts/pages/enrollment.html (accessed 20 October 2003).

23. Marikah Mancini, phone interview by author, December 2000.

24. St. Joseph's University, "St. Joseph's University," http://www.sju.edu.html (accessed 17 July 2001 and 20 October 2003).

25. Susan Casey, "Philadelphia City Council Unanimously Votes to Pass Resolution Supporting Area University Student's Fight Against Sweatshop Labor," *Philadelphia Students Against Sweatshops* News Release, 9 December 1999, http://dolphin.upenn.edu/~psas/press/releases/PressRelease120999.html (accessed 17 July 2001).

26. Melanie Tamblois, "Penn Protests Spread to St. Joe's," *The Hawk,* Feb. 2000, http://dolphin.upenn.edu/~psas/press/SJU022000.html (accessed 17 July 2001).

27. Melissa Byrne, phone interview by author, 18 January 2001 and 24 May 2001.

0 of 248

28. "UW–Madison and Sweatshops: Position Statements," http://www.news.wisc.edu/positions/sweatshops/ (accessed 17 July 2001).

29. Molly McGrath, phone interview by author, 6 February 2001.

30. University of Oregon, "University of Oregon Factbook, 2000–2001," http://darkwing.uoregon.edu/~uocomm/factbook (17 July 2001).

31. University of Oregon, "Planet Eugene: Community Guide to Lane County and Beyond," http://darkwing.uoregon.edu/~uocomm/factbook/ (accessed 17 July 2001).

32. Sarah Jacobson, telephone interview by author, tape recording, Rockville, Md., 11 March 2001.

33. Eric Brakken, phone interview by author, 15 July 2001.

34. National Conference of Catholic Bishops, "Communities of Salt and Light: Reflections on Parish Social Mission," *Origins* 23, no. 25 (December 2, 1993): 447.

35. Mark Asher, "Campus Activists Target Offshore Sweatshops: Schools Are Pressuring Companies That Make Collegiate Athletic Apparel to Monitor Factory Conditions," *Washington Post*, 28 March 1999, D7.

Appendix: Resources

WEBSITES OF CATHOLIC SOCIAL JUSTICE, SERVICE ORGANIZATIONS, AND INITIATIVES

United States

Association of Catholic Colleges and Universities
Peace and Justice Initiative
update.accunet.org/paj/
This website, and the accompanying resource card, "A Campus Guide To Catholic Social Teaching In Action," represent a collaborative effort of the Association of Catholic Colleges and Universities (ACCU), the Catholic Campaign for Human Development (CCHD), Catholic Relief Services (CRS), and the Departments of Social Development and World Peace and of Higher Education and Campus Ministry at the United States Conference of Catholic Bishops (SDWP/USCCB).
The inspiration for this collaboration is credited to the 1998 U.S. Catholic document, *Sharing Catholic Social Teaching: Challenges and Directions* and the accompanying report by the Task Force on Catholic Social Teaching and Catholic Education.
www.usccb.org/sdwp/projects/socialteaching/contents.htm

Catholic Campaign for Human Development (CCHD)
www.usccb.org.org/cchd
The Catholic Campaign for Human Development (CCHD) is the domestic anti-poverty, social justice program of the U.S. Catholic bishops. CCHD's mission is to address the root causes of poverty in the United

States through promotion and support of community-controlled, self-help organizations and through transformative education.

CCHD's Poverty USA Awareness Campaign
www.povertyusa.org

By sponsoring this website and its Spanish equivalent (www.pobrezausa.org), by promoting the observance of National Poverty in America Awareness Month each January, by preparing Public Service Announcements concerning this serious problem in our country, and by supporting community-based, self-help organizations with low-income leadership, the Catholic Campaign for Human Development is offering its contribution to breaking the cycle of poverty in America.

Catholic Charities USA (CCUSA)
www.catholiccharitiesusa.org/

Founded in 1910, Catholic Charities USA is the membership association of one of the nation's largest social service networks. Catholic Charities agencies and institutions nationwide provide vital social services to people in need, regardless of their religious, social, or economic backgrounds.

Catholic Health Association (CHA)
www.chausa.org/

The Catholic Health Association of the United States represents the combined strength of its members, more than 2,000 Catholic health care sponsors, systems, facilities, and related organizations. Founded in 1915, CHA strengthens the Church's healing ministry in the United States by advocating for a just health care system, convening leaders to share ideas and foster collaboration, and uniting the ministry voice on critical issues.

Catholic Relief Services (CRS)
www.catholicrelief.org/

Catholic Relief Services was founded in 1943 by the Catholic bishops of the United States to assist the poor and disadvantaged outside the country. The fundamental motivating force in all activities of CRS is the Gospel of Jesus Christ as it pertains to the alleviation of human suffering, the development of people, and the fostering of charity and justice in the world. CRS provides direct aid to the poor and involves people in their own development, helping them to realize their potential. Catholic Relief Services assists persons on the basis of need, not creed, race, or nationality. CRS also educates the people of the United States to fulfill their moral responsibilities toward our brothers and sisters around the world by helping the poor, working to remove the causes of poverty, and promoting social justice.

Migration and Refugee Services (MRS)
www.usccb.org/mrs/
Migration and Refugee Services carries out the commitment of the Catholic bishops of the United States to serve immigrants, refugees, and other people on the move. This commitment is rooted in the Gospel mandate that every person is to be welcomed by the disciple as if he or she were Christ himself and in the right of every human being to pursue without restraint the call to holiness. Migration and Refugee Services contributes to this commitment.

National Catholic Rural Life Conference (NCRLC)
www.ncrlc.com/index.html
The National Catholic Rural Life Conference seeks a living community in which people and the natural world are given the respect deserving of their creation by a loving God. In such a society, every person is valued, the Earth is carefully stewarded, the poor are fed, and community life is nourished by public and private deeds. The National Catholic Rural Life Conference serves the mission of the Church by communicating a Catholic perspective and urging public action on rural life and environmental issues.

NETWORK
www.networklobby.org
NETWORK, A National Catholic Social Justice Lobby, educates, lobbies, and organizes to influence the formation of federal legislation to promote economic and social justice. Founded as a contemporary response to the ministry of Jesus, NETWORK uses Catholic social teaching and the life experience of people who are poor as lenses for viewing social reality. As a women-led membership organization, NETWORK values participation, mutuality, cooperation, and stewardship.

Office for Social Justice, Archdiocese of St. Paul and Minneapolis os-jspm.org/cst
This website for the Archdiocese of St. Paul's Social Justice Office includes a very accessible and engaging overview of Catholic social teaching.

Social Development and World Peace (SDWP)
www.usccb.org/sdwp/
The Department of Social Development and World Peace is the national public policy agency of the U.S. Catholic bishops. The Department's goals are to help the bishops; share the social teaching of the Church;

apply Catholic social teaching to major contemporary domestic and international issues which have significant moral and human dimensions; advocate effectively for the poor and vulnerable and for genuine justice and peace in the public policy arena; build the capacity of the Church (national and diocesan) to act effectively in defense of human life, human dignity, human rights, and the pursuit of justice and peace.

International

Caritas Internationalis
www.caritas.org
Caritas Internationalis is a confederation of 162 Catholic relief, development, and social service organizations working to build a better world, especially for the poor and oppressed, in over 200 countries and territories. Caritas works without regard to creed, race, gender, or ethnicity, and is one of the world's largest humanitarian networks. The Caritas approach is based on the social teaching of the Church, which focuses on the dignity of the human person. Caritas' work on behalf of the poor manifests God's love for all of creation.

Catholic Agency for Overseas Development (CAFOD)
www.cafod.org.uk
Britain's Catholic Relief Agency
CAFOD's work is one of the ways in which the Church expresses and enacts its belief in human dignity and social justice. It is inspired by Scripture ("to bring good news to the poor," Luke 4:18), by Catholic social teaching and by the experiences and hopes of the poor, marginalized, and often oppressed communities it supports. CAFOD is funded and supported mainly by the Catholic community in England and Wales to assist poor communities, regardless of creed.

CIDSE: International Cooperation For Development And Solidarity
www.cidse.org
CIDSE is an alliance of fifteen Catholic development organizations from Europe and North America. The aim was to coordinate the work of national Catholic development organizations and thus provide more effective aid to the countries in the Southern Hemisphere. The seven founder members of CIDSE (from Germany, Austria, Belgium, United States, France, The Netherlands, Switzerland) were organizations sponsored by their national episcopates that carried out Lenten fundraising and education campaigns to support development initiatives in Southern countries. The current CIDSE member organizations base themselves on the social teaching of the church—in particular the two

Encyclicals on development: *Populorum Progressio* and *Sollicitudo Rei Socialis.*

Trócaire: Ireland's Catholic International Relief Agency
www.trocaire.org
Trócaire is the official overseas development agency of the Catholic Church in Ireland. It was set up by the Irish Catholic Church in 1973 to express the concern of the Irish Church for the suffering of the world's poorest and most oppressed people. Trócaire, which means "Compassion" in the Irish language, draws its inspiration from Scripture and the social teaching of the Catholic Church. The agency strives to promote human development and social justice in line with Gospel values.

COMMUNITY ORGANIZING NETWORKS AND RESOURCES

Association of Community Organizations for Reform Now (ACORN)
www.acorn.org/
ACORN, the Association of Community Organizations for Reform Now, is the nation's largest community organization of low and moderate-income families, with over 150,000 member families organized into 750 neighborhood chapters in more than 60 cities across the country.

Direct Action and Research Training Center (DART)
www.thedartcenter.org/
The Direct Action and Research Training Center, Inc. (DART) and Network are a national network of grassroots, metropolitan, congregation-based, community organizations spread throughout the United States. DART was founded in 1982 in South Florida to develop congregation-based community organizations.

Gamaliel Foundation, An Organizing Institute
www.gamaliel.org
The Gamaliel Foundation is a network of grassroots, interfaith, interracial, multi-issue organizations working together to create a more just and democratic society. The Foundation and Network teach ordinary citizens to effectively participate in the political, environmental, social, and economic decisions affecting their lives.

Industrial Areas Foundation (IAF)
www.iafnw.com/portland.asp
The IAF was organized in 1940 by Bishop Bernard Shield of the Chicago Catholic Archdiocese, retailer Marshall Field, Kathryn Lewis (daughter of

labor leader John L. Lewis), and Saul Alinsky. The "modern" IAF emerged in the 1970s. There are over sixty affiliated organizations in the United States, Great Britain, and South Africa. The IAF works to build broad-based organizations, which are large scale (city-wide or metropolitan) and based in mediating institutions of church, synagogue, mosque, union, school, strong civic, environmental, housing, and health groups.

National Training and Information Center (NTIC)
www.ntic-us.org
Based in Chicago, NTIC's mission is to build grassroots leadership and strengthen neighborhoods through issue-based community organizing.

Pacific Institute for Community Organizations (PICO)
www.piconetwork.org/
PICO is a national network of faith-based community organizations. PICO's mission is to assist in the building of community organizations with the power to improve the quality of life of families and neighborhoods. PICO carries out its mission through leadership training seminars; the recruitment and development of professional community organizers; and ongoing consultation and technical assistance.

Policy Link: Beyond Gentrification Project—Equitable Development Toolkit, Community Mapping
www.policylink.org/EquitableDevelopment/ (Go to "Controlling Development" link.)
Community mapping is the visual representation of data by geography or location, the linking of information to place. Community mapping does this in order to support social and economic change on a community level. Mapping is a powerful tool in two ways: (1) it makes patterns based on place much easier to identify and analyze and (2) it provides a visual way of communicating those patterns to a broad audience, quickly and dramatically. The central value of a map is that it tells a story about what is happening in a community. This understanding supports decision making and consensus building and can translate into improved program design, policy development, organizing, and advocacy.

SERVICE AND JUSTICE OPPORTUNITY LISTINGS FOR STUDENTS

Catholic Network of Volunteer Service (CNVS)
www.cnvs.org
CNVS, a national association of faith-based volunteer programs, promotes opportunities for men and women of all backgrounds and skills to re-

spond to the Gospel through domestic and international volunteer service to people in need.

Catholic Worker
www.catholicworker.org/communities/volunteers.cfm
Volunteer opportunities with Catholic Worker communities across the country.

The Pallotti Center
www.pallotticenter.org
The mission of the Saint Vincent Pallotti Center is to promote lay volunteer service that challenges the laity, clergy, and religious to work together in the mission of the Church. The Center supports lay volunteers before, during and after their term of service.

Parish Without Borders
www.parish-without-borders.net/volunteer.htm
Parish Without Borders is a global awareness ministry and resource for parishes sponsored by Pastoral Arts Associates of North America.

University of Minnesota's Learning Abroad Center
www.umabroad.umn.edu
This new office offers a database of overseas volunteer opportunities.

SOME BOOK RESOURCES

Aubert, Robert, and David A. Boileau. *Catholic Social Teaching: A Historical Perspective.* Milwaukee: Marquette University Press, 2003.

Coleman, S. J., John A., ed. *One Hundred Years of Catholic Social Thought: Celebration and Challenge.* Maryknoll, N.Y.: Orbis Books, 1991.

Curran, Charles E. *Catholic Social Teaching 1891–Present: A Historical, Theological, and Ethical Analysis.* Washington, D.C.: Georgetown University Press, 2002.

DeBerri, Edward P. and James E. Hug with Peter J. Henriot and Michael J. Schultheis. *Catholic Social Teaching: Our Best Kept Secret,* 4th revised and expanded ed. Maryknoll, N.Y.: Orbis Books, 2003.

Donders, Joseph, ed. *John Paul II: The Encyclicals in Everyday Language.* Maryknoll, N.Y.: Orbis, 1995.

Dorr, Donal. *Option for the Poor: A Hundred Years of Vatican Social Teaching.* Maryknoll, N.Y.: Orbis, 1983.

Dwyer, Judith A., ed. *The New Dictionary of Catholic Social Thought.* Collegeville, Minn.: The Liturgical Press, 1994.

Himes, Kenneth R. *Responses to 101 Questions on Catholic Social Teaching.* Mahwah, N.J.: Paulist Press, 2001.

Hogan, John P. *Credible Signs of Christ Alive: Case Studies from the Catholic Campaign for Human Development.* Lanham, Md.: Rowman & Littlefield Publishers, Inc., 2003.

Hollenbach, David, S.J. *The Common Good and Christian Ethics (New Studies in Christian Ethics).* Cambridge, U.K.: Cambridge University Press, 2002.

Kammer, Fred, S.J. *Doing Faith Justice: An Introduction to Catholic Social Thought.* Mahwah, N.J.: Paulist Press, 1991.

Land, Philip S., S.J. *Catholic Social Teaching: As I have Lived, Loathed, and Loved It.* Chicago: Loyola University Press, 1994.

Massaro, Thomas, S.J. *Living Justice: Catholic Social Teaching in Action.* Come and See series. Franklin, Wis.: Sheed and Ward, 2000.

Mich, Marvin L. Krier. *Catholic Social Teaching and Movements.* Mystic, Conn.: Twenty-Third Publications, 1998.

O'Brien, David J. and Thomas A. Shannon, eds. *Catholic Social Thought: The Documentary Heritage.* Maryknoll, N.Y.: Orbis Books, 1992.

———, eds. *Renewing the Earth: Catholic Documents on Peace, Justice, and Liberation.* New York: Doubleday, 1977.

Williams, Oliver F., C.S.C., and John W. Houck, eds. *Catholic Social Thought and the New World Order: Building on One Hundred Years.* Notre Dame, Ind.: University of Notre Dame Press, 1993.

Index

AFL-CIO, 179
African Americans, 21–25, 136, 138
AFSCME (American Federation of State, County, and Municipal Employees), 165, 167
After School Challenge, 147
Alinsky, Saul, 127–29, 142, 143
Alliance Schools, 147
America: elastic v. inelastic cities in, 18–20, 37nn6–8; external/internal migration of, 16–17; as first global society, 16–17; metropolitan areas of, 18; as racially/ethnically diverse, 16–17; "real cities" of, 18, 37n4; regional land use planning in, 28–29, 38n17; suburbanization of, 18, 37n5; as urbanized country, 17–18
America, concentrated poverty in: children's education and, 27; as not "color-blind," 21; pull factors created by, 19–21; push factors created by, 19–21; social/geographic problem of, 19–21
America, urban trends/issues of: racial/economic segregation as, 16; social exclusion as, 16, 37n3

American Federation of State, County, and Municipal Employees. *See* AFSCME
American Indians, 116–17, 118
Annapolis, 169
Aquinas, Saint Thomas, 62, 68, 74
the Archdiocese of Chicago, 105, 110
Asbed, Greg, 154, 160, 162
Asians, 126
Augustine, Saint, 43

Back of the Yards, neighborhood of, 105–14
Baltimore: BUILD and the Solidarity Sponsoring Committee: background of, 164–65; Baltimore City Council and, 164; Catholic social teaching and, 163, 174; organizations of, 165. *See also* BUILD
Baltimore: BUILD and the Solidarity Sponsoring Committee, challenges of: crime as, 165; health issues as, 165; housing as, 165; isolation as, 163; job security as, 163; living wage as, 163; "payday loans" as, 163, 168–69; temporary workers as, 163; unemployment as, 165

Baltimore, redevelopment of:
convention center's expansion as,
165; Harborplace as, 165; sports
stadiums as, 165
Baltimoreans United in Leadership
Development. *See* BUILD
Baltimore City Council, 164
Baltimore Sun, 164
Baumann, John, 125, 127–28
Benevides, Albert, 143
Benitez, Alejandro, 160
Benitez, Lucas, 157, 159, 161
Bernardin, Joseph Cardinal, 105, 110
black Protestants/Catholics, 138
Bourgeois, Roy, 189
Brakken, Eric, 194
Bronx/Bronx River. *See* Project ROW;
RIVER Team; YMPJ, locations
relating to
Brown, Renee, 172, 173
BUILD (Baltimoreans United in
Leadership Development), 173, 174;
AFSCME joined with, 167; Child First
campaign as initiative of, 172; as
coalition of churches/leaders/
workers, 165; IAF affiliated with,
166; living wage bill forced by, 167;
service workers' issues identified
by, 166; social changes led by,
165–67
building coalitions: allies used in, 36,
39nn27–28; challenges of, 35–36;
faith-based groups in, 36; social
equity as part of, 36
Bush, Jeb, 158
Byrne, Melissa. *See* Melissa Byrne: St.
Joseph's University, Philadelphia

Campaign for Dignity, Dialogue, and a
Living Wage, 159
Canalas, Maria. *See* Maria Canalas:
University of Notre Dame
Cara Hayes: Georgetown University:
Catholic social teaching relating to,
181; challenges of, 181; CLC with,
180; FLA with, 179–80; GSC with,
179–81; Licensing Implementation

Committee relating to, 180; Witness
for Peace program relating to,
180–81
Caritas International, 52
Carter, Jimmy, 158
case studies. *See* Students Against
Sweatshops, case studies of
Catholic Campaign for Human
Development. *See* CCHD
Catholic Charities for the Diocese of
Venice, 153
Catholic Charities USA, 52
Catholic Healthcare Association, 52
Catholic Relief Services, 79, 85n59
Catholic social teaching: action taken
(pastoral plan) as, 46; Baltimore:
BUILD and the Solidarity
Sponsoring Committee relating to,
163, 174; Catholic educational
programs and, 3; "circle of praxis"
as, 46; data gathered as, 45;
"hermeneutical circle" as, 46;
judgments made as, 45; "pastoral
circle" as, 46; The Resurrection
Project (TRP) relating to, 113–14;
YMPJ (Youth Ministries for Peace
and Justice) relating to, 93–94, 97,
103–4
Catholic social teaching, case studies of.
See Students Against Sweatshops,
case studies of
Catholic social thought, and NDC,
122–24
Catholic social tradition, 9–12; Catholic
social teaching as, 3; Coalition of
Immokalee Workers and, 152, 157;
essays of, 4, 12; modern beginnings
of, 9, 14n27; practical/theoretical
riches of, 4; "social question" as, 3
Catholic social tradition, case studies of,
4, 12; Baltimore: BUILD and the
Solidarity Sponsoring Committee as,
163–74; Coalition of Immokalee
Workers as, 151–62; COPS: Putting
the Gospel into Action in San
Antonio as, 139–50; introduction to,
89–91; Neighborhood Development

Center as, 115–24; Oakland
Community Organization as, 125–38;
The Resurrection Project as, 105–14;
Students Against Sweatshops as,
175–96; Young Visionaries in the
South Bronx as, 93–104
Catholic social tradition, challenges of,
43–52; current generations' role as, 4,
52; educational institutions as, 4
Catholic social tradition, focus of:
economy's globalization as, 53–54;
natural environment as, 54; women's
equitable treatment as, 54
Catholic social tradition, inclusion of:
Catholics' lives as, 3; Jesus'
life/teachings as, 3, 9; Old Testament
as, 3, 9; papal/conciliar/episcopal
writings as, 3
Catholic social tradition, initiatives of:
"charity path" as, 53, 115;
diocese/parish projects as, 52;
individual projects as, 52; "justice
path" as, 53, 115; national
organizations' projects as, 52
Catholic social tradition,
issues/concerns of: faith in everyday
lives as, 3; "incarnational" principles
as, 55–56; justice as, 11–12; politics
as, 10–11; questions asked as, 10;
"social Catholicism" as, 49; tradition
engaged as, 9–10
Catholic social tradition, ministry of:
evangelization in, 44–45; resources
used in, 44–45; social responsibility
in, 44, 56; urban, 56; works of mercy
in, 44
Catholic social tradition, resources of,
45; Vatican documents as, 46, 47–49,
49–52, 57n6
The Catholic Worker, 54
Catholic Worker Movement, 183
CCHD (Catholic Campaign for Human
Development), 12, 52, 79–81, 90–91,
130, 161
Centesimus annus, 56, 60, 66, 69, 71,
73, 74
The Challenge of Peace, 77, 78

Chambers, Edward, 142
charity, 53, 115
Chavez, Cesar, 160
Chicago Housing Authority, 26–27
Child First campaign, 172
Chiles, Lawton, 158
Christ. *See* Jesus
"circle of praxis," 46
cities, elastic American, *20*, 37n7;
college student population increased
in, 18–19, 37n8; immigrant
population increased in, 18–19; land
acquired in, 18–19, 37n6; new
development of, 18
cities, inelastic American: city
neighborhoods' decline in, 18–19;
examples of, 19; suburban
expansion in, 18–19
City of God, 43
Clarke, Mary Pat, 167
CLC (Collegiate Licensing Corporation),
178, 180
Clinton, Bill, 168
Coalition of Immokalee Workers, 154,
160, 161; Campaign for Dignity,
Dialogue, and a Living Wage and,
159; Catholic social tradition relating
to, 152, 157; ethnic background of,
154; farm worker population in, 151;
growth of, 158–59; Our Lady of
Guadalupe Parish working with, 153;
Religious Leaders Concerned
working with, 158; roots of, 153–54,
162; St. Ann's Catholic Church
working with, 157
Coalition of Immokalee Workers,
achievements of: fair
wages/dialogue campaign as, 161;
food cooperative as, 162; labor
cooperative as, 162; leadership
training as, 161; membership
strengthened as, 161; network built
as, 162; quality of life improving as,
162; slave-labor convictions
assistance as, 162
Coalition of Immokalee Workers,
actions of: hunger strike as, 156–58;

negotiations helped by, 155–57; public awareness/support of, 157–58; statewide march as, 159; work stoppage as, 151, 155–56

Coalition of Immokalee Workers, challenges of: cost of living as, 152; isolation as, 154; language as, 154; poverty as, 151; transportation as, 152; trust as, 154; violence as, 151; working conditions as, 151

Coalition of Immokalee Workers, core themes of: awareness as, 159; change as, 152, 159; commitment as, 159; dignity as, 152; popular education as, 160; solidarity as, 152

Collegiate Licensing Corporation. *See* CLC

the common good, concept of: communion as, 60, 65; individual rights/dignity as, 61, 82n9; interdependence as, 60–61; social nature as, 59–61

the common good, fulfillment conditions of: classic economic theories relating to, 66–70; classic political theories relating to, 66–70; democracy relating to, 69; egalitarianism relating to, 67–70, 83n28; right of v. use of property relating to, 68; social spheres relating to, 65–70, 82n23, 83n29

the common good, fulfillment of: definition of, 62–65; divine harmony as, 62–63; equality practiced in, 69–70; moral obligation of, 61–64; salvation as form of, 62; solidarity practiced in, 64–65, 70, 82n18

the common good, themes from: option for poor as, 72–73; peace as, 77–81; private property and consumer society as, 73–75; rights and duties as, 70–72, 84n42; subsidiarity, 75–77, 84n53, 93, 105

Communities Organized for Public Services. *See* COPS

Community of Sant'Egidio, 79

Cooper, Allan, 140

Cooper, Scott, 169, 173

cooperatives, 111, 154, 162, 171

COPS (Communities Organized for Public Services), 142–44, 149; as IAF's oldest member, 139; Metro Alliance merging with, 139; San Antonio as home to, 139–50

COPS: Putting the Gospel into Action in San Antonio, 139–50, 163

COPS/Metro Alliance, 144; as grassroots association, 140; public officials held accountable by, 139

COPS/Metro Alliance, concerns of: cost of living as, 140–41; ethnicity as, 140–41; flooding as, 139; poverty rate as, 140–41

COPS/Metro Alliance, projects of: drainage as, 143–44; Human Development Fund as, 146–47; job training as, 139; living wage as, 147–49; Project Quest as, 144–46

Cortés, Beatrice, 141, 149

Cortés, Ernesto, 142–44

crime: Baltimore: BUILD and the Solidarity Sponsoring Committee's challenges of, 165; Neighborhood Development Center's challenges of, 117; as push factors, 19; The Resurrection Project's challenges of, 105, 107

Dahm, Chuck, 106, 109, 110, 111, 113, 114

Daley, Richard M., 108, 110

Day, Dorothy, 12, 54–55, 183

DeBerri, 3

Democracy in America (de Tocqueville), 127

demographics: in Baltimore, 164–65; Neighborhood Development Center and, 116–17; in OCO "Faith in Action," 126–27

de Paul, Saint Vincent, 54

de Tocqueville, Alexis, 127

D'heedene, Walter, 142, 148

dibujos, 161

discrimination: economic practices of, 24–25; exclusionary zoning as, 24–25

Dives in misericordia, 69
"The Divine Law of Harmony," 63
Downs, Anthony, 25
drugs, 106, 127
Duke University, 178

economic globalization, of urban areas, 15, 16
economic inequality, in The Resurrection Project, 106, 107
economic practices, of discrimination, 24–25
economic restructuring, of urban areas, 15
economic segregation, 16, 24–25, 37n10
economic theories, of the common good, 66–70
education: Catholic programs for, 3, 4; for Coalition of Immokalee Workers, 160; Human Development Fund's focus on, 147; Neighborhood Development Center and, 117, 119–20; popular education as, 160; poverty in America relating to, 27; "transformative education" as, 7–8; YMPJ, programs of, 97–98
Elizondo, Virgil, 132
employment: Baltimore: BUILD and the Solidarity Sponsoring Committee's challenges of, 165; Neighborhood Development Center's achievements of, 120–21. *See also* The Resurrection Project; SSC
Eppig, Eileen, 153
Esperanza Familiar, 110–11
Ethnic Entrepreneur Training Program (EETP), 118
Exodus 3:7-12, 60
Exodus, story of Moses and Pharaoh, 136

Fair Labor Association. *See* FLA
Fair Labor Task Force, 182
faith/faith-based. *See* building coalitions; Catholic social tradition, issues/concerns of; OCO "Faith in Action," foundation of; PICO

Favorite, Antoinette, 145
Federal Clean Air and Water Acts, 101
Federal Environmental Protection Agency (EPA), 101
Federation for American Immigration Reform, 6
FLA (Fair Labor Association), 178, 179–80, 182–83, 184–85, 186, 188, 193
Florida Rural Legal Services: Asbed working with, 154, 160, 162; Germino working with, 154, 155–56, 157, 159, 162; Immokalee workers aided by, 154, 162
Flynn, Elizabeth Gurley, 191
Francis of Assisi, Saint, 54
Freire, Paulo, 145
Frost, Tom, 144
Fruitvale, neighborhood of, 126

Gallego, Beatrice, 144
Gandhi, Mahatma, 160
Gaston, Maria Teresa, 153
Gaudium et spes, 10, 64, 77
Georgetown Solidarity Committee. *See* GSC
Germino, Laura, 154, 155–56, 157, 159, 162
Gifford, Kathie Lee, 178
Glendening, Paris, 168
global-local world, 4–6, 13nn5–6; immigration in, 5–6; as troubling, 5; urbanization in, 5–6
God, 60, 61, 63, 65
Grass Roots Organizing Workshops (GROWS), 189
Greeley, Andrew, 9
GSC (Georgetown Solidarity Committee), 179–81
Guadalupano Family Center, 110
Guadalupe Social Services: under Catholic Charities for the Diocese of Venice, 153; Coalition of Immokalee Workers assisted by, 154, 162; food kitchen run by, 153; meetings of, 154–55; social-service center as part of, 153

Guatemalans, 154
Guerrero, Andrés, 132

Haitian Peasant Movement, 153, 154
Harborplace, in Baltimore, 165
Hayes, Cara. *See* Cara Hayes:
  Georgetown University
health issues: Baltimore: BUILD and
  the Solidarity Sponsoring
  Committee's challenges of, 165;
  The Resurrection Project's
  challenges of, 107; YMPJ's
  problems of, 94
"hermeneutical circle," 46
Hernandez, Raul, 109, 112
Hidalgo, Father, 132
Higher Education Research Institute at
  the University of California at Los
  Angeles, 8–9
Hispanics/Latinos, 21–25, 37n9, 116–17,
  118, 126
Hmong, 116–17, 118
Hobbes, Thomas, 61
HOPE VI grants, 26, 38n14
housing, Baltimore: BUILD and the
  Solidarity Sponsoring Committee's
  challenge of, 165. *See also* regional
  mixed-income housing; The
  Resurrection Project
Human Development Fund: focus of,
  147; programs of, 147
Human Rights Alliance (HRA), 192
hunger strike, 156–58

IAF (Industrial Areas Foundation),
  139–40, 163; BUILD affiliated with,
  166; COPS as member of, 139;
  leadership training provided by,
  140; The Resurrection Project (TRP)
  and, 109; as watchdog/advocacy
  group, 140
Immokalee. *See* Coalition of Immokalee
  Workers
Immortale dei, 59, 62
Industries Areas Foundation. *See* IAF
Isaiah 32:7, 77

Jackson, Kenneth T., 6
Jacobson, Sarah. *See* Sarah Jacobson:
  University of Oregon
Jerusalem, 43
Jesuit Refugee Service, 52
Jesus, 3, 9, 43, 50, 55, 56, 60, 65, 89,
  114, 124, 143, 186, 194
Jim Crow. *See specific segregation
  headings*
Jobs with Justice, 183
job training: COPS/Metro Alliance's
  projects of, 139; Project Quest as,
  144–46
John Paul II, 56, 60, 64, 65, 66, 67, 69,
  71, 73, 74, 75, 78, 89–90, 177
John XXIII, 60, 62, 63, 69, 73, 177
Joshua 6, 136
justice. *See* Catholic social tradition;
  PICO, faith-based process of; *specific
  YMPJ headings*
Justice in the World, 11

Kalil, Carmine, 94, 96, 103
Katz, Bruce, 6
Keady, Jim, 188
Kennedy, Ted, 61
Kernaghan, Charles, 177–78, 190
King, Martin Luther, Jr., 160
Kirley, Kathleen, 157
Knight, Phil, 193
Koinonia Baptist Church, in Baltimore,
  166

labor: cooperatives, 111, 154, 162, 171;
  work stoppage, 151, 155–56
Lange, Jonathan, 172
Latinos. *See* Hispanics/Latinos
Lee, Marvin, 169, 171, 172
Leo XIII, 9, 45, 49–50, 59, 62, 63, 72, 73,
  74, 176
Leon, Ramon, 118, 121, 124
Licensing Implementation Committee,
  180
Little Village, neighborhood of, 105–14
LOC (local organizing committees),
  125–38

Locke, John, 61, 66
Lofton, Michael, 107–8
Lopez, Peter, 154
Luke 4:18-19, 114

Malloy, Edward, 184
Mancini, Marikah. *See* Marikah Mancini:
Purdue University
Maria Canalas: University of Notre
Dame: Catholic social teaching and,
185–86; FLA relating to, 184–85;
issues of, 185; Progressive Student
Alliance (PSA) and, 184; Task Force
on Anti-Sweatshop Initiatives relating
to, 184; WRC working with, 184–85
Marikah Mancini: Purdue University:
Catholic social teaching and, 187;
FLA relating to, 186; news media
relating to, 187; opposition to, 187;
Purdue Students Against Sweatshops
(PSAS) working with, 186–87; USAS
working with, 186–87; WRC working
with, 186–87
Martinez, Elizabeth, 191
Maryland Senate Finance Committee,
169
Massaro, Thomas J., 9, 12, 93, 105, 106,
115, 126, 139, 151, 163, 175
Mater et magistra, 60, 62, 177
Matthew 14:13-21, 135
Matthew 25:40, 56
McCallum, Tim, 148–49
McGrath, Molly. *See* Molly McGrath:
University of Wisconsin-Madison
Melissa Byrne: St. Joseph's University,
Philadelphia: accomplishments of,
188–89; Catholic social teaching and,
189; FLA relating to, 188; Grass Roots
Organizing Workshops (GROWS)
relating to, 189; No Sweat formed by,
188; St. Joseph's Students Against
Sweatshops relating to, 188; USAS
organized by, 188–89; WRC relating
to, 188
metropolitan areas: of America, 18; "civil
religion" in, 42; Jerusalem as, 43;

religious historical context of, 41–43,
57n2; religious institutions in, 42–43.
See also specific urban areas
Mexicans, 154
Miles, Doug, 166, 167, 174
ministry. *See* Catholic social tradition,
ministry of; National Farm Worker
Ministry
Minneapolis, 115–24
Missionaries of Charity, 52–53
Molly McGrath: University of Wisconsin-
Madison: accomplishments of,
190–91; Catholic social teaching's
influence on, 191; issues of, 190;
University of Wisconsin Labor Center
directed by, 190; USAS working with,
191; WRC working with, 191
More, Saint Thomas, 43
Muth, Joe, 166, 173, 174

National Farm Worker Ministry, 162
National Guard, 101
National Immigration Forum, 6
National Labor Committee for Worker
and Human Rights (NLC), 177–78
National Society for Experiential
Education, 7
Neighborhood Development Center
(NDC): Catholic social thought and,
122–24; ethnic groups of, 116–18;
mission of, 117, 124n1; Temali
forming, 115, 118, 120, 122–23;
Western Initiatives for Neighborhood
Development (WIND) setting up, 116
Neighborhood Development Center,
achievements of: employment
opportunities created as, 120–21;
local leaders/role models formed as,
120–21; neighborhoods revitalized
as, 120; "sense of community"
developed as, 121
Neighborhood Development Center,
challenges of: abandoned buildings
as, 117; education/experience as, 117;
immigrants/poor as, 117, 122;
language/cultural barriers as, 117,

118; poverty rate as, 117; relationships established as, 121–22; rising crime rate as, 117

Neighborhood Development Center, community of: demographic changes in, 116–17; industries of, 116; Minneapolis as, 115–24; population of, 116–17; St. Paul as, 115–24

Neighborhood Development Center, programs/services of: education/assistance as, 119–20; Ethnic Entrepreneur Training Program (EETP) as, 118; financial support as, 120; long-term support as, 119–20; RECIPES for Business Success as, 119

Neighborhood Entrepreneur Training Program (NETP), 118

Neighborhood Housing Services (NHS), 108

Nesmith, Virginia, 162

Nevins, John, 158

Nike/Champion, 178

Nivola, Pietro, 28

No Sweat, 188

Oakland Community Organizations. *See* OCO

Oakland Community Organizations' "Faith in Action": Locating the Grassroots Social Justice Mission. *See specific OCO "Faith in Action" headings*

OCO (Oakland Community Organizations), 125; Alinsky's organization as model for, 125, 127–29; lay people trained by, 125, 127; as neighborhood-centered, 125, 126–27; as network, 125

OCO "Faith in Action:" challenges of, 127; ethnic groups of, 126, 138

OCO "Faith in Action," achievements of: consultation meetings' success as, 132–34; first Oakland charter school as, 137; "On Road to Tepeyac" as, 131–32; parents/children's

involvement as, 132; Spanish choir as, 132; "village center" formed as, 132, 137

OCO "Faith in Action," areas of: demographic changes in, 126–27; Fruitvale neighborhood in, 126; Lake Merritt in, 126; Oakland in, 125–26, 129–30, 133, 135, 138; Oakland Public School District in, 125, 126, 130, 136, 137; parish of St. Anthony's in, 125–26, 127, 129, 131, 136; San Antonio District as, 125–26, 137

OCO "Faith in Action," foundation of: civic skills as part of, 130–32; empowerment as, 138; faith-based community as, 127–30; PICO training as, 127–30; recruitment of members as, 132–34; St. Anthony's as, 131

OCO "Faith in Action," organizations of: LOC as, 125–27, 129–32, 134–35; OCO as, 125–27, 129–38; PICO as, 125, 127–30, 133–38

Octogesima adveniens, 51, 70

"On Road to Tepeyac," 131–32

On War (von Clausewitz), 78

Our Lady of Guadalupe, 131–32

Our Lady of Guadalupe Parish, 153

Pacem in terris, 63, 64, 73, 162

Pacific Institute for Community Organization. *See* PICO

Parkinson, Michael, 15–16

"pastoral circle," 46

"Pastoral Constitution on the Church in the Modern World," 10

Paul VI, 51, 64, 67, 69, 70, 73, 74, 177

Pedagogies for the Non-Poor, 7

pedagogy and social change, 4, 6–9, 14n22; case methods of, 6–7; experiential education of, 7–8; macro-changes/micro-level of, 8; theories of, 8

Pentagon, 77

Personal Responsibility and Work Opportunity Reconciliation Act of 1996, 168

Piccione, Mary, 142
PICO (Pacific Institute for Community Organization), 125–38, 163; civic behaviors/skills of, 128–29; civic participation modeled by, 130–32; educative mission of, 128–29; faith-based process of, 134–38; methodology of, 129–30
PICO, faith-based process of: African American preachers as part of, 136; organizational culture as part of, 135–36; prayer as part of, 136; social issues as part of, 135; social justice principles as part of, 135
Piderit, John, 182
Pilsen, neighborhood of, 105–14
Pius XI, 59, 61, 62, 68, 69, 73, 74
Pius XII, 63, 64, 68, 69, 73
popular education: drawings (dibujos) as, 160; theater as, 160; videos as, 160
Populorum progressio, 177
poverty: Coalition of Immokalee Workers' challenges of, 151; COPS/Metro Alliance's concerns of, 140–41; Neighborhood Development Center's challenge of, 117; The Resurrection Project's challenges of, 105; as YMPJ problems, 93, 95–96. *See also* America, concentrated poverty in
private property, 73-75
Progressive Student Alliance (PSA), 184
Project Quest: enrollment criteria for, 145; graduates placed by, 145; job-training program as, 144–46; relationships formed by, 146
Project ROW (Reclaiming our Waterfront): Bronx River Greenway developed by, 99; diesel bus use decreased by, 100; Edgewater Road designated "brownfield site" by, 99–100; mass transit increased by, 100; Sheridan Expressway decommissioned by, 99; Starlight Park renovated by, 99
prostitution, 127

protest march, 152, 156
pull factors, 19
Purdue Students Against Sweatshops (PSAS), 186–87
push factors, 19

Quadragesimo anno, 68, 75

racial. *See* segregation, racial
Ramirez, Ramon, 193
Ramirez, Virginia, 145
Ransom, Avis, 170–71, 172
Rawls, John, 61
Raymundo, Raul, 113–14
RECIPES for Business Success, 119
Redemptor hominis, 65, 74
regional competition, in urban areas, 15
regional land use planning: America v. Europe and, 28–29, 38n17; federal land development relating to, 29–30, 38nn18–19; free market forces relating to, 28–29, 38n16; reform of, 33; state land development relating to, 30–33; suburbanization relating to, 28
regional mixed-income housing: exclusionary zoning practices and, 26–27; federal public housing policy and, 25–26; HOPE VI grants and, 26, 38n14; inclusionary zoning policies and, 26–27
regional tax base sharing, 33–35, 38n26; American reliance on, 34; political coalitions relating to, 35; property taxes' importance in, 34–35; state legislatures relating to, 35
Religious Leaders Concerned, 158
Rerum novarum, 9, 11, 45, 49–51, 59, 60, 177, 183
Resurrection Construction Cooperative, 111
Resurrection Employment Center, 111
Resurrection Loan Fund, 111
The Resurrection Project (TRP), 106–14; Catholic social teaching and, 113–14; future challenges of, 111–12; housing

as focus of, 105; IAF working with,
109; six parishes forming, 105, 106;
St. Vitus Church bought by, 105, 110;
United Power for Action and Justice
and, 109

The Resurrection Project, areas of: Back
of the Yards neighborhood as,
105–14; ethnic, cultural, class
divisions in, 107; Little Village
neighborhood as, 105–14; Pilsen
neighborhood as, 105–14; southwest
Chicago as, 105–14

The Resurrection Project, challenges of:
affordable housing as, 105, 107;
crime as, 105, 107; drug use as, 106;
economic inequality as, 106, 107;
employment as, 105, 107; gang
violence as, 106, 107; health care as,
107; poverty as, 105; racism as, 106;
residents' reluctance as, 105

The Resurrection Project, community
center of, 106; after-school program
at, 106, 110; arts center at, 106, 110;
day care at, 106, 110; Guadalupano
Family Center as, 106, 110

The Resurrection Project, successes of:
community business encouraged as,
106; cultural heritage nurtured as,
106; Daley's "New Homes for
Chicago" program and, 108, 110;
employment opportunities promoted
as, 106, 111; *Esperanza Familiar* as,
110–11; housing improved as, 106;
local block clubs as, 106, 109;
marginalized women/children
supported as, 106, 110;
Neighborhood Housing Services
(NHS) working with, 108;
networks/institutions formed as, 106;
rental units increased as, 108;
Resurrection Construction
Cooperative as, 111; Resurrection
Employment Center as, 111;
Resurrection Loan Fund as, 111

Richards, Ann, 146

RIVER Team: assessments of, 98–99;
Bronx River section cleaned by, 101;
National Guard helping, 101; Project
ROW developed by, 99–100

Rodriguez, Jeannette, 132

Rodriguez, Manuel, 160–61

Romero, Archbishop, of El Salvador,
185–86

the rules of the game: building coalitions
as, 35–36; regional land use planning
as, 27–33; regional mixed-income
housing as, 25–27; regional tax base
sharing as, 33–35, 38n26

Rusk, David, 12, 93–94, 105, 115, 163

Salgado, Juan, 112

San Antonio Education Partnership,
147

Sanders, Richard, 153

Sarabia, Andres, 142, 143, 144

Sarah Jacobson: University of Oregon:
Catholic social teaching relating to,
193; FLA relating to, 193; future goals
of, 193–94; Human Rights Alliance
(HRA) led by, 192; issues/setbacks
of, 192–93; WRC relating to, 192–93

Schmoke, Kurt, 167

"School Counts," 172

Second Vatican Council, 10, 45, 60, 62,
64, 67, 69, 74, 77

segregation, economic, *22*, 37n10; of
African Americans, 21–25; of
Hispanics, 21–25; of poor whites,
23–25; racial segregation relating to,
16, 24–25; statistics of, 21–24

segregation, racial: of African
Americans, 24–25; economic
segregation relating to, 16, 24–25;
public policies of, 24–25, 38nn11–12

segregation, residential, *22*; of African
Americans, 21–25; of Hispanics,
21–25, 37n9; statistics of, 21–24

September 11, 2001, 77–81

Seton, Saint Elizabeth Ann, 54

"Sharing Catholic Social Teaching:
Challenges and Directions," 3–4

Sharry, Rank, 6

Shuffler, David, Jr., 94, 96, 98–99, 100,
102–4

"Signs of the Times," reading of, 10, 12, 45, 47, 52–56, 163
Smart Start, 147
Smith, Adam, 66
social change, 4, 6–9, 14n22, 165–67
social equity, 36
social exclusion, 16, 37n3
social/geographic problem, 19–21
social issues, 135
social nature, 59–61
social services. *See* Guadalupe Social Services
social spheres, 65–70, 82n23, 83n29
social teaching. *See* Catholic social teaching
social tradition. *See* Catholic social tradition
Solidarity Sponsoring Committee. *See* SSC
Sollicitudo rei socialis, 60, 64, 69, 74, 177
Somalians, 116–17, 118
SSC (Solidarity Sponsoring Committee), 171–73; banks working with, 169; BUILD and AFSCME joined as, 165, 167–68; community relationships formed by, 172; Maryland Senate Finance Committee working with, 169
SSC (Solidarity Sponsoring Committee), challenges of: check-cashing industry as, 168–69; low wages as, 168; organizational goals as, 174; "payday loans" as, 163, 168–69; recruitment as, 173; sustainability as, 173; trust as, 173; welfare-to-work participants as, 168, 172
SSC (Solidarity Sponsoring Committee), employment agency of, 172; CCHD working with, 170; decision-making model of, 171; development of, 169–71; part-time employment as issue of, 169–70; temporary employment as issue of, 169–70; as worker-owned cooperative, 171
St. Ann's Catholic Church, 157
state land development, impacts on: state annexation laws as, 31–32; state municipal planning laws as, 32–33;

38nn20–22; state transportation policy as, 30–33
Stein, Daniel, 6
St. Joseph's Students Against Sweatshops, 188
St. Matthew's Catholic Church, in Baltimore, 166
St. Paul, 115–24
Strunk, Tom. *See* Tom Strunk: Loyola University Chicago
Students Against Sweatshops, background of: AFL-CIO's role in, 179; Collegiate Licensing Corporation (CLC) in, 178; Duke University's role in, 178; Fair Labor Association (FLA) in, 178; Gifford's clothing line in, 178; National Labor Committee for Worker and Human Rights (NLC) in, 177–78; Nike/Champion in, 178; sweatshop history in, 176–79; United Students Against Sweatshops (USAS) as, 178–79; U.S. retailers in, 177; White House Apparel Industry Partnership (AIP) in, 178; Worker's Rights Consortium (WRC) in, 179
Students Against Sweatshops, case studies of: Cara Hayes: Georgetown University as, 179–81; Maria Canalas: University of Notre Dame as, 184–86; Marikah Mancini: Purdue University as, 186–87; Melissa Byrne: St. Joseph's University, Philadelphia as, 187–89; Molly McGrath: University of Wisconsin-Madison as, 189–91; Sarah Jacobson: University of Oregon as, 191–94; Tom Strunk: Loyola University Chicago as, 181–83
St. Vitus Church, 105, 110
suburbanization: of America, 18, 37n5; regional land use planning and, 28
sweatshops. *See specific Students Against Sweatshops headings*
Synod of Bishops (1971), 11

Task Force on Anti-Sweatshop Initiatives, 184

Temali, Mihailo, 115, 118, 120, 122–23
Teresa, Mother, 12, 52–53, 185
theories: of economics/politics, 66–70; of pedagogy and social change, 8
A Theory of Justice, 61
Tom Strunk: Loyola University Chicago: Catholic social teaching relating to, 183; Fair Labor Task Force relating to, 182; FLA working with, 182–83; Jobs with Justice working with, 183; outcomes of, 183; UNITE working with, 183; USAS relating to, 181–83; WRC relating to, 182–83
Torres-Fleming, Alexie, 93–104
Tracy, David, 50
tradition. *See* Catholic social tradition

UNITE, 183
United Power for Action and Justice, 109
United States Conference of Catholic Bishops, 79
United States Department of Justice, 162
United Students Against Sweatshops. *See* USAS
University of Wisconsin Labor Center, 190
urban areas, 15–16
USAS (United Students Against Sweatshops), 178–79, 181–83, 186–87, 188–89, 191

Valdez, Elizabeth, 140
Vasquez, Susana, 113
Vatican Council II. *See* Second Vatican Council
Vatican documents, 46, 47–49, 49–52, 57n6
violence, 106, 107, 127, 151
Vitillo, Robert, 12
von Clausewitz, Karl, 78

wages, 167: BUILD and, 163, 167; SSC's challenges of, 168. *See also* Coalition of Immokalee Workers
Weigart, Kathleen Maas, 105, 175
welfare-to-work, 168, 172
Western Initiatives for Neighborhood Development (WIND), 116

White House Apparel Industry Partnership (AIP), 178
Whitmore, Todd David, 12, 105, 106, 125, 139, 140, 152, 163, 164
Winright, Tobias, 79
Witchger, John, 153
Witness for Peace program, 180–81
Worker's Rights Consortium. *See* WRC
World Trade Center, 77, 81
WRC (Worker's Rights Consortium), 179, 180, 182–83, 184–85, 186–87, 188, 191, 192–93

YMPJ (Youth Ministries for Peace and Justice), 115; Catholic social teaching's impact on, 93–94, 97, 103–4; environmental justice as focus of, 95; future visions for, 93–104; origins of, 96–97
YMPJ, issues tackled by: community empowerment as, 102–3; federal clean air/water acts as, 100–101; neighborhood zoning as, 100; police relations as, 101–2; policy enforcement as, 100–101
YMPJ, locations relating to: Bronx River as, 93, 94, 95, 99, 104; Bronx River Parkway as, 95, 100; Bruckner Expressway as, 93, 95, 100; Cross Bronx Expressway as, 95; Edgewater Road as, 99; Sheridan Expressway as, 93, 95, 99, 100, 104; Soundview/Bruckner neighborhoods as, 93, 94, 99; South Bronx as, 93–96, 101; Starlight Park as, 99
YMPJ, problems of: air pollution as, 94; asthma/other health issues as, 94; highly industrialized area as, 94; inaccessibility as, 94; poverty as, 93, 95–96; raw sewage as, 94
YMPJ, programs of: arts for activism as, 97–98; assessment and training as, 97–98; community organizing as, 97–98; education for liberation as, 97–98; RIVER Team as, 98–100
Youth Ministries for Peace and Justice. *See* YMPJ

Zamora, Virginia, 142

About the Contributors

William P. Bolan is currently an instructor of theology at the University of Notre Dame, where he is also a Ph.D. candidate in moral theology and Christian ethics. His areas of expertise include the Catholic social encyclicals and the requirements of Christian solidarity. His most recent writing deals with the theoretical and practical correlations between Catholic social teaching and the pedagogy of community-based learning.

Patrick J. Hayes has graduate degrees in education from the Teachers College at Columbia University and in theology from Yale Divinity School. In 2003, he completed doctoral studies in ecclesiology and ethics at the Catholic University of America. He employs the case study method as a visiting assistant professor of theology in the Department of Theology at Quincy University in Illinois. His current research interests include Catholic cultural relations in nineteenth and twentieth century America, the concept of nostalgia, and miracle stories.

Monika K. Hellwig, LL.B., Ph.D., is currently president and executive director of the Association of Catholic Colleges and Universities. She was formerly the Landegger Professor of Theology at Georgetown University where she taught for three decades. She has written and lectured extensively, nationally and internationally, both in scholarly and in popular contexts, in Catholic systematic theology and inter-faith studies, and is a past president of the Catholic Theological Society of America. Her published books include: *Understanding Catholicism, Jesus the Compassion of God, The Eucharist and the Hunger of the World, Sign of Reconciliation and Conversion*, and *Guests of God: Stewards of Creation*. Dr. Hellwig is the mother of three now-grown adopted children: Erica Hellwig Parker, Michael Hellwig, and Carlos Hellwig.

Alexia K. Kelley is currently program director at Environmental Resources Trust in Washington D.C., where she focuses on partnerships to support renewable energy, in particular a collaboration with Verdant Power, a sustainable tidal and river-flow "green" energy company. She has an M.T.S. from Harvard Divinity School with a focus on social ethics. For nine years she worked at the Catholic Campaign for Human Development in media, development, and outreach. She is also the author of a CCHD publication, *The Call to Family, Community and Participation* and serves on CCHD's Resource Development/Education Advisory Committee, and on the board of the Janelia Foundation.

Christopher C. Kelly is director of public affairs at the Armed Forces Institute of Pathology (AFIP) in Washington, D.C., where he oversees a comprehensive internal and external communications program and serves as spokesperson for the Armed Forces Medical Examiners. Since 1997, he has served as a volunteer lead writer for the Catholic Campaign for Human Development's newsletter "Helping People Help Themselves," profiling numerous CCHD-funded programs that help low-income residents across the United States address the root causes of poverty and determine effective solutions to bring about change in their communities. He also serves on CCHD's Resource Development/Education Advisory Committee, and since 1999 has been chair of the Social Concerns Committee at St. Mary's Church in Rockville, Md.

Thomas J. Massaro, S.J., a Jesuit priest of the New England Province, is associate professor of moral theology at Weston Jesuit School of Theology in Cambridge, Mass. He holds a doctorate in Christian social ethics from Emory University and other degrees in philosophy, theology, economics, and political science. He has published four books: *Catholic Social Teaching and United States Welfare Reform* (The Liturgical Press, 1998); *Living Justice: Catholic Social Teaching in Action* (Sheed and Ward, 2000); *Catholic Perspectives on Peace and War* (Sheed and Ward, 2003), co-authored with Thomas A. Shannon; and, as co-editor of *American Catholic Social Teaching* (The Liturgical Press, 2002). He writes and lectures frequently on topics of social justice, both in scholarly forums and for general audiences.

Joseph M. Palacios is presently assistant professor of sociology at Georgetown University, where he also teaches in the graduate program of the Center for Latin American Studies. At Georgetown he specializes in research and teaching courses in social theory, social justice analysis, religion and society, and culture and power in Latin America. Prior to academic work he worked for many years in pastoral ministry in California specializing in urban ministry for ethnic and immigrant minorities and faith-based community organizing. In addition he spent several years in Guadalajara and Mexico City doing ethnographic research focusing upon the effects of Catholic social justice teaching upon social change in urban Mexico.

Steven M. Rodenborn is currently a doctoral student at the University of Notre Dame and is living in Chicago, Ill. Following the completion of his comprehensive exams in systematic and historical theology in 2004, he plans to explore the intersection of discipleship and doctrine as it is addressed by contemporary Catholic political theology.

David Rusk is former mayor of Albuquerque and New Mexico state legislator. He has spoken and consulted on urban policy in over 100 American metropolitan areas as well as in Canada, England, Germany, The Netherlands, and South Africa. He is author of *Cities without Suburbs* (1993; 3rd edition, 2003), *Baltimore Unbound* (1995), and *Inside Game/Outside Game* (1999). Many of his speeches, articles, research reports, and community presentations may be found at www.davidrusk.com.

Kathleen Dolan Seipel is currently a mother and part-time social worker at Trinity Episcopal Parish in Wilmington, Del. From 2000 to 2002, she was an organizer with *Voces sin Fronteras* (Voices Without Borders), a faith-based community-organizing project in Delaware. Since 2000, she has served on the Diocese of Wilmington's local committee for the Catholic Campaign for Human Development. While studying for her master's degree in Social Work, she completed an internship with the national office of the Catholic Campaign for Human Development. She is a 1996 graduate of the University of Notre Dame, with a B.A. in theology and a concentration in peace studies.

Kathleen Maas Weigert is the first director of the Center for Social Justice Research, Teaching, and Service (csj.georgetown.edu) and research professor in both the Department of Sociology and Anthropology and the Program on Justice and Peace at Georgetown University. She co-edited *America's Working Poor* (University of Notre Dame Press, 1995); is one of the authors of *The Search for Common Ground: What Unites and Divides Catholic Americans* (Our Sunday Visitor, 1997), which received the "1998 Award for Excellence in Research" from the National Conference of Catechetical Leaders; and is co-editor of *Teaching for Justice: Concepts and Models for Service-Learning in Peace Studies* (American Association of Higher Education, 1999). She serves on the board of NETWORK: A National Catholic Social

Justice Lobby and on the Association of Catholic Colleges and Universities Interinstitutional Advisory Committee on Peace and Justice Education.

Todd David Whitmore is associate professor of social ethics, Department of Theology and Director of the Program in Catholic Social Tradition at the University of Notre Dame. He is also director of the Teaching Catholic Social Teaching project, funded by the Wabash Center for Teaching and Learning in Theology and Religion. The project has facilitated the development of programs and courses in Catholic social teaching in over a dozen schools. Professor Whitmore was named a Carnegie Fellow for his work in pedagogy and Catholic social teaching.